The Formation and History of Telangana

The Formation and History of Telangana

A Collection of Nine Critical Essays

Gautam Pingle

Orient BlackSwan

THE FORMATION AND HISTORY OF TELANGANA:
A COLLECTION OF NINE CRITICAL ESSAYS

ORIENT BLACKSWAN PRIVATE LIMITED

Registered Office
3-6-752 Himayatnagar, Hyderabad 500 029, Telangana, India
e-mail: centraloffice@orientblackswan.com

Other Offices
Bengaluru, Chennai, Guwahati, Hyderabad, Kolkata,
Mumbai, New Delhi, Noida, Patna

First published by Orient Blackswan Private Limited 2021
Reprinted 2021, 2022

ISBN 978-93-5442-048-1

038386

Typeset in
Goudy Old Style 10/12
by Shine Graphics, Delhi 110 094

Printed at
Thomson Press, New Delhi 110 020

Published by
Orient Blackswan Private Limited
3-6-752, Himayatnagar, Hyderabad 500 029, Telangana, India
e-mail: info@orientblackswan.com

DEDICATED

TO

SATISH KUMAR ARORA
(30 March 1932–27 August 2018)

Contents

Tables, Figures and Appendix

Tables

Figures

Appendix

Glossary

Afaqi	foreign-born elements
agraharams	whole villages
agraharas	tax-free villages
Akasalivaru	ironsmiths
ashvasahini	denoting cavalry
astadasamahapraja or *astadasapraja*	eighteen village groups
Atraf-e-Balda	district surrounding the city
Bangaru	Golden
bantu	an ordinary soldier
Chatur varna	the fourth caste
Chaturtha-panch-bhagikah	one who pays one-fourth or one-fifth share
chauth	a regular tax imposed by the Marathas on Mughal provinces
chauth	one-fourth
Circar	the state
circars	north-eastern Andhra
curmuns/karnams	village accountants
Dakhani	native-born or converted elements
dams	copper coins
dandanayaka	a term used to distinguish a military from a civil nayaka
Dbalanja Settigandru	traders
Desa	a specific administrative and political unit
deshmukhs	revenue administrators
dhimmi	non-Muslim subjects
diwani areas	a territory where the state collects taxes directly from landowners
doras	lords/a class of feudal landowners
durbar	court
emirs	Muslim rulers or kings

Enakaram	warriors
fay	the land surrendered by those defeated by Muslim power
gajasahini	denoting the elephant forces
gajasenapathi	general of elephant corps
Garuda	Vishnu's vehicle
ghalpadhi	a volumetric measure, also measured as one-quarter *padhi*
ghanimah	booty taken in battle in the form of weapons, horses, prisoners and movable goods
Gollavaru	shepherds
gotra	lineage
Hadiths	'traditions' of the Prophet many generations after his death, compiled into six books, of which *Sahih al-Bukhari* and *Sahih Muslim* generally have the highest status
hasil	the degree of collection
hun	a gold coin with a gold content of approximately 10.97 grams
Iddavaru	toddy tappers
ilaquas	whole districts conferred upon important nobles
inams	tax-free grants of land
Jaghire	the region surrounding Fort St George, or the present-day Madras/Chennai city
jagirdars	title-holders of *jagirs*
jagirs	fixed tenures of large estates
jati	sub-caste/caste
jihad	Islamic Holy War
jizya	Islamic canonical poll tax on non-Muslims
Kallam/ghalam	a variable volumetric measure
Kampulu	farmer caste
kani	a volumetric measure equal to 1.33 acres
Karnalu	Brahmin village accountants
karnam	village accountant
kharaj	land tax on non-Muslims
kharif	monsoon
Komatis	traders
kulas	sub-caste
lemka	*bantu*'s superior

lila	grace
mahamandaleshwaras	great lords of the regions, or governors
makta village	a grant of a village on specific concessional terms
mali patel	village tax collector
mandala	an administrative unit
mandaleshwara	the governor of a *mandala*
mandalika	a title and honour conferred by the king
mantri	minister
maund	a volumetric measure equal to 37.32 kilograms
mirasi	land by hereditary right
Nadu	the grant of a territory
nayaka	a military leader or a feudal chief
Nayakulu	*nayakas*
nayamkara units	military units of the *nayakas*
nayankara	the Kakatiya military system
Nayilu	washermen
Padilechina Telangana	*The Fall and Rise of Telangana*
paigahs	former military leaders
paigahs	military *jagirs*
pancha maha shabda	five types of sound
pangamu	one-fourth of a tax
para	one-eighth of a tax
parganas	districts
patwari	accountant
peshkash village	villages granted to nobles on the condition that they pay tribute
police *patel*	village law and order functionary
rabi	winter
rajahs/rajas	kings
Redlu	Reddys
ryotwari	small holder
ryotwari village	villages where the ownership of land and payment of revenue are by individual cultivators
sahinis	commander or general
Salevaru	weavers
samantha	chief feudatory
samasthans	little kingdoms
sarf-i-khas	the Nizam's crown estates
sarkar	an administrative unit consisting of *parganas*

seema	a territory or region
senani	the equivalent of a general
senapati	general
shadabhagin	one who is entitled to collect the *shadbhaga*
shadbhaga	one-sixth tax share due to a Hindu king
Sharia	Islamic law and practice
Shastra	canon
sirdeshmukhi	title for a revenue administrator; head of a set of *deshmukhs*
Srivaisnavulu	Srivishnava priests
suba	sub-region
taluk	an administrative unit
talukas	administrative divisions
tarafdar	governor
Telikivenurur	oil pressers
thanas	police stations
Turkas	Muslims
usher/ushr	one-tenth of a tax on Muslims
vamsa	genealogy
Varaha	God Vishnu's third avatar or incarnation as a boar
varnas	main four castes
Velamagaru	Velamas
veli	a measure of land extent (6.6 acres or 2.64 hectares)
vetti	unpaid labour from tenants as part of their obligations
visti	serve
zamindar	landowner
zamindaris	landownings

Acknowledgements

I have always been a connoisseur of the essay form. This is largely because I do not have a grand story to tell—only short and interesting ones. This also suits me as my interest shifts from one subject to another.

However, Telangana has been the main object of my studies since my PhD days. Gradually, it seemed that my works related in some loosely connected way to Telangana. It was through the suggestion of my friend Dr Satish Arora that I consider putting them together and making them available in a publication.

These set of essays have a chequered history. I got interested in the subjects because I did not understand them and wanted to know more. As my search continued, I discovered that much work had been done on them but very little was known. Taking the data, narrative sources, histories, epigraphically records and old published works, the essays gradually emerged as historical pieces with current relevance. Some have taken many decades in their making.

I classify these Essays as 'unknown knows'—in that much of what is made available in them has been known but not available to the contemporary reader. It is that I have put what is known together in narratives that, hopefully, makes sense and encourages readers to think and make up their minds.

It is my hope that scholars will be stimulated to use these essays to further extend their scope and/or challenge their narrative by work of their own.

I thank my wife, Rina, and my son, Mohan, who have put up with the time I have spent on these essays at their expense. Their tolerance and patience has been basic to my task. As John Milton said in another serious context, 'They also serve who only stand and wait'.

Publisher's Acknowledgements

For granting permission to reproduce copyrighted material in this volume, the publishers wish to make the following acknowledgements:

Oxford University Press, for J. F. Richards. 1975. *Mughal Administration in Golconda*. Oxford, England: Oxford University Press. Granted by PLSclear on 25 January 2021, PLSclear Ref. No.: 45825. Licensor: Oxford Publising Limited.

Deccan Chronicle, for *Exclusive Sundarlal Report on Hyderabad Police Action*, *Deccan Chronicle*, 18 March 2019[30 November 2013]. Available at https://www.deccanchronicle.com/131129/news-current-affairs/article/exclusive-sundarlal-report-police-action.

Introduction

The creation of Telangana as the twenty-ninth state of the Indian Union was a long-sought culmination of the aspirations of the people of Telangana. In the course of the movement and agitation, much has been written and many ideas have been canvassed to justify the demand for a separate state. I have authored articles in scholarly journals and daily newspapers aimed at intellectuals and policymakers to inform public opinion on the subject. These writings have been put together in the book, *The Fall and Rise of Telangana*, and its Telugu translation, *Padilechina Telangana*. Both the English and Telugu versions have become required readings for students appearing for the Telangana Public Service examination.

Despite the political, emotional and psychological basis for the popular aspiration for statehood, its historical necessity remained unclear. There was a need to explore, identify and reveal the historical sources that justified the formation of the state. A comprehensive history of Telangana needed to be set out, taking into account the most credible evidence and data that was available in this regard.

I intend to take up in this book the idea of the state of Telangana, the problems that occurred in the process of its formation, and then trace back its trajectory to its historical roots. I shall explore this history extensively as well as intensively in order to ascertain how the state of Telangana came into existence. This study has also led me also to explore different issues related to Telangana. The nine essays of this book are a result of this study and look at various aspects of the history of Telangana and its birth and eventual rise as a state.

Essay 1 is a comprehensive summary of the origins and growth of the Kakatiya empire from its modest origins in the Anamkonda Visaya. It recounts how the Kakatiyas began their historical role as vassals of the Chalukyas. Seizing the opportunity afforded by the collapse of the Chalukyan suzerain, the dynasty managed to incorporate other vassals into its growing domain. The Kakatiya empire emerged from a feudal phase into an imperial one and it united almost all the Telugu people and their land under one political entity. But in 1324 AD, the dynasty and the kingdom was conquered by Muslim power.

Essay 2 describes the feudal structure of the Kakatiya state. The narrative of resilience of the Kakatiya Nayaks, even after the collapse of the dynasty and the destruction of its capital Warangal, is an extraordinary history. The governance by the Kakatiya feudal elite, which was based on religious and cultural legitimacy, and often, on the notion of 'divine right', justified their historical role in maintaining the religious and cultural heritage of its people and safeguarding them from a hostile alien power. This role seems to have continued for nearly 700 years, in one way or another.

The historical legacy of the Kakatiya elite, which helped to maintain Telangana's identity more or less through the alien rule of the Bahmani, Qutub Shahi, Mughal and Nizam regimes as well as under representative democracy in the state of Andhra Pradesh, is explored in Essay 3. This essay also looks at the semi-feudal structure of Telangana as well as the similarity and differences between the semi-feudal structure of Telangana and Andhra Pradesh.

Essay 4 tackles the critical issue of the land tax, confining itself to South India and setting Telangana within the South Indian context. This essay formed my Presidential Address delivered at the first Conference of the Telangana Economic Association. This analysis is central to the history I chart in this book because land tax is a critical explanatory variable, which is determined by the type of governance in force, and it is also a critical factor determining the development process of agricultural societies and the condition of the peasant population.

The issue of agricultural productivity in India, generally, and in South India, particularly, was an open-ended question. I have been studying this subject over the last 40 years, the scope and depth of which intrigued me. Essay 5 takes into account the historical evidence on agricultural productivity in South India from the tenth century to the nineteenth century. An earlier version of this essay was published in the *Economic and Political Weekly* (Pingle 2017: 36–45). The core focus of this essay is on yields of paddy, the major crop, on which the data is relatively abundant across time and space. In the course of developing the hypothesis, I made many assumptions as well. However, my intention has been to lay the foundation for scholars to refine, criticise and develop the subject further.

Essay 6 aims at assessing the income, wealth and taxation system in Telangana for over a period of 700 years. It is somewhat impressionistic, especially with regard to the earlier periods for which data is scarce. This essay puts forward the real and potential wealth, income, and taxation capacity of land and the people of Telangana. The land and the people generated the income, which in turn paid the onerous taxes levied upon them. On the one hand, the alien state that ruled them became rich; but on the other hand, the people became poor. This diversion of funds, even in a democratic framework, has been one of the main justifications and rationale for the creation of a separate state of Telangana.

Essays 7 and 8 explore two reports, the Pundit Sundarlal Report and the Report of the Official Commission appointed to investigate the Mulki Riots of 1952. Essay 7, through the Pundit Sundarlal Report, describes the trauma and tragedies that followed the annexation of the Hyderabad state by the Indian Dominion in late-1948. It also takes the opportunity given by the recent availability of rough notes, drafts and final report to analyse the changes, deletions and additions that occurred in the Report, thus also emerging as an interesting case study in report writing. The Mulki Riots report studied in Essay 8 had been formally submitted to the Government of Hyderabad State and was then presented to the Legislative Assembly. The report was lost after that, but was retrieved and recovered from the library of the University of Wisconsin in 2013.

Essay 9 is a detailed study of differences in household income between Hindus and Muslims in Telangana. It examines the data sourced from the Sachar Committee and arrives at a conclusion that is vastly different from that of the Committee. It also examines the Kundu Report as well as the data gathered from surveys conducted in the Minority Concentration Districts. All of this data confirms that the differences between Hindus and Muslims in terms of household income are not significant. The essay concludes with an analysis of the Sudhir Committee that was set up to investigate the conditions of the Muslim population of Telangana. The sample survey conducted by the Committee was one of the most rigorous and robust surveys ever conducted concerning the Muslim minority in India. The data produced by the Committee Report unambiguously shows that Muslim household income equals to or exceeds that of Hindu household income across all geographical regions of Telangana. Considering the larger household size, a lower proportion of household falling within the working age, and lower worker participation ratio of women in Muslim households, the resultant high income levels are evidence of the Muslim enterprise and hard work.

Therefore, first three essays establish the Kakatiya base on which Telangana rests. The next three essays examine land productivity, land tax, and the income, taxes and wealth that the state of Telangana generated for over 700 years. The last three essays are concerned with the issue of the Great Minority, that is, the Muslims of India. It describes briefly the fall of Muslim power in Telangana in 1948, the massacres that followed the event, the brief outburst of violence four years later, and finally, the current economic well-being of the Muslim population in India, and especially, in Telangana. This book is a culmination of the various issues on the subject that have engaged me for years, and I hope now to get them across to the readers who might be interested in the same.

References

Pingle, Gautam. 2014. *The Fall and Rise of Telangana*. Hyderabad: Orient BlackSwan.

——. 2017. 'Paddy Yields in Pre-Industrial South India', *Economic and Political Weekly* 52(16).

1

The Kakatiyas

The Beginning

Indian history is plagued by a lack of documentation and availability of information. A series of invasions by Muslim powers as well as their iconoclastic drive for the destruction and desecration of temples and other forms of non-Muslim texts has been one of the major causes of this problem. Also, a structural problem relating to the recording of documentation on palm leaves, which required continuous renewal as the palm leaf deteriorated over time, also contributed to the difficulty. Much of Hindu chronicling as well as Hindu sacred texts have been part of the oral tradition and required state support for them to be maintained in palm leaf manuscripts. This support was usually by way of direct grants or grants of tax-free land and *agraharams* (whole villages) in perpetuity to individual or groups of Brahmin scholars and their successors.

Even as early as 1866, Max Müeller bemoaned the loss of Indian history that was occurring through the neglect of traditional manuscripts written on palm leaves. These manuscripts had to be regularly re-copied due to their natural deterioration. He compares the neglect of these archives to the loss of power of the *rajahs* (kings) and to how the succeeding British imperial government neglected the traditional state role of maintaining these archives. He was outraged when the East India Company rejected the archives that were offered to them (Müller 1903, Vol. 1: 345).

Thus, the recounting of Indian history depends massively on the existence of documentation made during the period in question, or even on records of the immediately succeeding periods. In order to get an understanding of what transpired in the past, historians had to put together various bits of information derived from inscriptions, travellers' tales and court chronicles. The credibility of many of these pieces of information has to be checked against other sources to ascertain their validity. The farther we look into the past, the more unclear the view becomes due to the shortage of credible information.

The period from 1000–1323 AD forms a critical 300-year period for the Kakatiya history. The early periods are scarce in information, although later periods get richer as documentation gets more extensive and is preserved. For Indian history, the period starting from 1000 AD is critical since north India was subject to massive and steady raids and invasions by Muslims from outside India. These raids and invasions resulted in the consolidation of Muslim rule in most of northern India, displacing the existing Hindu kingdoms. However, most of peninsular India, which was south of the Vindhya mountain range, was not affected by Muslim invasions till about 1200 AD.

When dealing with Kakatiya history, we have to acknowledge the significant contribution of P. V. Parabrahma Sastry (2016), whose work on the Kakatiyas is a classic and has not been excelled or challenged. In this work, we draw extensively and heavily on his book, *The Kakatiyas*, and try and summarise the narrative. The work of Venkatramanayya and Sarma (1960), Venkatramanayya and Sastry (1957), and Sastry (2016) are also important sources in this context.

During the period 1000–1200 AD, several Hindu kingdoms such as the Rashtrakuta and Chalukya kingdoms dominated the Deccan plateau. Further south, there were the Hoyasala, Pandya and Chola kingdoms. Initially, the Kakatiya rulers were tributaries of the Rashtrakuta empire. Later, when the Rashtrakuta empire succumbed to the Chalukyan empire, the Kakatiyas became tributaries of the new Chalukyan dynasty.

As per the norms of the feudal-tributary relationship with the rulers, the Kakatiyas acknowledged the sovereignty of the Rashtrakuta king, paid tribute, and provided troops for the Rashtrakuta army. Subsidiary rulers or vassals received titles in, and authority over, the areas that they held. They also attempted to expand the areas under their control by waging war or conspiring against neighbouring vassals. In such a situation, the vassals' relationship to the Rashtrakuta king was critical. In situations where members of the royal family disputed the Rashtrakuta succession, the Kakatiyas, like other vassals, had the opportunity of making the hard choice of backing one side or the other. Depending on the outcome and their commitment to the winner or loser, they either gained territory and status or lost everything they had in their possession.

Again, the Rashtrakuta empire was subject to attack, invasion and conquest by the Chalukya empire based at Kalyani. In the classical Hindu tradition, this did not seriously affect the vassals as they usually acknowledged the new paramount dynasty. The vassals would inevitably renew their loyalties to the new rulers and would be given confirmation regarding their status and territories. Rapidly, the balance would get restored.

We can estimate the extent of the Kakatiya empire at different periods from the location of inscriptions and their texts. Talbot (2001) provides exciting and useful maps of the Kakatiye empire, summing up her observations in the following words:

> [The period 1175–1324] marks the rise of the Kakatiyas to a hegemonic position within the region. Beginning with their base in northern inland Andhra, the Kakatiyas gradually built up a political network that at its very height encompassed roughly two-thirds of the territory of the modern state [of undivided Andhra Pradesh]. While the Kakatiyas were forced at times to repel invading armies, they were never subjugated by any other South Indian polity, unlike the Eastern Chalukyas (2001: 30–33).

She further says about the fate of the empire:

> The good fortune of the Kakatiyas resulted from the division of peninsular India in this period into four regional kingdoms that were equally balanced in power—the polities commanded by the Yadavas or Seunas of Southern Maharashtra and Northern Karnataka, the Hoysalas of Mysore, and the Pandyas of the Tamil country, in addition to the Kakatiyas of Andhra. Armed incursions of the Delhi Sultanate disrupted the peninsular balance of power beginning in the late thirteenth century and eventually brought about the collapse of all four regional kingdoms (ibid.: 26).

The occurrence and location of inscriptional evidence indicate that the Kakatiya domain included most of Rayalaseema as well as central and south coastal Andhra. Talbot's study is based on a meticulous analysis of inscriptions and it provides a broad account of the land and the people of Telangana.

The Kakatiyas: The Feudal Phase

The origin of the Kakatiya dynasty is shrouded in darkness, but it is clear from the inscriptions that they belong to the fourth caste; that is, they are Sudras, as are most of the ruling families in the region south of the Vindhya range. There has been some discussion in the existing literature on the subject about whether the Kakatiyas were Kshatriyas; but the overwhelming evidence suggests that they belonged to the Sudra caste.

The Bhotpur inscription of Malyala Gumda (Gundaya) *senani* (the equivalent of a general or *senapati*) dated 1259 AD clearly states: 'Among these were the fourth caste of innumerable greatness, honoured, the birthplace of wealth [i.e., the breeder of wealth] great in number, very pure like the milky ocean among the four oceans and having excellent men; In that [fourth caste] there is the praiseworthy Kakatiya dynasty' (His Exalted Highness [HEH] The Nizam's Government 1940: 159).

In this context, the inscriptions are more credible sources of information than later narratives such as that of Vidyanatha, which suggest a Kshatriya status for the dynasty. After reviewing the evidence, Sastry (2016) concludes: 'Therefore, instead of believing in the statements of the other records that are rather panegyric it is quite reasonable to accept the statements of Gundaya's records' (Sastry 2016: 29; Venkatramanayya and Sastry 1957: 197).

The name they took on comes from either a place called Kakati or is derived from their household goddess, Kakati, who is one of the forms of the goddess Durga. Their original home is in the present-day Kandhar in Nanded district of Maharashtra. The particular locality of their residence was named Kakatipura (Sastry 2016: 22–23). In many inscriptions, their subsequent capital, Orugallu or Warangal, was referred to as Kakatipura, by virtue of its being the capital city of the Kakatiya dynasty (Venkatramanayya and Sastry 1957: 197).

The founder of the Kakatiya dynasty, as per the historical record in the inscriptions, was called Venna, and he was born in the Durjaya family. He was one of the commanders in the Rashtrakuta army (Sastry 2016: 37). He lived in the early years of the ninth century. His descendants, Gunda I, Gunda II and Gunda III also functioned as commanders of the Rashtrakuta army. Gunda III participated in the successful attack by the Rashtrakuta ruler Krishna II on Vengi, on the Andhra coast, in around 895 AD. All of this information comes from inscriptions recording various victories of the time. However, after Gunda III fell in the battle of Peruvanguru (a village near modern Nidadavole), the Rashtrakuta king conferred the region of Korvai and Manukota on Gunda III's son, Erra. In due course, Erra was succeeded by his son, Betiya, and Betiya's son, Gunda IV, later succeeded him in around 956 AD (Sastry 2016: 37–39).

Soon, Vengi was in the throes of a civil war. The rulers of Vengi, Eastern Chalukaya king Ammaraja II and his half-brother the senior Prince Danarnava, fought for power. Krishna III, the Rashtrakuta king, and the overlord of Vengi, ordered his feudatory Gunda IV (r. 955–95) to intervene and help Danarnava, which the latter did successfully.

At his request, a Brahmin called Dommana, who had performed the ritual called Karpativara for Gunda IV's benefit, was gifted the village of Mangallu as an *agraharam*. This information has been detailed in the Mangallu Grant in about 956 AD. Gunda IV was instrumental in getting the Mangallu Grant issued by the Chalukya senior Prince Danarnava, which details the genealogy of the Kakatiya family for the previous three generations and it constitutes the earliest record of the Kakatiya chiefs (Sastry 2016: 14–15).

Thus, the Rashtrakuta empire began to yield its power to the Western Chalukya based in Kalyan. The Western Chalukya king, Tailapa II, replaced the Rashtrakuta dominance in Telangana with his own rule. Danarnava, lord of Vengi, was killed in the process. Taking advantage of this confusion in the west and the power vacuum in the east, Gunda IV proclaimed his independence instead of submitting to the Chalukya king. The original rulers of Korvai, whom Gunda IV had displaced with the support of the Rashtrakuta king, opposed this. The Korvai ex-rulers received help from the now dominant Kalyani Chalukyas. They, in turn, sent their general Viriyala Erra in support of the Korvai ex-rulers, and Gunda IV was killed in battle in 995 AD (Sastry 2016: 39–42).

Gunda IV's son, Garudanka Beta I (r. 1000–52), received the support of his maternal aunt, Kamavasini, who was also fortunately the wife of Viriyala Erra, who managed to secure the fief of Anamkonda for Garudanka Beta I, who thereupon acknowledged the sovereignty of the Kalyani Chalukyas, which was, in any case, conditional on his receiving the fief. Anamkonda Visaya included parts of present-day Warangal district and the Sanigaram region of Karimnagar district. Garudanka Beta I is said to have participated in the Kalyani Chalukya attack against the Chola capital at Kanchi. He continued to serve as the feudatory of the Kalyani Chalukyas till 1052 AD when his son Prola I succeeded him. Four inscriptions—at Gudur, Bayyaram, Sanigaram and the Kazipet Darga—enable the reconstruction of this part of the history (Sastry 2016: 42–444).

Prola I (r. 1052–76) conducted successful campaigns against Bhadranga of Chakrakuta-*vishaya* and the Kokana *mandala*. This extraordinary success resulted in his being granted the Anamkonda Visaya permanently as well as the right to issue coinage and to use the Chalukya emblem. Prola I adopted the *Varaha* (God Vishnu's third avatar or incarnation as a boar) or *Garuda* (Vishnu's vehicle) as his emblems, which continued till the end as the Kakatiya symbol on their banners, coins and cattle. With these rights and privileges, Prola I was on the way to becoming a semi-independent ruler. He annexed the nearby areas of Vemulawada, Gunhasagaram and Kadparthi, thus greatly enlarging his domain. He was also a shrewd ruler who had the Kesamudram tank constructed in the Warangal District, which is still in existence. Prola I died in 1076 AD, and his son Beta II succeeded him (Sastry 2016: 44–47).

By this time, the Chalukyan kingdom was on the brink of a civil war over the issue of succession to its throne. Beta II (r. 1076–1108) was lucky as he supported the eventual winner and received the neighbouring territories of Sabbimandalam and Munigonda, which resulted in further expansion of his domain. It also enhanced his status significantly. The diplomatic skills of his minister, Vaija, coupled with his armed might, allowed him to maintain his hold on the newly acquired territories. He was succeeded by his son, Durgaraja (r. 1108–16), who within eight years suddenly made way for his brother Prola II (r. 1116–57) (Sastry 2016: 47–50).

In 1138 AD, Jagdekamalla II succeeded his father, Bholukamalla, to the Chalukyan throne (Sastry 2016: 84). However, this provoked a revolt by Kumar Tailapa in Telangana against his nephew's accession. Kumar Tailapa had already been engaged in a 'silent revolt' against his brother Bholukamalla since 1127 AD (ibid.: 84). Soon after his accession to the throne, King Jagdekamalla II turned his attention to Telangana and led his army personally to crush the revolt. Prola II was the only loyal feudatory in the region who stood with the king against his uncle, Kumar Tailapa (ibid.: 81–85). The latter was captured and forgiven as per the the standard Hindu tradition. However, he lost his rights over Kandurunadu, which he had enjoyed for more than 25 years.

Prola II had intervened twice on behalf of his king (Sastry 2016: 84–85). From 1130–36 AD, the intervention was carried out in order to restore Udaya Choda to the Pangallu domain, resulting in Udaya Choda acknowledging Kakatiya suzerainty and becoming a Kakatiya vassal. Next, it was to help dispose of Kumar Tailapa himself. Even as the civil war continued to rage in the Chalukyan empire, Prola II maintained his loyalty to the Chalukyan king. The domains of Kanuduru, Polavasa, Pangallu and Mirayagudem revolted against the central power, but the revolts were put down by Prola II (ibid.: 86–87).

Accompanied by one of his generals, Inangala Bramhi Reddy, Prola II intervened to help the Chola king, Rajaraja II, to suppress a rebellion in the coastal area, but unfortunately died in battle (Sastry 2016: 88). His victors were many—Chadaraja of the Kota family, Manamasatya and Mallideva of the Haihaya family of Kona, the Suryavamsi chief of Mahadeva Raja, and a subordinate of the Eastern Chalukya king of Vengi, Malla Vishnuvardana (ibid.: 87). He had taken on the entire block of subordinates of the Vengi kingdom. It would not be the last time that the Kakatiyas of Warangal would engage in battle with the feudatories of Vengi.

The Kakatiyas were fortunate in that their general, Ivangala Bramhi Reddy, survived the disastrous battle and returned to proclaim Rudradeva, the eldest son of Prola II, as lord of Anamkonda Vishya (Sastry 2016: 88). Through all these events, by the time he died in 1157 AD after a 41-year-long reign, Prola II had laid the foundation of the Kakatiya dynasty. This development allowed his son Rudra to proclaim independence and direct his general, Racherla Rudra, to attack the Bottu chief of Korvai and take over the domain (ibid.: 83–87).

Fellow (Chalukya) Feudal Vassals

It is not as if the Kakatiyas exercised full dominance over the Telangana region, even if on behalf of the Kalyani Chalukyas. There were other equally powerful rulers of neighbouring domains, who acknowledged the Eastern Chalukya king of Vengi as their sovereign.

The Chalukyas of Modigunda ruled the neighbouring Korvai region (Sastry 2016: 51–57). They seem to have been a minor branch of the Eastern Chalukyas, and as such, may have enjoyed a higher degree of independence. They were also able to receive the support of the Western Chalukya king, Bhima II (934–44 AD), to become lords of Korvai, from which position the Kakatiya ruler Rudra displaced them in 1163 AD.

The Polavasa chiefs took their name from the domain of the Polas or Polavasa in Jagtial district, northwest of Warangal (Sastry 2016: 58–64). The Thousand Pillar Temple inscription and other epigraphs refer to Medaraja of the Polavasa family as an enemy of Rudra, the Kakatiya chief. The Polavasa domain extended from Polavasa to Narsampet, bordering the Anamkonda Visaya. Members of both families had initially been Rashtrakuta generals and were given adjacent domains in Telangana. When in 950 AD the Rashtrakutas were overpowered by the Kalyani Chalukyas, the new rulers allowed both the Kakatiya and the Medaraja chiefs to continue as *mahamandaleshwaras* (great lords of the regions, or governors) of their domains. There existed a peaceful relationship between the two families for many decades until they backed opposite sides in the succession crisis that overtook the Chalukyan kingdom. The Kakatiya rulers, Prola II and Rudra, backed the winning candidate, Jagadekamalla II, and jointly attacked the Polavasa chief, Gumda, and killed him, while his brother, Medaraja II, went into exile. The members of the Medaraja family were followers of the Jain faith. This incident is another illustration of how feudatories could suffer or benefit from the succession crises and battles.

The Kanduru Chodas were another dominant family holding the domain of Kandurunadu, comprising the Jadcharla and Achampet *talukas* (administrative divisions) of the present-day Mahboobnagar district, and the Nalgonda and Miryalguda *talukas* of Nalgonda district (Sastry 2016: 64–68). Their capitals were at Koduru and Pangallu. They ruled this domain for 100 years from 1060–1160 AD. In 1091 AD, when its ruler Bhima Choda II died, his ashes were carried all the way to Gaya on the Ganges for immersion! This extraordinary journey indicates the status and power of this feudatory family. During his lifetime, Bhima Choda II had acquired the domain of Kanduru Vishaya as a result of his support to Vikramaditya VI's successful effort to seize the Kalyani Chalukya throne from Someshwara II. Once again, this suggests the dynamic changes of feudal domains due to succession wars of their sovereigns.

By 1124 AD, the young Kalyan Chalukya prince, Kumar Tailapa, divided Kanduru *Nadu*, which was his appanage (a grant of territory for his maintenance), between the two Kanduru Choda brothers: Kanduru Vishaya in Mahboobnagar went to Bhima III, and Panagallu Vishaya to Gokarna Choda. This type of action once again illustrates how a great domain can be reduced in size and power by its sovereign. This arrangement continued till the Kalyani Chalukya emperor, Tribhuvanmala, died in 1126 AD, and following his death, Bholokamalla Someshwara III succeeded him. Bhima III withdrew his loyalty, but Gokarna's support to the new Chalukya ruler remained intact. In the ensuing power struggle, Gokarna Choda lost his life. His son, Udaya Choda, succeeded and continued to be a feudatory of the Kalyani Chalukyan emperor. However, later he acknowledged the supremacy of the Kakatiya rulers who had declared their independence in about 1158 AD. Udaya Choda lived till 1176 AD and was succeeded by his two sons, Bhima IV and Gokarna, who continued to be subordinates of the Kakatiyas; thereafter the family passed out of history.

We therefore see how feudal domains and their ruling families could disappear if luck and history were against them. There was hardly anything permanent about feudal domains as such, although the structure continued to be the only form of governance that was possible in that age, given the poor state of transport and communications, and the slow speed at which information, orders and reports travelled. When these aspects improved, centralised structures became viable, effective and efficient.

Jaggadeva was a prince of the Paramara royal family of Malwa in Central India (Sastry 2016: 69–73). He had been appointed *mahamandaleshwara* by the Chalukyan king, Vikramaditya VI, for four years from 1104–08 AD. His domain with his capital at Kollipaka consisted of 7,000 villages. In 1106 AD, he defeated the kings of Vengi, Dravida, Chitrakota and Mahira. However, this attracted the attention of his overlord, Vikramaditya VI, as Jaggadeva's expansion tended to be towards his Paramara home. In order to avoid this attempted consolidation of feudal entities, the king appointed his son, Kumara Someshwara, as the Viceroy of Kollipaka. Jaggadeva was forced to leave Telangana. This opportunity was seized by the Kakatiya ruler, Beta II, to align himself with the new *mahamandaleshwara*, Kumara Someshwara. Jaggadeva, in alliance with the Polavasa chief, Medaraja II, retaliated against the Kakatiyas. Medaraja II had been in exile, and together with Jaggadeva, he attacked Anamkonda, the Kakatiya capital. However, Beta II's brother, Prola II, defeated them. This set of events one again reveals the dynamics of feudal interaction with the sovereign, as well as the capacity and willingness of feudal rulers to fight with each other, with disastrous consequences for both the parties.

The Feudal Structure

It is one thing to have a feudal society, but given the exigencies of the government, this society had a complex structure with various levels of importance, power and status. Much depended on their ability to raise armed forces and to mobilise tax revenues. It was also vital that the feudal vassals owed and demonstrated loyalty to their overlord, for which he may have taken and received formal oaths.

The overlord not only granted them territories to rule and tax, but also imposed an obligation of providing fighting men and units as well as tribute. He also granted them symbols of status, such as the right to sit on a throne, have an umbrella held over their heads, use of fly whisks and palanquins, use of the overlord's emblem, the right to strike coin, and the right to have *pancha maha shabda* (five types of sound) played before them. In fact, this type of a feudal structure is common throughout India and other parts of the world.

Even though the ruler fixed the position of the individual vassal in the hierarchy, their positions were capable of being upgraded; though it would be a rash ruler who tried to downgrade a vassal from his position. In the Kakatiya pattern, titles (and power and responsibility) in ascending order were *Mahamandelswara*, *Mahamandalika*, *Mandalika*, *Mahasamanta*, and *Samantha*. The expression 'maha' was the type of upgrade before the move into a different category altogether (Ganapathi 2000: 14–15).

With respect to the bureaucracy, the terms *mahapradana*, *pradana*, *pregeddda*, *amatya* and *mantri* occur in the inscriptions. These were posts that were largely occupied by Brahmins, who were paid salaries by, and were responsible directly to, the overlord. They staffed the central government as well as acted as inspectors and negotiators with the vassals (Ganapathi 2000: 16). The Kakatiyas, under Ganapathideva, developed an elaborate bureaucracy consisting of 72 *niyogas* classified as *mahapradhani*, *sanadhivigraha*, *sarvadhikari*, *srikaranadhipathi* and *katakarakshapala*[1] as a way of centralising his administration (Pramila 2002: 30).

As far as the military was concerned, titles also denoted status and functions. The Kakatiya military system was called *nayankara* and it overlapped in some ways with the political feudal system because many personnel occupied positions in both systems. The ordinary soldier was called *bantu*, his superior was called *lemka*, and then there was a whole range of *sahinis* (commanders or generals). There were *ashvasahini* denoting cavalry, *gajasahini* denoting the elephant forces, while a simple *sahini* would be in charge of the infantry and archers. The term '*nayaka*' was a general term for a military leader and also for a feudal chief. It would seem that there was little distinction in terms of functions between a political feudal and a military general. However, the term '*dandanayaka*', often used, probably distinguished a military *nayaka* from the civil *nayaka*. As distinct from a *nayaka*, a *senapati* or *senani* would denote a general in command of a large body of armed forces (Ganapathi 2000: 130–43).

Many inscriptions state that consent was obtained from the *astadasamahapraja* or *ashtadasapraja* (18 *jatis* or sub-castes), or a request from them was considered, as they were representatives of the village. These 18 groups have been identified as: [1] *Namahajanulu* (priests), [2] *Enakaram* (warriors), [3] *Kampulu* (farmer caste), [4] *Dbalanja Settigandru* (traders), [5] *Komatis* (traders), [6] *Iddavaru* (toddy tappers), [7] *Gollavaru* (shepherds), [8] *Akasalivaru* (ironsmiths), [9] *Salevaru* (weavers), [10] *Srivaisnavulu* (Srivishnava priests), [11] *Velamagaru* (Velamas), [12] *Illaris*, [13] *Gandvaru*, [14] *Nayakulu* (*nayakas*), [15] *Redlu* (Reddys), [16] *Karnalu* (Brahmin village accountants), [17] *Telikivenurur* (oil pressers) and [18] *Nayilu* (washermen) (Pramila 2002: 158).[2] These records seem credible as they also reflect the current reality of Telangana's village demography. Names of many other communities appear as part of the *astadasamahapraja* in other inscriptions, and the total number goes up to 30 (Pramila 2002: 158–66).

Whenever the Kakatiyas invaded and absorbed independent neighbouring territories, they tended to re-establish the old ruler or his son, provided he acknowledged the Kakatiyas as overlords. In some cases, marriage with female members of the defeated family and absorption of the younger male members as generals in the Kakatiya army allowed for the build-up of personal relationships even after the trauma of defeat. Apart from this particular situation, the Kakatiya family also inter-married with some vassal families. In the case of the Natavadi family, the marital relationships were renewed over generations.

The Imperial Phase

As we have seen, Rudradeva (r. 1158–95) inherited the territorial base acquired and consolidated by his father, Prola II. Fortunately, Rudradeva was the eldest son and did not encounter any opposition from his brothers. This natural and easy succession, combined with the succession warfare for the Kalyani Chalukyan throne, offered to Rudradeva an opportunity to assert independence and establish the Kakatiya kingdom. Gradually, his kingdom expanded further in the next century to constitute a veritable empire. However, the core area for all this future development was Telangana.

Rudradeva continued the expansion of the Kakatiya domain by attacking Dommaraja, the leader of an aboriginal tribe located in Sabbimalam, with its headquarters in Nagunur (in the present-day Karimnagar district). Another target was Medaraja II, the ruler of Polavasa *Desa* (a specific administrative and political unit) (the present-day Jagtial), who had earlier been defeated by Prola II and had gone into exile. The third was Mailagideva, who was probably a Kalachuri prince. The three of them formed an alliance with the last two, Medaraja II and Mailagideva, being devotees of the Jain faith. However, as the inscription specifically states that Rudradeva, a staunch Shaivite, defeated this Jain alliance. Subbimalam came under the control of the Kakatiyas, and Rudradeva put his general and minister, Vellanki Gangadharam, who was the architect of the victory, in charge of this newly acquired domain.

The inscription states that Dommaraja, after the defeat by Rudradeva's forces, crossed the Godavari river and found refuge in the jungles there. As for Medaraja II, he was, after his defeat, 'unwilling to offer, it is said, his daughter to Rudra, and he sued for peace, and gave up his wealth, pride and family reputation' (Sastry 2016: 92). Maligideva, the Kalachuri prince (either the son or brother of Kalachuri Bijjala, who had usurped the Chalukyan throne), seems to have retreated to Kalyani. His territories up to Zaheerabad now became part of the growing Kakatiya kingdom. The consolidation of Telangana's western border at Zaheerabad and the northern border along the Godavari river seem to date from this event.

Rudradeva then turned his attention to the south. We can locate four kings from the Annumkonda record: Bhima, Gokarna, Chododaya and Tailapa, whose history is cited by Venkataramanayya and Sarma (1960) as follows:

> Gokarna was killed by Bhima; Chododaya died as a result of the "bewilderment born of the fear produced by the prowess of Rudradeva", and Tailapa "with body completely overcome by dysentery" died from the fear of Rudradeva. Then Bhima enjoyed the kinship for a short time. He had killed his brother [Gokarna] by poisoning his food or otherwise while he was dining, and took his stepmother for his wife. To put an end to his misdeeds Rudradeva invaded his territories, and Bhima fled to the forests with his mother, brothers, and wives ... (1960: 587–88).

It further states:

> Rudradeva's war with the Bhima appears to have been one event of outstanding importance which happened during the early years of his rule. The struggle between them is described at some length in the Annumkonda inscription, no less than 12 out of the total number of 50 verses being devoted to a description of it. In recounting the causes of the war the author of the inscription enumerates first the atrocious crimes committed by Bhima, which provoked Rudradeva to launch an attack on him (ibid.).

The narrative then delves into the exploits of Bhima in details:

> Bhima's first evil deed was the capture and execution of a person called Gokarna; he next appropriated the territories of the two chiefs named Chododaya and Tailapa, both of whom are said to have died of the fear caused by Rudradeva's military successes.... Bhima had gathered together a number of the petty chiefs around him, and proclaiming himself king became Rudra's rival for the sovereignty over Telangana. Therefore it became necessary for Rudra to declare war on Bhima in order to humble him and establish his own supremacy over the whole country (ibid.).

Two epigraphs, from Kishtapuram and Rachuru, established the identities of Rudradeva's enemies and also the approximate years when this conflict occurred, 1157 AD and 1162 AD. These conquests established the boundaries of the core Kakatiya empire, which now constitute those of the modern Telangana state (Sastry 2016: 91; Venkatramanayya and Sarma 1960: 588–90). Rudradeva found it more difficult to defeat Chododaya, as its capital, Kandur, was protected by forests as well as a strong fort. He destroyed the forest by fire and reduced the fort. He, however, built the big tank in the middle of the city and resettled it by bringing in population brought from elsewhere. He also built a large tank called Rudrasamudram at Panagallu. Rudradeva seems to have married Chododaya's daughter Padma (Venkatramanayya and Sarma 1960: 588).

Rudradeva's attention now turned east towards the Godavari delta and the kingdom of Vengi, where his father had met his major defeat and death. In 1181 AD, the Velnati king Koluttunga Rajendra Choda II died, and this was followed by a succession crisis (Sastry 2016: 98). At about the same time, civil war broke out in Palnadu, the cause of which is not clear. However, it was a fratricidal war and weakened the political conditions of coastal Andhra. This war presented an opportunity for Rudradeva, and he took it.

Rudradeva allied with Rajaraja II, the Chalukya-Chola king, and invaded the delta and established his hold on coastal Andhra without much resistance (Sastry 2016: 97). He subjugated Dharanikota, but refrained from annexing it; instead, he gave it to Kota II, the son of Bhima III, who had lost his life defending his domain from Rudradeva. This was a traditional tactic and strategy that allowed for minimal disruption and restoration of order after the conclusion of war.

Rudradeva then attacked the Kondapadumatis and fought the battle on the Krishna river, on the borders of Vengi, and routed his enemies. He placed his younger brother, Dugga Bhupa, in charge of governing the area, but the Velanadu rulers were able to re-acquire the area (Sastry 2016: 98). Rudradeva paved the way for his successors to expand towards the coast, which eventually they did.

Based on Deogiri inscriptions, Mahalingam (1957) suggests that soon after the death of its king, Bhillama, Rudradeva sent a force under his brother, Mahadeva, to attack Deogiri in 1191 AD (1987: 143). The attackers seem to have even reached Deogiri. But the new king, Jaitugi, retaliated in 1194 AD against the Kakatiya kingdom and Rudradeva died in the battle. Moreover, in this battle, Jaitugi captured Ganapatideva, Mahadeva's son, and took him back to Deogiri.

The state of the kingdom and the very confidence and enthusiasm displayed by its ruler, Rudradeva, are illustrated not only in the construction of the 1,000-pillar temple at Hanamkonda/Warangal, but also in the inscription found there:

> A capital city named Anumakonda which was like the capital of the goddess of fortune raised to a great state by the rise of the excellent and full grace [*lila*] of God Siva who was there: which was full of delight [Rati] like the city of Cupid: and it is like Mahendri in being possessed of temples Jishnu and Vishnu [as image in its temples] and [which was] beautiful with the charm of plantain trees [with the amorous play of Rambha] ... (Archaeological Survey of India, Hyderabad Circle, Blog Post).

The inscription further reads:

> Where, the women were indeed the metropolis of Cupid, having eyes like the petals of the blue lilies and slim bodies; ornaments to the women of the three worlds and had bodies weighed down by the weight of big and high breasts:
>
> [Where] in the houses of the excellent Brahmins clever parrots, though prevented join the students and study the Vedas [which contain] all the *Vedangas* all appropriate subjects, beautiful histories and [which are] in well studies *pada* and *krama* methods ... (ibid.).

And it concludes:

> [and where] in the house of courtesans the loud and sweet sound of young parrots make all the quarters resound–[parrots] imitating the sounds of amorous sports in sexual enjoyment, which are during day-time like full moon of the tremulous ocean of the excitement of love ... (Ibid.).

Rudradeva had died childless in 1195 AD, and his brother, Mahadeva who was born from the same parents, succeeded him (Sastry 2016: 103). Muppamamba, sister of the Natavadi chief, Guggaraja, was the mother of both Rudra and Mahadeva. Mahadeva, in turn, married his two daughters, Kunadamba and Mailambika, to their cousins, sons of Natavadi Buddha and future chiefs, Rudra I and Rudra II (Pakkidi Rudra), respectively (Ganapathi 2000: 39). Marriages of each generation strengthened political bonds between the two families. Venkatramanayya and Sarma, however, suggest that both the sisters were married to Rudra, implying that there was only one husband (1960: 599). Venkatramanayya and Sastry earlier wrote: '[T]he marriage of two sisters with that of Rudra still remains a puzzle. There is a possibility of there being stepsisters, Mailamamba [*sic.*] being Ganapathi's own sister and Mailambika a stepsister' (1957: 211). This confusion has been created by the similar names of the two Natavadi brothers. In their inscriptions, the Natavadi proudly proclaim their origin and social status as 'born of Brahma's feet, of the *chaturvarna*', or the Sudra caste (Hultzsch 1902: 157; Sastry 2016: 29).

Perhaps to recover his son, Ganapathideva, from captivity, and also to avenge his own defeat and Rudra's death by the Seuna/Yadavas, Mahadeva invaded the Seuna/Yadava kingdom of Deogiri. This invasion occurred while the Yadavas were engaged in a war with their southern neighbour, the Hoysalas. However, Mahadeva's attack failed, and he died in battle a mere three years after his accession (Sastry 2016: 103–04).

Mahadeva's death and the provocation to the Yadavas resulted in retribution, and the Yadavas were even able to take control of the administration of the Kakatiya territory from Deogiri itself. However, at this juncture, a new hero entered the stage. Racherla (Reddy) Rudra managed to organise the Kakatiya army and negotiate with the Yadavas for the release of Mahadeva's son, Ganapathideva, who was their captive. Racherla Rudra also managed to suppress revolts by feudal vassals in Telangana while awaiting Ganapathideva's release (Ganapathi 2000: 46–49; Sastry 2016: 103–07). Racherla Rudra also seems to have fought off an invasion by the Chola emperor, Koluttunga III, who had managed to capture Warangal (Venkatramanayya and Sarma 1960: 600). Due to Racherla Rudra's loyalty and efficiency, Ganapathideva (r. 1199–1262) was able to ascend the throne soon after his release from Deogiri.

The uncontroverted fact is that both the Kakatiya kings were killed in battle by Jaitugi, but Ganapathideva was not harmed while he was a prisoner of Deogiri for nearly eight years. It is therefore not surprising that Jaitugi claimed that he had placed Ganapathideva on his ancestral throne. Ganapathideva promised friendship between the two dynasties and their domains. The differences in the Deogiri and Kakatiya narratives are subtle, but they help to understand the situation and the confusion caused while recording this history.

The relationship between the Kakatiya and Seuna/Yadava dynasties should have been friendly and supportive, considering that they were neighbours and had together been Chalukyan vassals. Yet, it seems that the Kakatiya territorial ambitions took a northerly direction and were rebuffed brutally on two occasions. As we shall see later, the Seuna/Yadava dynasty took advantage of the death of Ganapathideva and the succession of a woman to the Kakatiya throne and attacked its southern neighbour.

On the strong foundations laid by his grandfather, Prola II, and his uncle, Rudradeva, and assisted by Racherla Rudra, Ganapathideva ruled for 62 long years. During this period, the Kakatiya empire reached its pinnacle in terms of peace and progress (Sastry 2016: 103–04). Ganapathideva commenced his reign with an invasion of the Velnadu kingdom, which his ancestors had always sought to conquer. He invaded it in 1201 AD and moved to take over Divi. His general, Malyala Chaumunda, managed to overcome the strong fortifications of Divi island and plundered its treasury 'full of diamonds' in 1203 AD. Once again, in keeping with the tradition, the territories were not annexed, and the Ayya chiefs of Divi were allowed to continue as Kakatiya subordinates. To further consolidate their relationship, the Ayya ruler, Pinna Choda, gave his two daughters, Naramba and Peramba, to Ganapathideva in marriage. The Ayya son, Jaya or Jayapa, was taken into the Kakatiya army and was known famously as *gajasenapathi* (general of elephant corps) (Venkatramanayya and Sarma 1960: 602, 616–17).

After Divi, Ganapathideva turned his attention to Velanadu, which he captured, but in 1208 AD, he had to withdraw his army as the Cholas had invaded the Kakatiya empire (Venkatramanayya and Sarma 1960: 602; 1957: 212). After tackling the Chola invasion, Ganapathideva returned to Velandu and defeated and killed its ruler, Prithiviswara, in 1210 AD. The inscriptions give credit not only to Ganapathideva, but also to the Telugu Choda king of Nellore, Tikkabhupala, and a *mahamandaleshwara* Ballaya of Kammanadu. Ganapathideva appointed his young Ayya brother-in-law, Jaya, *senapati* and the governor of Velnadu in 1213 AD. With this, Ganapathideva had completed the annexation of *Kammarastra* and Velanadu into his kingdom. He had also successfully intervened in Nellore, restoring Tikkabhupala to the throne of his father, Manumasiddhi I, who had been defeated by Kollatunga Rajendra Chola. Tikkabhupala's father's brothers, Nallasiddhi and later Tammusiddhi, occupied the throne, supported by, and owing allegiance to, the Chola king. The inscription of Jaya *senani* dated 1231 AD, the Mathwada inscription of 1228 AD, and the Chebrollu inscription of 1213 AD, all seem to suggest that Ganapathideva continued the invasion of the Chola territory and plundered the Chola capital at Kanchi (Sastry 2016: 107–08).

Having moved his frontier towards the east and the sea, and south into the Chola country, Ganapathideva then turned his attention towards the northeast–to Kalinga. The Velanti king, after his defeat in the central province, seems to have retreated north of the Godavari. Ganapathideva sent his army under the command of Soma-*mantri* (minister) of the Induluri family and Raja *nayaka*, the general of Racherla Rudra there. The inscriptions of Katte *nayaka*, son of Raja *nayaka*, dated 1236 AD, as well as other inscriptions of Jayapa *senani*, indicate that the Kakatiya armies penetrated Kalinga as far as Aska in the Ganjam district (Sastry 2016: 109–11).

It would seem that Ganapathideva's desire to annex Vengi from 1212 AD onwards did not materialise completely. However, the inscriptions suggest his conquest of the Kolanu region by his general, Induluri Soma-*mantri*, took place, which inscriptions of 1240 AD and other inscriptions dated 1237 AD also support. Induluri Soma-*mantri* finally affected the conquest of Vengi and was made Lord of Kolanu (Sastry 2016: 112).

Ganapathideva's attention was drawn to Nellore when his subordinate and the Telugu Choda king of Nellore, Tikkabhupala, died in 1248 AD, and the kingdom was in confusion. Tikkabhupala's son, Manumasidha II, appealed to his overlord, Ganapathideva, for help, which came in the shape of a powerful army under the command of the *samantha* (chief feudatory), Bhoja, who reinstated him on his ancestral throne. The army continued into the Chola territory under the command of Bhoja, who seems to have fought the final battle at Palaiyaru in Tanjore district and captured Kanchi in 1250 AD. However, it seems that it was difficult for Manumasidha II to re-establish power at Kanchi, although he had succeeded to do so in Nellore.

After that, the Kakatiya armies marched against the Vaidumba chief, Rakkasa Ganga, who had earlier defeated Gangaya-*sahini* (general), the Kayastha commander of the army of the Telugu Choda king. Notwithstanding this, the Kakatiya armies defeated Rakkasa Ganga, and the territory of Pottapinadu, which had been seized by him, was taken back and given to the Telugu Choda king. Recognising the ability of Gangaya-*sahini*, despite his defeat, it is recorded in 1250 AD that Ganapathideva appointed him as 'superintendent of the 72 niyogas'. He also conferred upon him the region of Marjavadi, which Gangaya-*sahini* had conquered from Rakkasa Ganga, as his estate.

Manumasidha II continued to have problems with the south due to the invasion of the Pandyan king, Jatavaraman Sundara Pandya I, in about 1257 AD, who invaded Nellore and attacked the subordinate rulers who had allied with Manumasidha II. As usual, Manumasidha II appealed to his overlord, the Kakatiya king, and others. This time, the Kakatiyas and their allies were unsuccessful, and the Pandyan empire annexed the Telugu Choda kingdoms of Nellore and Kanchi. With this military defeat, Ganapathideva retired from the active politics of his kingdom and seems to have nominated his daughter as the heiress-apparent. Venkatramanayya and Sarma suggests that 'the time was not yet propitious for celebrating her coronation. The political situation in the country was indeed critical; both internal and external danger threatened the stability of the kingdom' (1960: 621).

By the end, Ganapathideva had moved the capital from Anamkonda to Warangal, having constructed a formidable fort there with an inner wall of stone and a massive outer wall made of sun-baked mud. In the course of the 62 long years of his reign and a life of approximately 78 years, Ganapathideva does not seem to have produced a son and heir from his chief wife, Soma. Ganapathideva seems to have married her before his captivity in Deogiri in 1198 AD (Sastry 2016: 107). The records state that as a result of his Divi conquest, in around 1203 AD), he had also married the two Ayya princesses, Naramba and Peramba, daughters of the Ayya ruler, Pinna Choda (Sastry 2016: 108). An interesting comment on the king is given in the Bothpur inscription of Malyala Gumda, dated 1272 AD. It says, 'Kakatiya Mahadeva's son Ganapa satisfied himself with his own wedded wives' (Sreenivasachari 1940: 150). An inscription dated 1259 AD records that Ganapathideva gave his daughter Rudrama in marriage to the Chalukya prince, Virabhadra, grandson of the Vengi Chalukya king, Mahadeva I (also known as Vishnuvardhana). His other daughter, Ganapamba, was married to Kota Betaraju, but the marriage was short and childless, and she became a widow at an early age in 1218 AD. As a widow, she ruled the Kota kingdom as a principality of the Kakatiyas as a *mahamandaleshwara* (Ganapathi 2000: 86).

Mahadeva I had extensive contacts and relationships with the neighbouring chiefs, athough it seems that he acknowledged the Kakatiyas as his overlords. Virabhadra, as a result of his marriage, seems to have opted to be the son-in-law of the Kakatiyas rather than rule his paternal domain. He stayed with Rudrama and supported her while her father, the king, was training Rudrama as queen-designate. The inscriptions dated 1259 AD and one dated 1266 AD mention Virabhadra. His family's Vengi Chalukya kingdom was ruled by his brother, Mahadeva, and his son, Indusekhara II, who administered it as Kakatiya governors from their capital, Nidadavole.

The marriage of Rudrama also does not seem to have produced a male heir. Sastry (2016) says that the queen had three daughters, Mummadamma, Rudrama and Ruyyamba. The first was married to her cousin, the Kakatiya prince, Mahadeva. The second, Rudrama, was married to the Yadava prince, Ellanadeva, after the successful defence of the Yadava invasion and the Kakatiya counterattack. The youngest of the queen's daughters, Ruyyamba, was married to Induluri Annayadeva (Sastry 2016: 33, 128).

Ganapathideva's marriage to the two Ayya princesses lasted for nearly 60 years, and Ganapathideva had two sons, Harihara and Murarideva, by these junior wives. However, it seems he was determined instead to pass the kingdom into the hands of his daughter, Rudrama Devi. His sons were to later challenge the accession of Rudrama Devi and even shut her out of the capital, Warangal (Sastry 2016: 118). Sensing the tremendous future difficulty, Ganapathideva seems to have nominated Rudrama Devi as the queen-designate in 1259 AD, seven years before his death (ibid.).

Several questions arise concerning the twin succession issues. Ganapathideva had sons from his Ayya wives. Why did he not nominate the eldest son as his heir? Second, if he was determined to pass the throne to his daughter, why did he not confirm his son-in-law, Virabhadra, as his heir? He died quite early on in 1266 AD (Ganapathi 2000: 108). The latter decision would have united the two domains–Kakatiya and Chalukya–in practical terms. Third, when Rudrama had no sons, why then, having given her eldest daughter to a Kakatiya prince, not nominate him as her heir? Unfortunately, we do not have enough information to answer these questions, which seem to have affected the internal coherence of the Kakatiya dynasty and state.

It maybe that Ganapathideva neglected the sons born from his Ayya wives largely because the Ayyas were a part of an aboriginal tribe called Boya (Hanumantha Rao 1987). They were quite distinguished, and as part of the ruling feudal elite, they had been absorbed into the Kakaktiya governance and military structure, where they held important positions. Their uncle, Jayappa, held a high position in the Kakatiya armies as *gajasenapathi* and the family continued as chieftains of Divi. If their maternal family background had been the reason for bypassing their claim to the Kakatiya throne, it was unfortunate. Such a move would have consolidated the kingdom and avoided justification for revolt by Ambedeva, which created considerable uncertainty and crisis for the dynasty.

By 1504 AD, which marked 200 years of Ganpatideva's death, Chittapakhana alias Sitapati alias Shitab Khan, a Boya by caste, had defeated the Bahmanis and had wrested from them the beautiful city of Ekasilapuri, which was formerly ruled by the Kakatiya kings (GoAP 2016a: 291). He had a great army of 60,000 Boyas, including 'thousands of gunmen, many elephants and masses of infantry–Shitab Khan had become the virtual overlord of Telangana' (Sherwani 1973: 16–33). This shows the strength of the Boya community and its leaders (Sastri 1932; Talbot 1995: 692–772).

The succession of Rudrama was contested not only by her Ayya half-brothers, Harihara and Murarideva, but also by the other vassals, such as the Kayastha chiefs, Jannigadeva and his younger brother, Tripurari. However, the chief, Racherla Prasaditya, assisted her (Sastry 2016: 119). An inscription states,

> ... when Rudrama had gone to a village of Moglicherla to worship the deity Ekavira, her two step-brothers Harihara and Murarideva closed the gates of

> Warangal fort and refused her entry. She appealed to the loyalty of her people and brought the two brothers around tactfully. Army generals, accustomed to receiving orders from her since the reign of her father, supported and sustained her rule just as Recherla Prasaditya, had helped her during the accession. Having entered the Fort, she severely punished for the rebels (Jha 1994: 201).

Technically, the Kakatiya dynasty ended with Ganapatideva, as Rudrama would have been a Chalukya princess after her marriage. Rudrama's next problem was the Kalinga invasion. However, the Kakatiya army, commanded by Prolaya Nayaka and Poti Nayaka, defeated the invading force and established the Godavari river as the boundary between the two kingdoms (Sastry 2016: 120).

The threat from the north came from the Seuna/Yadava king, the Yadava Mahadeva, who invaded the Kakatiya territory and laid siege to its capital, Warangal. The epigraphs from the era state that Queen Rudrama fought for 15 days and destroyed the great Seuna/Yadava cavalry, and then chased Mahadeva up to the walls of the Deogiri fort. One of the epigraphs is even located in the southern Seuna/Yadava kingdom, testifying to Rudrama's rule as she seems to have annexed part of this territory. Mahadeva sued for peace and agreed to pay massive amounts of money (one crore gold coins) and horses as war indemnity. A Yadava prince, Ellana Deva, who had defected to her cause, married the third daughter of Rudrama, also called Rudrama (Ganapathi 2000: 108; Sastry 2016: 121, 128; Venkatramanayya and Sarma 1960: 625–26).

Mahalingam (1957) gives us the Seuna/Yadava perspective. Their inscriptions seem to suggest that Ganapatideva died in 1261 AD, and taking advantage of the confusion caused by the succession of a woman to the throne, Mahadeva invaded the Kakatiya kingdom. Their chronicler, Hemadri, claims that he was victorious and captured many Kakatiya elephants. Hemadri also claimed that after this victory, Mahadeva did not press his advantage because of Rudrama's gender. The last bit could be an understandable excuse for a defeat. In this context, the Kakatiya chronicles and inscriptions seem to be more credible. After Mahadeva's death, there was a disputed succession of his nephew, Ramachandra, to the Seuna/Yadava domains. Ramachandra, instead of attacking Rudrama, seems to have supported her dissident vassals led by Ambadeva. As a result, of course, Rudrama retaliated, and her forces conquered the southern Seuna territory, including Raichur. Again, as may be expected, we can see the subtle differences between the two narratives, that is, those of the Yadavas and the Kakatiyas.

Soon Rudrama was challenged by the Kayastha ruler, Ambadeva, who carried out a series of tactical moves by eliminating his neighbouring vassals and absorbing their territory. This strategy had its double effect in that it not only increased his power, but it also eliminated some of the vassals who were loyal to Rudrama, thus weakening her base. The inscriptions of Ambadeva claimed that he defeated 75 Kakatiya *nayakas*. For a certain period, it can be assumed that Rudrama allowed this to happen unchecked, until Ambadeva finally declared himself in full revolt. Following this, the entire southwest region of the Kakatiya kingdom below River Krishna formed the independent state of Ambadeva, and he even expanded east towards Nellore. In addition, Ambadeva defeated the Pandyan army that sought to intervene in 1286 AD (Sastry 2016: 123–24). The inscription found at Chandupatla village near Nalgonda, which is dated 27 November 1289 AD, declares the results of the final battle between Queen Rudrama and Ambadeva. It announces the death of Rudrama and her general, Mallikarjuna-*nayaka*.

The historical and romantic narratives about Rudrama, including that of Marco Polo, who describes her as the virtuous widow of the king, praise her virtue and competence. She assumed male titles and dressed in male garments, and did not hesitate to take the field in person and lead her troops. This unusual behaviour is lauded by current commentators, who seem to be carried away by the rare event of a reigning queen without noticing the fact that she needed to act like a man in order to establish her legitimacy to the throne. However, historians, while noting the hostility of male rulers–both of her father's vassals and her equals–do not see this as a violation of the values of the period in which she lived. Pratapa Rudra (previously known as Kumara Rudra), Rudrama's grandson and son of her daughter, Mummadamma, and Mahadeva, succeeded to both the Kakatiya Warangal and the Chalukya Vengi territories of his maternal grandparents, thus uniting the central core of the Telangana region with the Andhra coastal strip.

Prataparudra (r. 1289–1323) had to take some critical steps to reorganise the Kakatiya army, which had suffered a severe defeat and loss of morale. He seemed to have reorganised the *nayamkara* units (military units of the *nayakas*) and proceeded to attack Ambadeva, who had nevertheless taken necessary steps for defence, as he knew that he was no match against a full-fledged Kakatiya army. He entered into an alliance with the Seunas/Yadavas to the north of the Kakatiya kingdom and the Pandyas to the south of his kingdom. The Pandyas are stated to have assisted Ambadeva by sending their elephants and horses (Sastry 2016: 129).

However, Prataparudra, even in 1281 AD, that is, in the lifetime of his grandmother, had commenced the attack on Ambadeva. Manuma Ganayya, the son of Kolani Soma-*mantri*, and his cousin, Annayadeva, son of the Induluri Pedda Ganayya-*mantri*, led the attack. Ambadeva was forced to retreat south towards Mulikinadu. However, despite two attacks on Nellore and one on the Seunas in the north to punish them for their support to Ambadeva, Prataparudra was not able to consolidate Kakatiya possessions in the south (Sastry 2016: 130). What was even more puzzling was his attack on the Seunas in 1294 AD, when he should have actually been making an alliance with them to together meet the challenge from the Khilijis (ibid.: 131). His attack only distracted the Seunas from the northern threat. Soon, however, his own attention was taken up when the Muslim invaders had conquered Deogiri in 1295 AD, and would, in due course of time, envelop his Kakatiya domain.

Venkatramanayya and Sarma state that although Prataparudra had been aware of the Muslim danger years before he acceded to the throne, it was an attack by Garshap Malik on Devagiri that pushed him to restructure his army (1960: 643). Prataparudra reorganised the defences of his kingdom, toned up the *nayakmara* system of feudal levies, and organised an army of 900,000 archers, 20,000 horses and 100 elephants. This force enabled Prataparudra to fight off nearly seven incursions of Muslim armies from Delhi between 1303 and 1323 AD, beating some, buying off others, and eventually losing his kingdom and his life to the final seventh attack. In between, Prataparudra even helped the Muslim Khiliji armies to invade the Pandyan territory in 1311 AD. Prataparudra himself commanded his army and fought the decisive battle in the vicinity of Kanchi (Sastry 2016: 133–34). All of this was expediency, and temporary at that.

It seems obvious that the Muslim invasion and conquest of Deogiri did not receive an effective response from the Kakaitya rulers. The first invasion of Deogiri was carried out in 1295 AD. It was a surprise attack and resulted in payment of a huge tribute as well as handing over the Deogiri princess to Allaudin Khilji. When the crown prince returned hastily to the capitol with his army, he was outraged that the treaty had been signed. He commenced an attack but failed to carry the battle. The consequence was that a further amount of tribute had to be paid. Promises of annual tribute were made and kept till 1308 AD. The rift between the Deogiri king, Ramachandra, and his crown prince over their attitude towards Khilji was responsible for the breach of the treaty and resulted in the second attack. The second attack was led by Malik

Kafur, the eunuch slave and catamite lover of Khilji, who again defeated the Deogiri armies and sent the king to Delhi (Briggs 1989, Volume 1: 208; Lal 1980: 263). At Delhi, he was treated kindly since his daughter was Khilji's queen, and he was permitted to return after six months. This assured that Malik Kafur's expedition to Warangal would receive Deogiri support. This involved logistics, food and necessaries, as well as Deogiri military contingents.

In 1312–13 AD, Malik Kafur was sent to Deogiri by the Khiljis, as their loyal tributary, Ramachandra, had died and had been succeeded by his son, Singhana, who was opposed to them. This attack resulted in Malik Kafur seizing the king 'and inhumanly put[ting] him [to] (*sic.*) death' (Briggs 1989, Volume 1: 217). Harpal Deva, Ramachandra's son-in-law, was put on the Deogiri throne (Lal 1980: 44–47, 233–39, 246, 255–57). By 1318 AD, Malik Kafur had died and Deogiri was lost to the Delhi sultanate. This provoked the last and final expedition against Deogiri under Qutbuddin Mubark Shah, which was marked by Harpal Deva fleeing the battlefield. Ferishta writes in this context: 'A detachment was sent in pursuit, which brought back Harpal Dew prisoner, who was flayed [skinned] alive, decapitated, and his head fixed on the gate of his own capital' (Briggs 1989, Volume 1: 222; Lal 1980: 294). This was the first time that such a horrific atrocity was committed in the land, and it must have generated the terror intended.

A similar terroristic act was performed on a Hindu ruler when Sultan Mahmud Shah Bahmani attacked Telangana, and having defeated Nagadeo, son of the Raja of Telangana/Warangal, captured him and had him 'shot from an engine into a burning pile of wood'. This so provoked the Raja that he applied to Delhi to become a vassal of the emperor, but at that time, Emperor Feroz Shah was too occupied with internal matters to take up the offer (Gribble 2002: 37–38). Such acts as well as the destruction and desecration of temples, massacres of civilian population, and demands for Hindu princesses for the Muslim ruler's harem had a profound effect on both the willingness and capacity of the Hindu kings and feudal elite as well as the subject people to resist.

The historical narrative of this period is complex and is mostly dependent the views and biases of the Muslim chroniclers of the Delhi sultans. It is clear is that Prataparudra did not understand the nature of the invasion as he was unfamiliar with the ideological and religious motivation of the invaders. He seems to have treated them like he would have treated any other Hindu monarch and expected reciprocal treatment in return.

Despite this initial lack of understanding of the nature of the Muslim invasion, the *nayamkara* system rallied and coped for 20 years. Even after the final fall of Warangal, and without a central command of a monarch, the *nayakas* united and managed to eject Muslim power and re-conquer Warangal in less than 13 years under the leadership of the Musunuri Prola Nayaka. Prolaya Nayaka's cousin, Kapaya Nayaka, recaptured Warangal in 1336 AD. The account described in the Vilasa Grant of Prolaya Nayaka is the first-hand report from Hindu chronicles (Venkatramanyya and Sarma 1962: 239–68).

The development of a centralised monarchy reduced the power of its vassals and even absorbed vassal territory into the central core. This tendency had reached a high level, especially during Ganapatideva's long reign. Ganapatideva had reached such a degree of confidence that he even attempted to place a woman on the throne when other safer and more conventional alternatives existed. It would seem that the effects of centralisation, as well as the defiance of tradition, may have induced Ambadeva's revolt and subsequent instability. Prataparudra struggled to correct this, but he was hampered by having to cope with Muslim invasions without the support of the powerful erstwhile Kakatiya vassals in the south, who were led by the Kayastha chief, Ambadeva.

Let alone supporting Deogiri before and after the Khilji attack, Prataparudra attacked the southern part of the Seuna kingdom: 'the Kakatiya ruler Prataparudra annexed a sizable part of the Seuna kingdom in present-day Ananthapur and Raichur districts without much difficulty' (Mahalingam 1957: 154). In turn, the Deogiri rulers returned the favour by assisting Khilji in his attack on Warangal. Thereafter, both the Seuna and the Kakatiyas assisted Khilji in his attack on the Chola and Mabar countries. As they say, with the enemies such as these, Khilji needed no friends.

The Kakatiyas' inability to determine who the real enemy was seems to have been a vital weakness in Kakatiya policy when facing the Muslim invaders from the north. In the end, the monarchy collapsed due to the three elements: attack from outside by a hostile ideological power, the revolt, and the lack of support in the south.

Concluding Remarks

The above account of the Kakatiya empire, which traces the trajectory from its lowly origins and its steady growth, to the periodic defeats and final collapse, indicates how empires rose and fell in India. Much depended on the correlation of forces between the great kingdoms, their wars with each other, each empire's succession crisis, and revolt of powerful feudal vassals or groups of vassals. It is remarkable that the Kakatiya empire, in the very heart of the Deccan, could have become a political entity in order to sustain itself for nearly 300 years. Much of this development depended on an accepted cultural and religious tradition that ensured a low level of violence and a high level of accommodation even after victory and defeat.

The entire Kakatiya territory was liberated from alien control within 15 years of the fall of the Kakatiyas in 1323 AD. Following this liberation, the unitary character of Telangana ended, and it split into three regions ruled by former Kakatiya *nayakas*. By 1337 AD, the Musunuri Nayaks controlled the region around Warangal, the Padma Nayaks controlled the region around Rachakonda; and the Panta Reddis, that around Kondavedu. In 1347 AD, the Muslim kingdom of Bahmani annexed the western territories of present-day Telangana, stretching from Kaulas up to Bhuvanagiri, forced payment of annual tribute upon Musunuri Kapaya Nayak, and later extended their territories up to Golkonda.

In 1366 AD, the Padma Nayaks threatened Kapaya Nayak's territory, and in 1367 AD, they killed him in battle. The Padma Nayaks, based in Rachakonda and Devarkonda, held the eastern districts of present-day Telangana. However, the Padma Nayaks were a constant challenge for successive Bahmanis, and they did not take long to subdue the Padma Nayaks. By 1425 AD, the Bahmanis made the Padma Nayaks their tributaries, and by 1468 AD, they annexed the latter's territories.

The coastal Andhra districts, mostly lying to the south of the Krishna river, were under the control of the Reddis of the Kondavedu kingdom. The Reddis ruled the region comprised of the present-day districts of Guntur, Prakasham, Nellore, and parts of Kurnool district from their capital at Addanki. The Gajapathi of Orissa from the north and the Vijayanagar rulers from the south attacked the kingdom. As a result, its rulers split into two groups: one at Rajahmundry, and the other at Kondavedu. The Kondavedu rulers aligned with Vijayanagar, while the Rajahmundry rulers aligned with the Orissa Gajapathi king.

Eventually, Vijayanagar annexed Kondavedu in 1425 AD, and the Gajapathis of Orissa took over Rajahmundry in 1448 AD. Thus, by the mid-1400, the Kakatiya kingdom of Telangana was divided among three neighbouring kingdoms whose capitals and ruling dynasties were outside Telangana. This physical detachment of the rulers from the land and the people would have inevitable political and economic effects; as for the psychological distance, the effect is incalculable.

A thousand years later, in 1956, an attempt was made to reunite the Telugu people and their lands in much the same territorial area occupied by the Kakatiya empire when it was at its height. However, this resulted in the political and cultural developments that tore the region apart after 60 years. In 2014, the core inland Kakatiya territory emerged as the Telangana state.

Notes

1. These are official titles relating to posts in specific areas and to specific bureaucratic levels, which have no English equivalents; moreover, we have no clear understanding of the structure.
2. For *Illaris* and *Gandvaru*, the translations cannot be provided as the names of these sub-castes are not identifiable.

References

Briggs, John (trans.). 1989. *History of the Rise of Mohammedan Power in India*, Four Volumes. New Delhi: Atlantic Publishers and Distributors.

Ganapathi, Racherla. 2000. *Subordinate Rulers in Medieval Deccan*. New Delhi: Bharatiya Kala Prakashan.

Government of Andhra Pradesh (GoAP). 2016a. *Inscriptions of Warangal District*, ed. N. Venkatramanayya, *Epigraphical Series* no. 6. Hyderabad: Department of Archaeology and Museums.

Government of India, Archaeological Survey of India, Hyderabad Circle. Blog Post. Available at http://www.asihyderabadcircle.nic.in/warangal_monuments.html.

Gribble, J. D. B. 2002. *History of the Deccan*, New Delhi: Rupa Publications.

Hanumantha Rao, B. S. L. 1987. *The Boyas in Medieval Andhra History*, in *Journal of the Andhra Historical Society*, eds Dr N. Venkatramanayya Commemoration Volume, R. Subramanyam, and V. V. Krishna Sastry, Volume XXXVIII, Part IV. Hyderabad: Government of Andhra Pradesh (GoAP).

HEH the Nizam's Government. 1940. *Corpus of Inscriptions in the Telangana Districts*, Part II, *Hyderabad Archaeological Series*, Volume 13. Calcutta: Baptist Mission Press for HEH the Nizam's Government.

Hultzsch, E. 1902. *Epigraphica Indica*, Volume VI, Archaeological Survey of India. Calcutta: Government Printing Press.

Jha, Bishwambhar. 1994. *The Kakatiyas of Warangal* New Delhi: Janaki Prakashan.

Lal, Kishori Saran. 1980. *History of the Khaljis*. New Delhi: Munshiram Manoharlal Publishers.

Mahalingam, T. V. 1957. *The Seunas of Devagiri*, in *A Comprehensive History of India*, Volume 4, Part 1, eds R. S. Sharma and K. M. Shrimali. New Delhi: New Delhi Peoples Publishing House on behalf of the Indian History Congress.

Muller, Georgina Max. 1903. *The Life and Letters of the Right Honourable Friedrich Max Muller*, 2 Volumes. London: Longmans Green.

Pramila, K. 2002. *Economic and Social Conditions of Andhra Desa [AD 1000 to 1323 AD]*. New Delhi: Bharatiya Kala Prakashan.

Sastri, Hirananda. 1932. *Shitab Khan of Warangal, Hyderabad Archaeological Series*, No. 9. Calcutta: Baptist Mission Press for HEH the Nizam's Government.

Sastry, P. V. Parabrahma. 2016. *The Kakatiyas*. Hyderabad: Department of Archaeology and Museums, Government of Telangana.

Sherwani, H. K. 1973. 'The Bahmanis', in *History of the Medieval Deccan [1295–1724]*, eds H. K. Sherwani and P. M. Joshi, Volume 1. Hyderabad: GoAP.

Sreenivasachari, P. 1940. *Corpus of Inscriptions in Telingana Districts of HEH The Nizam's Dominions*, Part II, *Hyderabad Archaeological Series*, No. 13. Calcutta: Baptist Mission Press for HEH the Nizam's Government.

Talbot, Cynthia. 1995. 'Inscribing the Other, Inscribing the Self: Hindu-Muslim Identities in Pre-Colonial India', in *Comparative Studies in Society and History*, Volume 37, No. 4, 692–772. Cambridge: Cambridge University Press.

———. 2001. *Pre-colonial India in Practice: Society, Region and Identity in Medieval Andhra*. New Delhi: Oxford University Press.

Venkatramanayya, N., and P. V. Parabrahma Sastry. 1957. 'The Kakatiyas', in *A Comprehensive History of India*, Volume 4, Part 1, eds R. S. Sharma and K. M. Shrimali. New Delhi: People's Publishing House on Behalf of the Indian History Congress.

Venkatramanayya, N., and M. Somasekhara Sarma. 1960. 'The Kakatiyas of Warangal', in *Early History of the Deccan*, 2 Volumes, ed. G. Yazdani. London: Oxford University Press for GoAP.

———. 1962. 'Vilasa Grant of Prolaya Nayaka', in *Epigraphica Indica*, Volume XXXII, eds D. C. Sircar and D. C. H. Chabra. New Delhi: Manager of Publications, Government of India.

Appendix A

Genealogy of the Kakatiya Rulers

As Feudatory Chiefs

Nripa Venna, born in the family of Durjaya (r. 800–15)
Gunda I (r. 815–)
Gunda II (r. –865)
Gunda III (died before r. 900)
Nripati Erra
Betiya
Nripati Gunda IV alias Pindi-Gunda (r. 955–95)
Nripati Beta I alias Garuda Beta (r. 996–1051)
Prola I (r. 1052–76)
Beta II alias Tribhuvanamalla (r. 1076–1108)
Tribhuvanamalla Durgaraja (r. 1108–16), son of Beta II
Prola II (r. 1116–57), son of Beta II, who married Muppama
His children included Rudra, Mahadeva, Harihara, Ganapati and Repolla Durga

As Sovereign Rulers

Rudra (r. 1158–95), son of Prola II, became a sovereign in r. 1163
Mahadeva (r. 1196–99), son of Prola II, married Bayyama
Had three children, including Ganapathideva, Mailamba and Kundamba
Ganapati-deva (r. 1199–1262), son of Mahadeva, married Somala Devi
Had two children, including Ganapamba (married Kota Beta) and Rudrama Devi
Rudrama Devi (r. 1262–89), married Chalukya Virabhadra
She had three girls in birth order:
Mummadamba (married Kakati Mahadeva), Ruyyama (married Induluri Annaya-*mantri*) and Rudrama (married the Yadava prince, Ellana Deva)
Prataparudra Deva (r. 1289–1323), son of Mummadamba

2

Telangana Elites through the Ages

This essay attempts to identify and describe the elites of Telangana from the time of the Kakatiya dynasty (1163–1324 AD) to the formation of Telangana as the twenty-ninth state of the Indian Union. After the fall of the Kakatiya kingdom in 1324 AD, till 2014, the rulers of Telangana were alien to its land and people. Throughout these 700 years, Telangana elites alternatively contributed to, supported, and revolted against alien rule. The early history is sparse, as we have to rely on surviving inscriptions and travelogues of foreigners, Muslim court chroniclers, and family and village narratives. A reasonable picture emerges, but at the same time indicates the need for further research on Telangana's history.

The Kakatiya Kingdom and its Elite

A specific Telangana identity began to develop during, and more vigorously, after the period of Kakatiya rule. It was the first time in history that the ruling elite and the people of Telangana came from a common stock. The Kakatiya dynasty united in itself three elements–religion, ethnicity and language–of the people of Telangana. This one factor, the recognition of a common identity, has led to the retention and regard for the memory of Kakatiya rule till the present day.

The Kakatiya dynasty entered history through inscriptions during the Chalukyan rule over Telangana. The first significant inscription of 1053 AD at Sanigaram (in Karimnagar) records a grant by the Kakatiya, Prola I. According to the Kazipet inscription of Tribhuvanamalla Durga Chalukya (1093 AD), Prola I obtained Hanamkonda *visya* from Trilokamalla Chalukya (r. 1064–92) as a permanent domain (Pramila 2002: 26). In the Rudrasevaram inscription of 1163 AD, the Kakatiya, Rudradeva, proclaimed his independence (ibid.). Through his victories in the field, Radradeva's kingdom 'embraced almost the entire Telangana. At this time the Kakatiya kingdom was bounded by the sea in the east, Srisailam in the south, Kalyan in the west and Malyavanta hills [probably the Nirmal hill ranges on the banks of the Godavari in the north' (ibid.). After this, the Kakatiya kingdom based at Warangal/Hanamkonda began to dominate Telangana and the Telugus until its final collapse in 1323 AD. In this context, Cynthia Talbot, who has worked on inscriptional evidence, notes the following:

> While the Kakatiyas were nominally subordinate to the Western Chalukya dynasty of Karnataka, the bulk of their records are in Kannada, the language of Karnataka. Once the Kakatiyas ceased acknowledging Chalukyan overlordship, they immediately stopped issuing inscriptions in Kannada. The Kakatiya shift to Telugu and Sanskrit inscriptions had a certain political significance, of course, but was also a symptom of a solidifying Telugu ethnicity. (Talbot 1995: 713–14).

Out of the nearly 1,518 inscriptions during the period from 1175–1324 AD, 1,385 were in Telugu, while only 133 were in other languages such as Kanada, Grantha or Nagari (Talbot 2001: 25). The fact that the Kakatiya dynasty was Telugu-speaking is therefore quite clear. However, one must ask: what were they in social terms? In fact, the importance of this question lies in the answer to it, which is that there is some debate over the issue of the caste identity of the Kakatiyas.

The narrative history of Vidyanatha and one inscription of 1291 AD at Kundavaram, Jangaon, Warangal refer to the Kakatiya king as a Kshatriya (Government of Andhra Pradesh [GoAP] 1973: 57). The evidence was meagre; however, it somewhat advanced the claim of Kshatriya status for the Kakatiyas.

In neither of their inscriptions do the Kakatiyas claim to belong to any caste; moreover, they do not refer to their *gotra* (lineage),which is an essential characteristic of the three higher *varnas* (castes). Again, it is evident that there are marital relationships between the Kakatiya family, and the Natavadi and Kota chiefs, who proclaim their status as being of the fourth caste, that is, Sudra (Sastry 2016: 27–29):

> In the Bayyaram tank inscription, it is said that, according to the words of the ministers of the king Mahadeva, that his daughter Mailamba deserves the hand of the Natavadi Rudra in marriage as the latter belong to the same caste as the bride.... In an inscription at Amravati, the Natavadi chiefs are stated to be of the fourth caste. Both the records state in unmistakable terms that the Kakatiyas were born of the fourth caste. (2016: 29).

Moreover, the following three authoritative early inscriptions state this fact clearly:

1. Dharmasagar inscription (n.d.): 'Born of the Lotus of the Navel of the Lord of Lakshmi, the Creator, after creating the world was desirous of creating an excellent caste and accordingly created the Kakatiya dynasty of valorous Kings [who were verily] the Kalpa trees on earth' (HEH the Nizam's Government 1940: 3).
2. Kazipet inscription in the Dargah dated 1090 AD: 'There is Beta of the feudatory family of the working class [*sic.*] [Sudra],[1] lord of the Kakati city, [one] who had earned Goddess Lakshmi by churning the ocean of the army of the Chola Kings' (HEH the Nizam's Government 1940: 28–30).
3. The Malyala family inscription dated 1246 AD: 'In the fourth varna arose several royal families and in one of them was the Kakatisvara-kula' (GoAP 1956: 98).

The Kakatiya vassals proclaimed in their inscription that they were of the Sudra *varna* ('born at the feet of Vishnu', or 'of the fourth *varna*') (GoAP 1994a: 203). The statements are made as a matter of fact and without any particular emphasis. The subordinate rulers and *nayakas*, such as the Racherla chiefs of Rajakonda, supported Kakatiya rule. They were also Sudras who proclaimed that they were the 'purest of the Sudra caste which sprang from the feet of Brahma of the Lotus navel of Narayana, Lord of the Universe' (GoAP 2016a: 276–77). The inscriptions provide confused references to either Brahma or Vishnu as the originator of caste (Manu 1886: Chapter 1, Verses 5–11, 31).[2] Either way, they claim to be born from the feet of the Lord.

Marriages in each generation strengthened political bonds between two families. In their inscriptions, the Natavadi proudly proclaimed their origin and social status as 'born of Brahma's feet, of the *chaturvarna*', that is, the Sudra *varna* (Hultzsch 1902: 157; Sastry 2016: 29).

The Bhotpur inscription of Malyala Gumda (Gundaya)-*senani* dated 1259 AD clearly states in this regard: 'Among these were the fourth caste of innumerable greatness, honoured, the birthplace of wealth [i.e., the breeder of wealth] great in number, very pure like the milky ocean among the four oceans and having excellent men; In that [fourth caste] there is the praiseworthy Kakatiya dynasty' (HEH The Nizam's Government 1940: 159).

In this context, the inscriptions are more credible sources of information than later narratives, such as that of Vidyanatha, which suggests a *Kshatriya* status for the dynasty. After reviewing the evidence, Sastry argues in favour of the credibility of the Gundaya records: 'Therefore, instead of believing in the statements of the other records that are rather panegyric it is quite reasonable to accept the statements of Gundaya's records' (2016: 29).

Kakatiya Feudal Vassals

The Kakatiya state depended on a set of *nayakas* or feudal vassals who acknowledged Kakatiya suzerainty and assisted in the governance of the kingdom as well as in its defensive and offensive military campaigns. Sastry provides an exhaustive description of the Kakatiya elite and its relationship to the royal family (2016: 143–71). The relationship between the king and his *nayakas* could be quite substantial. The 1203 AD inscription at Kondaparthi describes the relationship between the Malyala family, one member of which was made Commander-in-Chief by King Ganapatideva (GoAP 2016a: 131). These relationships could result in marriage, as in the case of the Natavadi chief, Rudra, who married Mailama, the daughter of King Ganapatideva and the sister of King Mahadeva. Mailama constructed three temples to Shiva at Inugurthi and endowed a village towards the cost of its upkeep (ibid.: 138).

The Viriyala Chiefs

These chiefs were the earliest associates of the Kakatiyas, even before the assertion of Kakatiya sovereignty. It was Viriyala Erra who persuaded the Chalukyas to reinstate the Kakatiya, Bottu Beta, in the Koravi territory and secured his succession with Garuda Beta I, who was the nephew of Erra's wife, Kamavasani. These chiefs played a foundational role in establishing the Kakatiya dynasty and extending its authority in the early stages.

The Malyala Chiefs

The Malyala chiefs were born in the same family as the Kakatiyas, and they were lords of the town of Malyala. One of their members, Malyala Chaunda, was the Commander-in-Chief of the Kakatiya armies in the early years of Ganapatideva's reign. He gets the credit for subjugating Coastal Andhra after defeating Prithivisvara, the Velanati chief who held sway over the entire coastal districts at that time. Malyala Chaunda celebrated his great victory by building a temple to God Chaundesa at Kondaparthi near Warangal in 1193 AD.

The Natavadi Chiefs

The Natavadi chiefs and their family shared a close familial relationship with the Kakatiyas. Over generations, they had sequential marital links with each other. Their earliest record is dated 1101 AD at Narsampet in Warangal district. Initially, like the Kakatiyas, they were vassals of the Western Chalukya empire. The Bayyaram inscription states that they are of the same caste as the Kakatiyas (Sastry 2016: 29). The Amaravati inscriptions of 1234 AD, while recording an offering to Buddha, state that the family is of Sudra stock, and also suggest that the Kakatiyas are Sudra (Hultzsch 1902: 157; Sastry 2016: 29).

The Cheraku Chiefs

These chiefs got their name from the small town of Cheraku and its associated group of 12 villages in the Eruva region. This region extended on both sides of River Krishna in present-day Nalgonda and Prakasham districts. They were the vassals holding these 12 villages in Eruva-*mandala* (an administrative unit). They belonged to the Sudra *varna* and were Reddi by name. They were initially subordinates to the Telugu Choda kings, but changed their loyalty to the Kakatiyas, who made them hereditary *maha-samanthas*. They seem to have played a significant part in the Kakatiya victory over the Choda kings. In all the military undertakings of the Kakatiya kings, the Cheraku chief's participation ensured victory. Cheraku Rajanna married the daughter of Kayastha Ambadeva and received the town of Nandanapura as dowry. His role in the clash between Ambadeva and Queen Rudrama, which resulted in the death of the queen, is a matter of speculation (Sastry 2016: 154).

The Kota Chiefs

The Kota chiefs were close relatives of the Kakatiyas, and they came from Dharani-Kota near Amravati, from which they take their name, Kota. They are said to be 'Lords of the 6000 country' on the southern bank of River Krishna, which they obtained through the favour of Trinayana-Pallava. It seems that these chiefs were first enemies of the Chalukya Chola sovereign, but were influenced by their intermarriages with the Kakatiyas, and then switched sides after being attacked by Rudradeva in 1185 AD.

The Induluri Chiefs

The Induluri chiefs are of the Brahmin *varna*, which is exceptional because the Kakatiya dynasty, and most, if not all, their vassals were Sudra. The family had held a long record of distinguished and fruitful service to the Kakatiya dynasty. Rudrama Devi even gave her daughter, Ruyyama, in marriage to Induluri Annaya, who later became one of the loyal ministers of Pratapa Rudra. Annaya commanded the fifth battalion of the Kakatiya army, which consisted of 100,000 foot soldiers and 12,000 cavalry-men. Induluri Annaya was the Chief-General in the campaign against the Kayastha king, Ambadeva, and seized 70 of the enemy's forts (Sastry 2016: 162–63). He was also later entrusted with the defence of the Warangal inner stone fort during the Muslim attacks. Both as a result of his capacity and his relationship to the dynasty as its son-in-law, Induluri Annaya ruled the whole of the Vengi region and the regions beyond the Godavari river.

The Chalukyas of Nidadavole

After the subjugation of the Kolanu region, Ganapatideva proceeded to attack the Chalukyas of Nidadavole. However, he offered his daughter, Rudrama, in marriage to the Chalukya chief Indushekara's son, Virabhadra. The Chalukyas of Nidadavole thereafter served the Kakatiyas under Rudrama and Prataparudra as governors of the Nidadavole province. Rudrama, in her turn, married her two daughters to their Chalukya first cousins, and one of the alliances–that of Mahadeva II and Mummadamma–produced Pratapa Rudra, Rudrama's grandson and successor, the last king of Warangal. It is interesting to note that in a formal and legal sense, the Kakatiya dynasty ended with Ganapatideva, as both Raudrama and Prataparudra belonged to the Chalukya family, the first by marriage and the second by birth. Venkatramanayya and Sarma suggest that the Eastern Chalukyas of Nidadavole were Kshatriyas, but he does not advance any evidence for this assertion (1960: 639). The inscriptions of these Chalukyas do not refer to the *varna* or *gotra*, which would have been expected of a Kshatriya.

The relationship between the *nayaka* vassals and the king could also deteriorate. Such a situation usually occurred when a *nayaka* became more powerful than some other vassal *nayaka*. With a certain amount of skill and manoeuvrability, and a degree of violence against the neighbouring *nayakas*, an ambitious *nayaka* could take on central leadership. When such a crisis occurred, the royal leadership would be in disarray. In the case of the Kakatiyas, such a crisis happened when the sovereign who succeeded to the throne was a woman. Under Queen Rudrama Devi, as noted earlier, the full-fledged revolt of the *nayaka*, Ambadeva, of the Kayastha family in what is now Rayalaseema, broke out.

The Kayastha Chiefs

The Kayasthas are very important chiefs controlling what is now known as the Rayalaseema region. They played a decisive role in weakening the Kakatiya empire by attempting to break away to form an independent political entity. Their inscriptions describe five chiefs of this family, who ruled the Kurnool-Cuddapah region of the Kakatiya kingdom. Gangaya-*sahni* (commander of the cavalry) was the earliest member who became popular in the service of Ganapathideva. Cavalry seems to have been this family's military strength. Inscriptions dating to 1239 AD and 1242 AD state that as a subordinate of Ganapatideva, Gangaya-*sahni* ruled as the chief of 72 *niyogas*, that is, he was the chief of 72 branches of administration in the Kakatiya kingdom. His titles and position indicate the prominence to which he had risen and the power that he yielded. In this capacity, he even led a Kakatiya invasion of the Yadava kingdom in the far north of the Kakatiya domain. He received the title and rank of a *mandaleshwara* (the governor of a *mandala*).

In 1272 AD, Ambadeva II, who was the most ambitious, active and powerful chief of this family, defied the authority of the Kakatiya queen, Rudrama Devi, and proclaimed himself the king of Marjavadi and other regions. To reach this situation, he progressively eliminated all his neighbouring vassals who were loyal to Rudrama Devi. Finally, he fought with the Kakatiya army led personally by Rudrama Devi and defeated it in the battle in which Rudrama Devi died. However, Pratapa Rudra managed to root out the Kayasthas and re-establish his authority over the area only after eight years. Pratapa Rudra committed much attention and resources to quell this rebellion and re-establish his rule in the far south of the Kakatiya domain. This campaign distracted his attention from the events in the north, where Muslim power had invaded and subjugated the Seuna/Yadava kingdom of Deogiri.

Between 1290 and 1292 AD, Ambedeva's inscriptions in Cuddapah, by its lack of reference to any Kakatiya ruler, indicate his independent status (GoAP 1977: 219–22). Even after his death, his son, Tripurarideva, continued to rule effectively (ibid.: 229–32). This revolt continued successfully for about 10 years, after which Queen Rudrama was killed in battle with the rebels. She was succeeded by her grandson, Pratapa Rudra, who eventually restored central rule in 1309 AD (ibid.: 235–39). This set of events is evidence of how revolting feudal notables have always been a threat to their sovereigns throughout history.

Racherla Family—Velama or Reddi?

An important issue concerns the Racherla Nayaks, who were one of the most important supporters of the Kakatiya dynasty throughout the period of its existence. Unfortunately, it seems that the issue of the *jati* (sub-caste) status has been confused largely by family bards of the medieval period and has been assisted by later historians. This has, in turn, added a political dimension to an issue which, when examined closely as it has not been in the past, is quite simple and clear. In all of the inscriptions of the period, there is occasional mention of *varna*, and that, too, in order to emphasise the Sudra status of the issuer of the inscription. Usually, he describes himself as one of the *chaturvarna*, that is, of the fourth caste. There is usually a reference to the allegorical birth of that caste from the feet of Vishnu, and sometimes, of Brahma.

The Racherla chiefs were of the Sudra *varna* and carried Reddi as their name. Many inscriptions cite this name as well. This allows for a link to the modern Reddy *jati*, which is the dominant caste in Telangana and Rayalaseema, with a strong presence in Coastal Andhra. However, the inscriptions do not describe the Reddis as a *jati*, but rather, the person concerned only adds that name at the end of his given name. It is possible, therefore, that this is a proto-*jati*, or a *jati*-in-making. This possibility, of course, stimulates other current proto-*jatis* to attempt a linkage to the Kakatiya period in order to claim genealogical legitimacy. Although this dichotomy is commonly found in various historical narratives, the only problem is that it confuses and distorts the historical narrative to suit and substantiate modern requirements and demands.

The 1213 AD Palampet inscription of Rudra Reddi furnishes a lengthy account of the Racherla family. Their name seems to have originated from their native village, Recheruvala, or from their family name, Rechadi.

The Racherla chiefs served the Kakatiyas for many generations as military commanders with unfailing loyalty. Their record begins in 1052 AD with Bramha-*senani*, who served the Kakatiya king, Beta I, and helped him in the capture of Kanchi.

Racherla Rudra was responsible for extracting the Kakatiya heir after the disastrous attack on the Yadava kingdom. He negotiated with the Yadava king and obtained the release of the crown prince, Ganapatideva, who had been captured in battle. In the interregnum period, he was responsible for suppressing revolts against the Kakatiya dynasty by some vassals. The famous Ramappa temple and its large and unusual tank was built under the instructions of Rudra-*senani* in 1213 AD. He also seems to have built a temple at Ghanapura.

The Racherla chiefs were Reddis by *jati*, as distinct from the other Racherla family, who were of the Velama *jati*. Ganapathi (2000) states,

> ... the Racherla chiefs ruled over their principalities at Elkurti and Amanagallu for about 250 years from about 1000 AD and very faithfully served the Kakatiyas as feudatories up to the regnal period of Ganapatideva .... It is clear that the Racherla chiefs maintained good relations with the Kakatiyas and were rewarded suitably with positions as commanders-in-chief and, in turn, they maintained law and order in the country under the instruction of the imperial kings. They also acknowledge the kings in all of their inscriptions though they were issued to record some grants made by the Racherla families (2000: 51).

However, somehow, historians have concluded that this Racherla Reddi family left the historical scene after or during the time of Ganapathideva. Ganapati concludes that there was a loss of prominence of the Racherla Reddis at the imperial court during Ganapathideva's reign (2000: 118). They are succeeded by what historians have labelled the Racherla Velamas, who play a distinguished role in Kakatiya, Telangana and Andhra history. However, this is only probable if one assumes that there are two Racherla families–one Reddi and the other Velama.

In none of the relevant inscriptions cited (with one exception) is there any reference to the word 'Velama', either as a name or a *jati* (Talbot 2001: 191). It would seem, therefore, that the category of Velama evolved much later, and this more modern category was projected backwards into history in order to establish it as an older category. As Talbot (2001) concludes,

> It is all too easy to project the castes of the modern ethnography back into the medieval period on the basis of resemblance in terminology. In the case of the Velamas, however, even this excuse does not stand because the name Velama appears only once in the source material from Kakatiya Andhra. On that occasion it identifies a collective body, the Thousand Velamas, who act in concert with collectives of weavers and herders in assessing religious levies on their own communities (2001: 191).[3]

This occurrence is, in fact, unlike a lot of inscriptions where the name 'Reddi' appears, but again, without it being attributed to a *jati*. Just as the Racherla vassals named Reddi played a significant role in the earlier part of Kakatiya rule, the Racherla 'Velamas' were a significant group and played a decisive role in the later and post-Kakatiya phase. They are also treated as part of the Padma Nayaka community, which is identified as 'Velama', probably a later sub-*jati*.

The 'Velama' attribution rests largely on the fact that there is a substantial dominant *jati* in Telangana and Andhra that calls itself 'Velama'. Among the members of this *jati* are a dozen families ruling *samasthans*, or 'little kingdoms' of great social and political importance. One of these 'little kingdoms' is that of Venkatagiri in Nellore district of Andhra. The family of this particular kingdom, the Veligotu family, through adoption and marriage, is connected with all the great 'Velama' *samasthans* of the region.

The *Velugotivari-Vamshavali* has provided the narrative regarding this family, its offshoots and activities. Much depends on the credibility of this later chronicle, and the validity of its claims, as many of the current Velama royal families claimed descent from this family. The bardic poems are the foundational source of this chronicle. The publication of the text in Telugu and English was funded by the Venkatagiri Raja. Sarma (1948) provides an account of this work, citing it as a significant work studying the history of the Veligotu family, which was a branch of the Racherla line:

> So we have to depend on the *Velugotivari Vamshavali*, an anthology of verse composed and sung in ancient times by itinerant and family bards called Bhattu Rajus in praise of the different chiefs of the Racherla family, recounting their heroic deeds and great charities in their usual extravagance time, with this the sense of proportion (Sarma 1948: 11).

While the oral tradition may have been much older, the *Velugotivari Vamshavali* was recorded and composed in Telugu in the 1920s and was translated into English in by Sastry in 1922, and was published by the twenty-ninth Raja of Venkatagiri. This text provides an interesting genealogical list of the first 10 members of the Veligotu family. They all have Reddi as their last name. The founder, its most important member, is named Chevvi Reddi, and he lived while Ganapatideva ruled. He is also called Betala *nayaka*, as he was said to have confronted Betala in order to get access to a treasure hidden by his first ancestor, Hemadri Reddi. This treasure was the primary source of the family fortune. He is named in inscriptions dated 1195 AD, 1203 AD and 1208 AD (Sastry 1922: 3). He was perhaps a native of Amanagallu in Miryalguda in Nalgonda district. In fact, as the *Velugotivari Vamshavali* suggests, they probably derived their family name from their original village, Velugodu, in Kurnool district (ibid.: 2).

Chevvi Reddi's elder brother, Nami Reddi, 'served as a general under Rudradeva also and he is remembered by the Thrikutam built in 1195 AD and the temple of Nameshwara in 1202 AD' (Sastry 1922: 8). The dates of the inscriptions and their content indicate that this family was active during the early Kakatiya period, when both brothers played significant roles. However, at the very outset, *Velugotivari Vamshavali* makes contradictory claims in this regard, stating that Chevvi Reddi lived during the reign of Ganapatideva, then paradoxically citing the instance of a battle where he showed courage, fighting at a time which did not coincide with Ganapatideva's rule:

> ... Report of this incident soon reached the ears of the King of Vijayanagar who .... praised him for his bravery and gave him a reward of the tract of territory known as Lakshaseema, bordering on his own Amanagallu Estate, besides valuable jewels, horses and elephants .... His life-time seems to have been spent on account of his courage and skill in fighting in the battlefield rendering assistance to the Kings of Vijayanagar or the Manumasiddhi Rajahs of Nellore (Sastry 1922: 7–8).

If Chevvi Reddi lived during the reign of Ganapatideva (r. 1199–1262 AD), he could not have been involved with any Raja of Vijayanagar, since the founder of the Vijayanagar empire, Harihara Raya I, reigned after this period, between 1336 and 1356 AD. Moreover, Manumasiddhi II (r. 1248–63) also is not contemporaneous with any Vijayanagara king, although he was indeed assisted by Ganapatideva. Thus, it can be gathered that Chevvi Reddi lived approximately between 1208 and 1263 AD. This only indicates that the Bhatt Rajus, who composed this narrative, were eager to establish the Venkatagiri legitimacy by linking its early origins to the Vijayanagara sovereigns, who came nearly 200 years later. This record has not been altered for accuracy by Sastry (1922) or by any modern historians, the exception being Talbot (2001: 191). Talbot (2001) deals extensively with the issue of *Velugotivari Vamshavali* and its associated implications for the 'Velama' genealogy (2001: 190–94).

Chevvi Reddi began his reign in 1208 AD, when, during the reign of the Ganapatideva, he was appointed as the ruler of Pillalamarri and Amanagallu (1922: 3). He was also known as Pillalamarri Chevvi Reddi (Sastry 1922: 8). Incidentally, Amanagallu is also the seat of the Racherla Reddi family. If there existed only one family, then the mystery of the disappearance of the Racherla Reddis from history and the appearance of the Racherla 'Velama' brothers, Nami Reddi and Chevvi Reddi, at the same time, does not remain a mystery any longer. In fact, the undated Somavaram inscription of Recervula Raddu-Raddi greets Ganapathideva as king (Sreenivasachari 1940: 137). This establishes the Racherla Reddis as having existed during the reign of Ganapathideva.

Pramila (2002) provides a list of 26 inscriptions of grants of fiefs to government officials, military officers and soldiers from 1100–1325 AD. Among them is the inscription relied upon by the *Velugotivari Vamshavali*, which is dated 1195 AD. It was issued at Pillalamarri and cites Racherla Nami Reddi as both *senani* and *mandalika* (a title and honour conferred by the king), and as having received a military fief. Pramila further remarks that the Racherla Reddi family got divided into two branches, the Palampet and the Pillalamarri (2002: 34). In the inscription dated 1234 AD, issued at Nagulapadu, Racherla Kat Reddi, the son of Nami Reddi, also titled *senani* and *mandalika*, is said have held a subordinate fief. Pramila concludes from this particular evidence that it seems that the Pillalamarri region was subdivided into two smaller areas, one of which could have been the fief of Racherla Kat Reddi.

The possibility of large fiefs being split up either by division among the male adult heirs or by the sovereign attempting to cut his vassal's power to size is inherent in the system of feudalism. Inheritance through adoption and marriage compensates this tendency. Inheritance by primogeniture, where the eldest son inherits to the exclusion of all younger sons, is another traditional and legal measure to maintain assets and power across generations. Thus, it is possible that the Racherla family divided itself, as is apparent, and took different contemporary trajectories, which over time have led to social differentiation, to the extent of the branches evolving into two separate *jatis*, the Reddi and the Velama. It would therefore seem from an examination of this family that the evolution of *jatis* as a critical part of the existing *varna* distinction may have stemmed from the need for differentiation within the *chaturvarna* or the Sudra *varna* category, which was almost universal among the Kakatiya vassals. This possibility and hypothesis needs more rigorous examination despite the evidence that has been presented here.

Sastry attributes the name, Racherla, to a village of Recheruvula, from which the 'Reddi' family originated, and to a man called Rechadi. In the case of the 'Velama' family, which is not substantiated by the *Velugotivari Vamshavali*, Sastry says that according to the *Velugotivari Vamshavali*, Racherla is the family *gotra* (1922: 1). Incidentally, the *Velugotivari Vamshavali* records that a Mala (a Scheduled Sub-caste) servant of Chevvi Reddi, called Rechan, offered his life as a ritual sacrifice to Betala, so that Chevvi Reddi could get hold of the fortune hidden by his ancestor, Hemadri Reddi. Rechan offered his life on the condition that his descendants' marriages would have to be performed before any of the descendants of Chevvi Reddi, and at their expense as well. This condition has apparently been 'strictly complied' to by the Venkatgiri family since then (ibid.: 4–7). Perhaps the name and *gotra* has also been adopted in appreciation of the Mala Rechan's sacrifice.

Much reliance has been placed on narratives and poems praising local dynasties, which were in existence in the oral tradition, and were converted into text from the fifteenth century onwards. The poet, Srinatha, for instance, 'mentions in his *Bhimeshvara Puranum* the different communities comprising the *Caturtha varna.* They are Padma Nayakas, Velamas, Kammas, Sarisarlas, Ontaris, etc. It is interesting to notice the omission of the Reddi community in this list' (Sarma 1948: 50). This exclusion seems to have been an attempt to classify the Reddis as part of Kshatriya *varna*, whereas in the earlier inscriptions, they clearly identify themselves as part of the Sudra or the fourth caste.

Some of Sarma's speculations are based on other narratives that indicate that there is no difference between Velama and Reddi. Sarma quotes compositions, which suggest the expressions that Reddi and Velama are synonyms (1948: 50). Obviously, the separate categorisation of this community occurs in the modern period. It is important to determine when this differentiation occurred and why it was necessary, as current divisions are obvious and apparent. However, he does concede the difference between Padma Nayakas and Velamas. Moreover, Talbot deals extensively with this issue (2001: 187–94).

As for the Reddis, they seem to be part of the Kapu community, evident from the ambiguous expression, 'All Reddis are *Kapus*, but all *Kapus* may not be Reddis'. Whatever may be said about the narratives composed by the Bhatt Rajus in praise of their paymasters, historians have to rely on the inscriptions. The inscriptions only mention *varna*, if at all. None of what we call castes today, which are *jatis* or *kulas*, seem to have been in existence in the period in question here. To take the present *jati* distribution and superimpose it on the past is an act of foolishness or has to be seen as a way of enhancing the current social status by linking it to historical figures of heroic dimension. However, it seems that in the Kakatiya period, neither *varna* nor *jati* had the importance that they had much later; and their political and social dimension to which we currently give so much credence today was not significant at that time.

From the evidence, it is clear that after the defeat of the Kakatiya dynasty, this vassal family, Padma Nayak vassals, and other Reddi vassals managed to eject Muslim power from Warangal and restore Hindu rule. They also established their independent rule over much of inland Telangana at Rachakonda and Devarkonda. As the historian, M. Rama Rao (1947) states,

> It is thus clear that various parts of Andhradeśa were rescued from the Muslims at various dates–Rajahmundry and the coastal region in 1324, the territory south of the Krishna in 1325 AD, the Rekapalli region in 1330 and western Andhra between 1330-35 AD. Several individuals–Prolaya Vema Reddi, Musunuri Prolaya nayaka, and Arviti Somadeva liberated these parts and they had no political connection with each other (Rao 1947: 297).

The account further continues:

> After the example of these chieftains, Musunuri Kapaya Nayaka conquered Warangal in 1336 AD and liberated Telangana. There is no evidence to indicate that Prolaya Vema and Arviti Somadeva were in any way his subordinates at any time. The liberation of Andhradeśa from Muslim occupation was the result of a series of individual efforts by the chieftains of the time and not of a planned and coordinated movement directed by Kapaya Nayaka (ibid.).

Major Village Groups

In many inscriptions, in 1228 AD, 1310 AD, and 1323 AD, respectively, the *ashtadasaprajas* (eighteen groups) are said to have contributed to donations or offerings made to the temple gods or are portrayed as an important part of decision-making, who were consulted in the process and whose approval was required (GoAP 1994a: 61–66; GoAP 2016a: 186–87).

An interesting expression in many inscriptions is of the *ashtadasaprajas*, whose consent was obtained or request was considered, as they were representatives of the village. These 18 groups have been identified by Pramila, already discussed in the previous essay, Essay 1. It would appear that Pramila has put together this list from references in various inscriptions and narratives, her primary source being a set of four inscriptions (2002: 166).

However, Pramila says, 'Actually we find many more communities mentioned in the inscriptions and literary works of the period. Table XVI represents the communities, their professions and guilds they formed' (2002: 158, 164–65). When we examine Pramila's Table XVI, we find 30 groups which have been mentioned, which have been sourced from at least 46 inscriptions. Out of the 30 in this list, there is one inscriptional reference to Velamas, two to Reddis and one to *nayakas*. An interesting characteristic of historians has been to concentrate on the number, that is, the 18 groups denoted by the word, *asthadasa*, in *ashtadasapraja*. That there were 18 different types of services and that each are provided by separate corporate groups is a matter of some speculation. This is further complicated by the reference to 30 groups. Sircar (1966), in the *Indian Epigraphical Glossary*, records the entry in this manner:

> *Astadasa-jati*, same as *astadasa-praja*; the 18 castes. Kittel enumerates the 18 castes of the Kannada-speaking areas as *Brahamana*, *Ksatriya*, *Vaisya*, *Lingavanta*, *Banajige*, *Gandaikara-vokkaliga*, *Madivali*, *Lelasiga*, *Besta*, *Holeya and Madiga*. But the number 18 means 'all' in such cases. The number 36 has the same meaning in the Bengali expression *chatris-jati*, '36 castes'. *Astadasa-prakriti*; all classes of tenants, tenants belonging to all communities (1966: 31–32).

This is equally confusing and simple. Sircar falls into the same trap of caste, but permits Kittel to combine *varna* with *jati* in the group. However, by labelling '*asta*' to mean 'all', not only has he opened up the group, but he has also destroyed the very idea of a group. If it means 'all', then it would include the entire village. Interestingly, Kittel includes Madiga in the group, which is currently the dominant Schedule Caste (SC) in Telangana, and now appears in history probably for the first time.

A significant inscription seems to mention all of the 18 groups simultaneously. This describes the *ashtadasapraja* as constituting the following groups: [1] *Brahmana*, [2] *Kshatriya*, [3] *Vaisya*, [4] *Sudra*, [5] *Vayaharika*, [6] *Panchala*, [7] *Kumbhakara*, [8] *Tantuvaya*, [9] *Vastra-behdeka*, [10] *Tilaghatika*, [11] *Kurantaka* [12] *Vastra-ksaka*, [13] *Devanga*, [14] *Pereka*, [15] *Goraksaka*, [16] *Kirataka*, [17] *Rajaka*, and [18] *Ksuraka* (Sastry 2016: 180). Critically, this classification is stated on a single copper plate inscription, which is obviously not a public document, unlike stone inscriptions. Here, *varna* and *jati* are mixed up together, making no sense as such.[4]

Yet, this record is from the late-sixteenth century Vijayanagar period—a much later period than when the Kakatiya records were made. It is clear that the Vijayanagar society was becoming more diverse, as also more conscious of the need to explicitly cover the four *charturvarnas* (which do not find such a place in the Kakatiya *ashtadasapraja* inscriptions). Sastry thinks otherwise, although he does not comment on the non-specification of the *jatis* in the Vijayanagara inscription (2016: 180).

The absence of the Kshatriya varna in Telangana is a remarkable and continuing feature of Telangana polity, as is the presence of the Sudra ruling elites. It is clear that Vijayanagar adopted a distinct Hindu characteristic and philosophy, perhaps in contrast to the Islamic threat that it faced for 200 years. In a sense, therefore, Vijayanagar constituted the Hindu response to the Islamic challenge. This may have been a strong component in the Vijayanagar empire, but it seems that in Telangana, which was outside the direct influence of Vijayanagar, the *jati* differentiation within the Sudra varna evolved. This may have even driven dominant and powerful families such as the Racherla to break up and adopt different *jati* appellations as a way of distinguishing themselves from the other branches.

To the extent that social status was recognised (although not emphasised), it was the idea of *jati* that later supplanted *varna* as a social marker. Talbot therefore writes: 'On the rare occasions when the term *jati* figures in the epigraphic sources, it has a general meaning. The phrase *padunenmidi jatula praja*, literally meaning "the people of eighteen *jatis*" is equated with the more frequently occurring *astadasapraja* or "the 18 [kinds of] people"' (2001: 52). However, the inscriptions note *kula* and *vamsa* in the sense of genealogy (the current usage of *kula* as denoting *jati* is a late phenomenon, and was not in use in Kakatiya Telangana). This issue needs much closer attention, work and analysis, as it reflects the dominant hierarchy in Telangana and Vijayanagar villages at that time.

Military Groups

With the establishment of the Kakatiya dynasty, Telangana ensured the establishment of strong, well-structured state apparatus, both in administrative and military sectors. Its bureaucratic-cum-military structures assumed central control by the Kakatiya monarchs. The social base was by the dominant Telugu Sudra *nayakas*–mainly Reddis or Velamas–who controlled, administered and defended fortified villages and larger administrative units. By the end of the thirteenth century, the principal Kakatiya *nayakas* numbered to approximately 75, each of whom received an estate from the king, held under military tenure. *Nayakas* also commanded most of the 60 or more fortresses, which formed the primary means of internal control and external defence of the kingdom.

The economic base was agriculture, and this was supported by massive and extensive investments by the state and its notables in irrigation tanks. The religious aspect also meant the construction of temples alongside tanks and grants of *agraharams* in order to maintain temples and religious scholars. At the base, this system would continue into the twentieth century despite the alien conquest of Telangana and its rule by a Muslim state.

Some issues regarding the ordinary military manpower have been raised by Richards (1975):

> In addition to the *nayaks*, who formed a basic corporate group, the Kakatiyas relied on hereditary military slaves [*lenkas*] for manpower. *Lenkas* were predominantly ordinary soldiers, but they could, on occasion, rise to fill military posts comparable to those held by the *nayaks*. In such cases, *lenkas* holding high offices received military estates under the same conditions as those held that (*sic.*) the great *nayaks*. However the *lenkas*, unlike *nayaks*, were clearly bondsmen with servile social status. As slaves they could have different masters; *nayaks* served only the king (1975: 4–5).

However, Richards seems to have made an error. As he later quoted the authority on the subject:

> The *lenkas* were slaves who entered into a covenant with the lord to devote themselves exclusively to his service. They took an oath [*basa*] to look on their lord as their guru and deity in this world and the next, to have no regard either for their own property or for their lives in furtherance of his interests, to stand by him in the hour of danger ... either to perish with him in the clash of arms or to kill themselves if they should chance to survive him (Venkatramanayya and Sarma 1960: 668, quoted in Richards 1975: 6).

Further, many *lemkas* or *lenkas* appeared in inscriptions, and the expression was a descriptive term or title (Talbot 2001: 7). As early as 1314 AD, an inscription describes a governor as a son of *lemkas*, and the term is attached to the name of the person:

> During the reign of Prataparudra, some dignitaries with the *lemka* designation are noticed in the inscriptions. Juttaya-*lemka* Gonkareddi mentioned above was one of them. His brother was Rudraya-*lemka*. Other members of this category were *Maharaya-sakala-senadhipathi* Somayya-*lemka* and his son Pochu-*lemka*. Mayideva-*lemka* was holding Kondur *sthala* as *nayamkara*. A group of four *lemkas* named Tikkaya Rudra-*lemka*, Marayya-*lemka*, Picchaya-*lemka* and Rudraya-*lemka* were stated in the Kopparam inscription to be holding that *sthala* as *nayamkara* (Sastry 2016: 170–71).

Thus, it appears that *lemkas* could also have been generals, or Commanders-in-Chief, such as Gomkayareddi and Somayya-*lemka*, as indicated by his title, *Maharaya sakala-senadhipathi*, or could have also held territories as *nayakas*. It is clear that the idea of *lemkas* as being 'slaves' is a misnomer and a misunderstanding. Given the description, they are more likely comparable to the samurai of medieval Japan. Large groups of such men could hardly have remained constant and brave if they were mere 'slaves'. The fact that the *nayakas* were able to mobilise tens of thousands of spearmen and others throughout the period of Muslim rule would indicate a constancy of high order. It may be moot to remind ourselves that despite the fact that the *nayakas* were of the Sudra caste, they commanded the loyalty of the *lemkas*. There is a lack of reference to cavalry in the Kakatiya period. Their primary constraint in fighting Muslim armies seems to have been the lack of horses for cavalry operations. In this area, the Muslims had superior striking power and mobility which won them almost all their battles.

Sudra Dominance

It seems clear from the inscriptional evidence that the Kakatiya state was a Sudra-dominated state from top-to-bottom, and as such represented the vast spectrum of the population. However, this Sudra dominance did not exclude occasional Brahmin families also attaining power and prestige. In this sense, the stability of the Kakatiya state, despite the Muslim attacks, and even after the collapse of the dynasty, is a product of this inclusion of the main elements of Kakatiya society in its governance and military structure. It would take another 700 years before this pattern was re-established; but throughout this period, the stability of Telangana, whosoever its alien rulers might have been, depended on the inclusion of this elite that originated from the land and the people. All in all, these and other features of the Kakatiya feudal system indicate a reasonably close resemblance to feudal systems elsewhere in Europe and Japan.

While the capital city and towns were under alien rule, outside the urban areas, it was the native Hindu rural elite that delivered local governance, taxes and armed men even to the alien rulers. It was also these individuals on whom all economic development was based, whether in agriculture, industry, textiles or trade. For ordinary people, the native Hindu elite constituted their direct rulers. Ganapathi (2000) describes the roles and activities of these elites during Kakatiya rule and after the collapse and re-conquest of the kingdom. The basic structure of the Kakatiya kingdom rested on the *nayakas*, who may have numbered anywhere from 71–77. There is a list of names of 71 *nayakas* (ibid.: 135–37). The *Sivayogasaramu* gives a figure of 72. The *Kuluvacheru* grant of Avitali mentions 75 *nyakas*. *Prataparudracharita*, *Velugotvari Vamshali* and *Siddheshvari Charita* of Kase Sarvappa *nayaka*, all mention 77 *nayakas*. Ganapathi further states that each *nayaka* had 15,000 soldiers under his command (2000: 135). This would indicate a potential fighting force of 1,155,000 soldiers. This seems to be a very high figure.

It is reasonably clear that the *nayakas* migrated with parts of the defeated Kakatiya elite to establish their rule in Vijayanagar. These *nayakas* constituted the bulwark of that empire for 300 years, and after its fall, continued to dominate the governance structure of South India till modern times. Their continued defiance of alien rule indicates the strength and vitality of this decentralised and hierarchical *nayaka* structure in the state and society. It is also evident that the strength came from the fact that the *nayakas* were a part of the people and the land, and their Sudra status was more of an advantage than what an absence of Kshatriya *varna* status may imply. The *nayaka* system upturned the higher *varna* model, as Sudras occupied positions that were theoretically meant for Kshatriyas.

In fact, in the Mahabharata's *Santi Parva*, such a situation is envisaged. Yudhishthira asks Bhisma whether in crisis or chaos, a person who is a Brahmin or a Vaisya or a Sudra—not a Kshatriya—succeeds in protecting the people, the law permits him to do so. Bhisma says:

> Be he a *Sudra* or be he the member of any other orders, he that becomes a raft on a raft-less current, or a means of crossing where means there are none, certainly deserves respect in a way. That person, O king, relying upon whom helpless men, oppressed and made miserable by robbers, live happily,

> deserve to be lovingly worshipped by all .... The person .... that dispels the fears of others, always deserves respect .... That person who always protects the good and restrains the wicked deserves to become a king and to govern the world (Ganguli 2003: 172).

The Kakatiya polity of Telangana reflected this situation and designed a compatible, stable state structure that served South India for nearly 700 years. Its effectiveness continues to determine politics and governance in contemporary South India. The fact that South India is a largely Sudra-dominated polity is not widely known, as most of the rest of the country has laboured under a more standard *varna* polity.

The *nayaka* system showed its resilience and strength during the raids of Malik Kafur or subsequent major Muslim invasions. While Muslim chroniclers and Hindu historians differ on the specific details, it was clear that the Kakatiya royal armies offered stiff resistance and many raids were defeated, and the invaders were turned back with heavy losses. Even when agreements for tribute were reached and the tribute was paid, the Muslims never captured the fortress of Warangal. The last and disastrous Muslim raid caught the Kakatiya forces by surprise. The Kakatiya forces had earlier defeated the invaders. However, they were surprised by the quick return of the Muslim forces. Prataparudra had not expected such a move. The *nayaka* forces would have been sent home, and supplies run down when the Muslim armies suddenly turned up. This time, after a siege of only five months, Warangal and Prataparudra surrendered, and the Kakatiya dynasty ended in 1323 AD.

However, the *nayaka* system, now without a guiding royal dynasty and king at Warangal, rose to the occasion:

> Within five years after the fall of Warangal and the capture of Prataparudra, a Confederacy of Hindu chieftains under the leadership of Prolaya Nayak was established .... Western Andhra country [Telangana] thus slipped out of the control of the Delhi authorities by 1328–29, i.e., within five or six years of the fall of Warangal .... the chiefs of the Warangal area rose in rebellion in Saka 1258–59 [1336–37 AD], defeated the occupying army and recaptured the fort of Warangal .... The main work of the liberation of the entire Andhra land was thus accomplished within 15 years of the fall of Warangal (Ramesan 1973: 520–22).

After the restoration of Hindu *nayaka* rule, the Tughlaq sultanate's attempts to recover Telangana proceeded fitfully. Sherwani describes the process thus: 'The Sultan had appointed Malik Maqbul as governor of Warangal.

But he was not left long in the control of the region and was driven away by Krishna Nayak or Kapaya Nayak, who successfully asserted his independence' (1973: 145). This illustrates the resilience of the *nayaka* system as well as the weakness of the distant Delhi rulers.

Land Taxation

The problem was not only of alien rulers hostile to Hindu religious practices and worship, but taxation had also been based on the canonical Hindu rate of one-sixth of the output of land established as far back as the Mahabharata. The Hindu canonical rate was replaced by the Islamic canonical rate, which required non-Muslims to pay 50 per cent, while Muslims paid only 10 per cent of the gross output of land (see Essay 4).

The Kakatiya government collected taxes from irrigated land at the rate of one-eighth of the crop, and from dry land, one-fourth (Venkatramanayya and Sarma 1960: 684). Other epigraphical evidence even suggests one-twentieth as the land tax (Sastry 2016: 216). The Vilasa Grant of 1330 AD refers to one-sixth as the tax rate restored after Muslim rule (Venkatramanayya and Sarma 1962: 242).

The Islamic canonical rate for non-Muslim farmers was one-half of the produce, which was enforced by Allauddin Khilji after his conquest of the Deccan (Gune 1974: 559, 561). This canonical rate remained despite changes in Muslim rulers: 'The structure of Allauddin's innovations crumbled before his death. His successor, Ghaisuddin Tughlaq, was a moderate. He does not seem to have reduced the state demand for one-half of the produce, but he prevented any further increases and removed the levy on pastures' (Rizvi 2005: 183–84).

Thus, the inscription seems to suggest that 16 per cent was the standard tax rate on the gross produce of the land before the Muslim conquest; the Hindu tax rate was restored on Hindu re-conquest. Taking into account the different rates estimated (one-eighth, one-sixth or one-fourth), it would have been a relief from the forcible collection of the Islamic canonical rate of 50 per cent of the crop collected from Hindu farmers. But as long as Muslim rule remained, this canonical rate was applied and enforced.

Restoration of Status Quo

The *nayakas*, even after the collapse of the central Kakatiya rule, continued to support and enlarge religious and other structures. Kapaya *Nayaka*, in

1357 AD, even proclaimed himself not only as the restorer of idols destroyed by the Muslim invaders, but also as a '*brother of other's women*' (GoAP 1994b: 198). Many inscriptions of the period testify to the zeal of the *nayakas*. In 1365 AD, the Velama chieftain, Anavota, in four inscriptions, records the construction of forts, wells, and a temple at Rachakonda (GoAP 1992: 302–06). In 1367 AD, the chief Madanedu reported the installation of the idol of God Chennakeshava, the construction of a tank, and gifts of land to the deities and Brahmins at Domalapalli (ibid.: 307–08).

In 1369 AD, Chief Anapota of the Racherla family declared at Ayanavolu that he was ruling over Warangal, Rajakonda, and other parts of the Telugu country, and was performing the *digvijaya*. In 1375 AD, Venna, the Racherla Velama chief, constructed a temple for God Janardhana and also granted land for its upkeep. By 1377 AD, Annavema Reddi built the *sikhara* of the temple of Agastyesvara and also carried out other repairs of the temple at Vaddapalli (GoAP 1994a: 199–200). In the same year, the Racherla chief, Madana *Nayaka*, recorded the construction of the *mandapa* of the Maheshvara temple at Umamaheswara in Achampet (GoAP 2003: 94–102). At the same place in 1398 AD, the same chief records the establishment of a religious centre (ibid.: 102–03). In 1399 AD, the Recharla chief, Vedagiri I of the Devarakonda branch of the family installed an inscription that he had made a grant of an *agrahara* named Morrupunutala (GoAP 1992: 309–12). These inscriptions, made over an extended period (1357–99 AD), after the fall of the Kakatiya dynasty, indicate the strength and resilience of the basic structures of the Kakatiya polity.

Thus, it can be seen that even in the immediate aftermath of the collapse of the Kakatiya dynasty, the *nayakas* continued to exercise their usual roles and carry on traditional rituals without any reference to the Kakatiya disaster, except that they no longer acknowledged the presence of the Kakatiya king. In the centuries that followed, the inscriptions record the continuation of this tradition of *nayaka* chieftains. These records would indicate the measure of autonomy and independence at the local level throughout Muslim rule in Telangana.

This resistance to alien rule indicates the resilience and organisational capacity of the *nayaka* system and their effectiveness in driving out Muslim invaders from their land despite the absence of a legitimate dynasty to guide them. No better example, in victory, defeat as well as re-conquest, can be offered to establish the *nayakas* at the helm of Telangana, and in due course, in South Indian history of this period. As Richards (1975) sums up:

> Finally, perhaps most important was the unbroken continuity between society and state: the village tank and the royal reservoir, the village temple and the Saivite *matha*, the Reddi and Velama village headman and the Reddi and Velama *Nayak* in service of the crown. This bundle of characteristics suggests a strong capacity for resistance. Invasion and conquest of the eastern Deccan by the Muslims, who appeared early in the fourteenth century, were to be difficult, time consuming and expensive (1975: 6–7).

It is not as if only certain feudal and aristocratic classes (apart from the sovereign and his/her family) appeared in the historical record. A scan of the inscriptions recorded in Telangana produces fascinating results. Interestingly, an inscription of about the tenth century records the name of an individual shepherd, Ranayi; an inscription of 1271 AD records the donation by a man of his two granddaughters to the temple and the fact of how 'their progeny required to serve the god for generations'; an inscription of 1418 AD records the construction of a well as a gift by the jeweller of the Bahmani queen; and a 1529 AD inscription of a servant of the son-in-law of the Qutub Shahi king records the permission to donate funds for the construction of a tank (GoAP 1994b: 227; GoAP 2001: 208, 225). Moreover, inscriptions from the Kakatiya period (GoAP 2016b: 106) as well as from 1416 AD (GoAP 2001: 262) record donations by trading communities such as Komatis, Chetti, Setti and Virabalijas. A sixteenth-century inscription by a blacksmith, Agasala Timmoju Devoju, records his gift to the temple of God Samgameshvara at Alampur (GoAP 2003: 192–93). Another interesting inscription of 1608 AD records that 19 village poets/bards, who participated in the wedding of a Komati, donated part of their fees to the temple (GoAP 1994b: 220). The record of the donations by the trading community shows the emergence, strength and acquisition of its status. Talbot (2001) provides a comprehensive and exciting quantitative, social and spatial analysis of the inscriptions in the Telugu country. She also draws some interesting conclusions from this exercise.

Telangana Elite under Bahmani, Vijayanagara and Orissa

The Tughlaq sultans of Delhi were unable to retain control over Telangana despite the efforts of their local governors. Meanwhile, some of the Kakatiya *nayakas* migrated to the southwest and established the kingdom of Vijayanagara, which began to offer resistance to Muslim power in the south. As the Tughlaq state began to unravel, their governors in the Deccan broke away to form the Bahmani empire under Bahman Shah. The contest between these two great empires–one Hindu and one Muslim–set the scene in the Deccan and the south for the next 200 years. The intervention of the Orissa Gajapati kings complicated the contest over Telangana. The Telangana *nayakas* had to cope with three empires seeking to extend the domination over the region.

The issue is relatively simple. The Tughlaq conquest of 1323 AD resulted in the takeover of the Hindu Kakatiya kingdom by a Muslim power based in Delhi. By 1337 AD, Tughlaq power and its 15-year occupation had ended, and three Hindu kingdoms were established as successors to the Kakatiya kingdom. Not only was the Telangana region liberated from Muslim power, but a new power, Vijayanagar, which was based on the structure of the older Kakatiya polity, also began to build its imperial structure that would last for over 200 years. Vijayanagar generals, in 1364 AD, extinguished the sultanate of Mabar (Madura), which had been established in 1323 AD. All of South India was liberated from Muslim occupation, following which it experienced 200 years of Pax Vijayanagara; this was the major factor that differentiated South India from North India at that time.

Sherwani (1973) sees the period from 1323–37 AD as a 'rebellion' against a legitimate monarch who faced recalcitrant governors appointed by him. It could also be seen as a 're-conquest' by the *nayaka* elites, who had accommodated the alien regime until their forces were ready to remove it. These interpretations of facts are a matter that the readers will have to decide for themselves. In a clash of an alien Muslim power descending on South India and conquering a Hindu polity established for centuries, the matter is clear enough, although as we see that at least two not-so-subtle interpretations are possible. In understanding and comprehending the history of Telangana (and India), this is a vital factor.

Another fact again illustrates the resilience of the *nayaka* system. After the expulsion of Tughlaq power from the Deccan, the residuary Muslim power consolidated under the Bahmani kingdom. By 1345 AD, Zafar Khan and the Muslim *emirs* (rulers or kings), encouraged by the treacherous massacre of 89 emirs of Gujarat and the Deccan by the Tughlaq governor, rebelled against their sovereign and established the Bahmani kingdom at Daulatabad. This move by the generals and governors was a decisive rebellion, as they were part and parcel of the Tughlaq set-up. Finally, and oddly, Zafar Khan and his *emirs* were helped by Hindus to destroy the Tughlaq army. Sherwani, relying on Ferishta, says: 'His [Zafar Khan's] army was reinforced by contingents from the Raja of Tilangana, and the joint forces made a massive attack, completely defeating the Delhi army' (1973: 148). Sherwani, for his own reasons, underestimates the degree of help from Telangana, while Ferishta, on the other hand, is more informative on the numbers involved, which are not quite 'contingents', on the rebels' manifest distress, and puts a far different emphasis on this episode:

> Zuffer Khan also marched with twenty thousand horse[s] to Bidur, then occupied by Imad-ool-Moolk Tubrezy; but owing to the superiority of the royalists he dare not engage them. At last, being joined by fifteen thousand infantry, sent by the Raja of Tulingana, and five thousand horse[s], detached by Nasir-ood-Deen Ismael from Dowlutabad to his assistance, Zuffer Khan made the attack (Ferishta 1989: 177–78).

Thus, nearly half of the rebel's forces were Telangana warriors, who, with their Raja, must have concluded that the rebels could not be any worse than the Tughlaq sultan. As Sherwani states:

> It was easy now [i.e., after the battle] to overcome the Tughluq army which was centred in far off Delhi but it was more difficult to overcome internal enemies. There were the local rajas, partisans of the Tughluq cause, and finally, those who had secret sympathies with the downgraded Ismail who was now given the title of Shamsu'ddin (Sherwani 1973: 149).

As for Telangana, the Bahmani rebels entered into a treaty with Kapya Nayak the Raja of Warangal. As has been have observed, the military support that the *raja* (king) of Warangal provided ensured Bahamani victory over the Delhi sultanate. At the same time, Pocha Reddi Nayaka supported the Delhi rulers and fought the Bahmani forces (Sherwani 1973: 150). Hindu *nayakas* of Telangana fought on both sides! However, by 1350 AD, the issue had altered entirely as the new Bahmani sultan then became expansionist:

> In the east, he swept over southern Telingana and penetrated as far as Nellore, but he could not remain in occupation even of Warangal from where he seems to have been ousted by Kataya Vema. In fact, he could exercise his authority only as far as Bhongir in the east (Sherwani 1973: 151).

Bhongir was in northern Telangana, and it was the farthest point under the effective occupation of Bahman Shah; and beyond that was the dominion of Kapaya Nayak, who was on friendly terms with him (Sherwani 1973: 151).

The ebb of the border between Muslim and Hindu rule in Telangana depended on circumstances based on the changing fortunes of the respective rulers of the region. Finally, Bahmani Telangana, consisting of Indur and Kaulas (and perhaps, Bhongir) was established. The Kakatiya *nayakas* and the Bahmani administration would have had to come to mutually acceptable terms in order to ensure law and order, peace, easy tax collection, and flow of supplies of men and material to military operations. Kapaya Nayak and his successors became vassals to the Bahmani king, although they occasionally revolted or allied with the Vijayanagar empire across River Krishna.

Although much diminished in power and territory from that of the Kakatiyas, the Velama kings of Rajakonda and the Reddi kings of Kondavidu did provide a focus of authority and cohesion for each sub-region. Constant warfare ensured that the military ethic of the *nayakas* and *lenkas*, became more intense if it changed at all. However, Richards (1975) says that by about 1500 AD,

> The confused conflict between the retreating Bahmani and advancing Orissan and Vijayanagar forces in Telangana left a large number of virtually independent *nayaks*. Each occupied one of the many strongholds with which the countryside was studded; each commanded a body of hereditary Telugu troops who garrisoned the fort and defended it and its surrounding territory. These *nayaks* probably paid tribute to or negotiated with Muslim generals or Vijayanagar governors–whoever was present to make demands (1975: 8–9).

The contest between Vijayanagar and Bahmani raged along the length of the Tungabhadra-middle Krishna river line, with the Raichur Doab (the land between the two rivers) becoming an annual battlefield. The first war was brutal primarily due to the indiscriminate killing of lakhs of prisoners of war and civilians, including women and children, by the victorious Muslims. After the initial terror, the Vijayanagar ambassadors took a stand against the merciless treatment of the innocent and the poor, and told Mohamed Shah Bahmani I that ordinary people could not be punished or be treated as 'accessory' to political crimes. Advised by the good sense of the ambassadors on this matter, and also realising that is was best to remain on peaceful terms with the princes of the Carnatic, since his successors would be neighbours with them in future, Mohamed Shah Bahmani I took an oath stating a complete avoidance of further cruelty: '... he would not, hereafter, put to death a single enemy after a victory, and would bind his successors to observe the same line of conduct. From that time to this, it has been the general custom in the Deccan to spare the lives of prisoners in war and not to shed the blood of an enemy's unarmed subjects' (Ferishta 1989: 197).

This Bahmani policy also extended their practice of not levying *jizya* (Islamic canonical poll tax) on non-Muslims, started by the first Bahmani king, Allaudin Hasan Shah Gungu Bahmani. Gradually, the Hindus and Muslims of the region moved towards civilised behaviour, which was broken by occasional outbreaks of terrorism. This accommodation probably explains why the Vijayanagar empire made little attempt to expand into inland Telangana and liberate it from alien rule. Vijayanagar's thrust was mainly towards the deep south in an attempt to consolidate the peninsula, and meanwhile also to strengthen and hold the line of the Tungabhadra and middle Krishna river. They, however, contested the control of the former Kakatiya coastal province of Andhra and Kakatiya's trans-Krishna Rayalaseema province not only with the Bahmani rulers, but also with the Gajapati kings of Orissa.

The two empires of Vijayanagar and Bahmani carried their respective expansions across the peninsula towards the east and west, till they both stretched from sea to sea and faced each other throughout. Occasional breaks across this line promptly resulted in corrective action from the other side, and the line was restored. The Bahmanis resorted to a kind of annual test of forces–usually held in the Raichur Doab–due to an Islamic invocation to perform *jihad* (Islamic Holy War) at least once a year. This meant that for the first time, Hindu armies had to be kept on permanent standing order at the river border to prevent any severe breach of the accepted line.

By 1363 AD, the Bahmanis had acquired Golkonda (then only a simple fortress), and by 1425 AD, they had annexed the kingdom of Warangal, which had been their subordinate ally (Joshi 1973: 12). After many Bahmani setbacks earlier and elsewhere, the sultan reasserted his dominance over Telangana: '... the Sultan [Shihabuddin Ahmed I], alert despite his old age, moved into Tilingana in 1433 with a large army, conquering many forts including the strong fort of Ramgir. Singa III of Warangal submitted without a struggle but was restored to his possessions' (Sherwani 1973: 169–70).

The 1427 AD grant of the Racherla chief, Lingamanedu II, at Charikona at Kalvakurthi, introduces the Racherla family as belonging to the fourth caste, that is, as Sudras. He claims, among other titles, that of the 'Hindu Suratrana [Sultan]' and that of 'Medini Varaha that is the uplifter of the earth which was taken away by the Yavanas [Muslims]'.

The grant also mentions the Gajapatis, Asvapatis (Bahmanis) and Narapatis (Vijayanagar) kingdoms (GoAP 2003: 105–12). There is an interesting formulation by Phillip Wagoner on the implications of such a division in terms of Hindu tradition and the conceptual basis for understanding the political and military situation in the Deccan (1993: 60–69). The Hindu *nayakas* of Telangana were claiming supreme power and success over the Muslim Bahmanis, and were at the same time balancing between the Orissa Gajapathi kings and the Vijayanagar empire.

There exists an interesting inscription of 1453 AD at Darpalli in Ramayanpet *taluk* (an administrative unit) of Medak district, which acknowledges the Bahmani sultan, Alauddin. It states that a family of Velamas gave a daughter named Kasavamba in marriage to the Bahmani king, Alauddin, and the marriage produced a daughter, Jayi, for whose prosperity the construction of the tank was ordered. The father of the queen, Panna, is said to have been ruling 'Davadri Pattana' and he called himself 'Hinduraya Suratrana' (Hindu Sultan), among other titles (GoAP 2001: 256–62).

In 1460 AD, however, the Orissa king, Kapileswara, sent his armies under his son, Ambiradeva Kumara Mahapatra, and his nephew, Virabhadra Raghudeva Narendra, to take over Telangana. The king's brother, Parasuramadev, father of Raghudeva Narendra, was already ruling the former Kakatiya province of Andhra from Rajamahendravara (Rajamandry). Assisted by the former Kakatiya *nayakas*, they defeated the Muslim rulers and captured Warangal (GoAP 2016a: 283, 284).

The background to this extraordinary move of the Orissa conquest of Warangal was triggered when the Sikander, cousin of the Bahmani Sultan Allauddin Humayun, rebelled against his sultan. The rebels had been helped by the Telangana *nayakas* led by Linga. The sultan marched an army into Telangana and besieged Devaronda. Linga then appealed to Kapileswar of Orissa for help, who had already made himself lord of coastal Andhra as far as Kondavidu. Kapileswara sent his general Hamivira to Linga's help, and the Bahmani army was surrounded on all sides and defeated with great loss. Hamivira now marched on to Warangal, which was captured in 1460 AD and ousted the Bahmani army from Rajachal, which he made his headquarters (Sherwani 1973: 177–78).

In Telangana some accommodation between the Bahmanis and the *nayakas* seems to have been devised, and a trade-off between high taxation, on the one hand, and non-interference with local order, on the other, was affected. Although there is no direct evidence, there is one piece of inscriptional evidence of taxation of land under Bahmani rule.

The inscription on a stone set up near the *karnam*'s (village accountant's) house at Malkapuram, Guntur *taluk*, that is, Guntur district in present-day Andhra Pradesh, is dated 1442 AD. This inscription

> ... [r]ecords the extent of land in each of the 19 villages included in the Ravipundi-sthalam as measured by the standard rope of thirty-eight cubits, the measurement having been made by the villagers themselves, by mutual agreement, under the orders of Bahim Shah [the titular name for the Bahmani rulers]. It further states that on the *gudikat* so arrived at; the *Kapus* [Hindu cultivators] should pay the full assessment, Muhammadans half the assessment and Brahmins no assessment. Brahmins and Muhammadans are exempt from the grazing tax (Ramayya Pantulu and Rao 1948: 385–86).

The Muslim elite that was ruled by the Bahmani empire was composed of three main elements: the immigrant Shia Persians, locally born or converted Muslims, and imported 'Abyssinian' black slaves converted to Islam. The interplay between these three groups that was mediated, and sometimes encouraged and aggravated, by the Bahmani sultans, regularly brought the court, army and royal household into a violent crisis. The internal royal family politics of succession also plagued the sultans. The three groups chose to back competing successors and embroiled the state in civil war. Apart from individual murder and assassination of the highest court and army officials, regular massacres of one group or the other took place, and sometimes the sultan himself ordered it. Issues of race, language and sect divided the Muslim elite. Neither did these types of disputes make for the stability of the state, nor for peace and order.

Considering that the Muslim elite had to govern and rule the Hindu population, the structure of the state was weak. The state depended mainly on the enormous tax revenues collected from the hardworking Telangana farmers through the agency of Hindu *nayakas*. In this sense, the accommodation worked, but it was to the complete detriment of agriculture and the livelihood of farmers. Without the cooperation of the Hindu feudal structure, the Bahmani empire was a non-starter despite its regular and occasional successes in the battles against Vijayanagar.

The siting of Vijayanagar on the Tungabhadra river and Bahmani at Gulbarga put both capitals within striking distance of each other's capitals, and at the same time, made them vulnerable. Later, the Bahmanis shifted their capital to Bidar to be further away from Vijayanagar and towards Telangana. This move is an indication of Bahmani weakness, as the Vijayanagara capital was never shifted despite having been besieged several times, each time unsuccessfully.

These gains and losses of territories and forts went on against the Bahmanis. When Qutb ul Mulk was appointed the Bahmani Governor of Telangana in 1495–96 AD, he was able to get effective control over Warangal, Rajakonda, Dewarkonda and Kovilkonda (Sherwani 1973: 199). However, by 1504 AD, Chittapakhana alias Sitapati alias Shitab Khan, a Boya by caste, had defeated the Bahmanis and captured Warangal. He reinstalled the images of Krishna and Siva, which had been 'removed by the Turukushas' (GoAP 2016a: 291). He allied himself with Ramachandra, now Raja of Orissa.

The defeat of Shitab Khan and his great army of 60,000 Boyas, including 'thousands of gunmen, many elephants and masses of infantry' was essential as Shitab Khan had become the 'virtual overlord of Telangana' (Sherwani 1973: 16–33). Sherwani seems to consider this campaign of Qutb-ul-Mulk against Shitab Khan as the birth pangs of the Qutub Shahi state of Golkonda (ibid.). This episode of Shitab Khan is a story by itself and illustrates the resilience of the *nayakas* of Telangana under Muslim rule (Sastri 1932; Talbot 1995: 692–72). This story also brings to light the role of the Boya community in providing the main battle force to the Kakatiya *nayakas*. They had been independent rulers of the Divi province, and when Ganapathideva conquered Divi, he married two of the Boya princesses of the Ayya family and the son was made the general of his armies. Ganapathideva's two sons by the Ayya princesses were his only male heirs, although they did not succeed him. They had rebelled against their half-sister, Rudrama, and she had reached an accommodation with them. The Boya community was a significant element in the Kakatiya polity.

Hanumantha Rao (1987) provides a detailed account of the rise of this aboriginal tribe to power and prestige. They were also active in the south-east in Kondavedu as part the Vijayanagar forces, and later gave Sultan Qutub-ul-Mulk a hard time (Sherwani 1973: 19). It is not clear what exactly their social status was, but the current Boya community of Telangana is known for its hunting and muscular activity. Talbot (2001) also points out that many inscriptions of Boya donations and endowments are available (2001: 57). The existence of these inscriptions indicates the high status and considerable wealth of this community.

Therefore, the Muslim hold on Telangana was rather tenuous, even after the collapse of the Kakatiya empire. The twin pressures of Vijayanagar and Orissa hemmed in Qutb-ul-Mulk's attempt to dominate Telangana. Finally, Sultan Qutub-ul-Mulk marched on Warangal and forced the Raja of Orissa to accept River Godavari as the interstate border (Sherwani 1973: 199). The Bahmani conquest of the Dewarkonda fort led to 'all of the Rayas, Chaudaris and Sardars of the country around brought costly presents and paid homage to him' (ibid.: 22).

Across the river border, Pax Vijayanagar and Pax Bahmanica had reigned for 170 years (from the time of the founding of the Bahmani empire in 1347 AD up to 1518 AD, when it split into five smaller sultanates). This uneasy 'peace' between the two rival empires allowed for their internal development and prosperity of their peoples living behind the river border. It is within this framework of a cold-hot war that the *nayakas* under Vijayanagar and Bahmani administered their land and their people, and rendered service to their immediate rulers, both native and alien.

The Bahmani empire broke up, as it inevitably would have, due to its internal contradictions, and extended reach over a diverse set of Hindu populations. Out of the successor sultanates, Telangana came under a Qutub Shahi dynasty, whose internal contradictions were less severe than that of the Bahmani sultanate. The Qutub Shahs ruled a more compact region and a homogeneous Telugu-speaking population. They had to deal with and fight off the Bijapur sultanate—the rump of the Bahmani Empire—and tackle the other Muslim sultanates, the Vijayanagar empire and the Gajapatis of Orissa. They could hardly afford the internal rebellion of a Hindu population, led by their natural elites, the *nayakas*, and their battle-hardened forces.

After the destruction of the Vijayanagar empire at Talikota by the combined forces of the sultanates in 1565 AD, the Mughal empire became the main danger to all the Deccan sultanates, as it advanced towards the south from Delhi. Golkonda was the last of the Deccan sultanates to fall.

Telangana Elite under the Qutub Shahs

In Telangana, the Qutub Shahi dynasty inherited most of the structures of the Bahmani empire, but was able to manage better due to the accommodation arrived at with the Hindu *nayakas*. The fact that Telangana was relatively homogenous in demographic, linguistic and religious terms contributed to the cohesive nature of the Qutub Shah's Golkonda sultanate. The Qutub Shahs did have the inevitable conflict among the Muslim ruling elite, divided between the immigrant Persian Shia and local-born/converted Muslims. However, unlike in the Bahmani empire and some of its successor states, the Qutub Shahs did not have to cope with an imported Muslim Abyssinian slave elite. The problem that arose later was a sectarian issue between the Shia and Sunni Muslim ruling elite, which (in the later phases) resulted in provoking Mughal intervention.

The founder of the Qutub Shahi dynasty, Quli Qutub Shah, was the *tarafdar* or governor of Telangana in 1496 AD. However, he controlled only the territory between the fortress of Golkonda and the old Kakatiya capital Warangal, while the territory between Warangal and the sea came to be occupied by local chieftains, Reddis or *nayakas*, who owed loyalty mostly to the Gajapati of Orissa. Purushottam of Orissa held the whole of the Godavari-Krishna doab right up to Vijayanagar territory and had driven the Bahmani forces as far south as Kondavidu (Sherwani 1973: 18).

Thus, Sultan Quli Qutub Shah had his work cut out for him, with the Hindu kingdom of Orissa in the east, north and north-east, and the Hindu empire, Vijayanagar, on his southern and south-western border. He was indirectly assisted by the internecine war between the Orissa and Vijayanagar kings, which devastated most of the area around Kondavidu:

> The capture of Kondavidu was preceded by the subjugation of minor forts in the district such as Vinukonda, Bellamkonda, Nagarjunakonda and other forts in the vicinity and the devastation of the country around about at the hands of the [Hindu] *Boya* chiefs and three lakhs of Vijayanagar foot soldiers. This activity must have alienated the sympathies of the local population and, perhaps, made it easier for Qutb-ul-Mulk to re-conquer the littoral later (Sherwani 1973: 19).

In 1536 AD, the Racherla chief, Chintakunta Padmanabha, stated in an inscription at Kommarapalli in Nagarkurnool that Sri Rangaraya, the Vijayanagar prince, and later, king of Penukonda from 1572–86 AD, re-established Sri Ramanujacharya's *Sri Vaishnavism*. He made the grants at Rayalagandi in Pratapagiri *seema* (a territory or region), over which he exercised authority. It also records that Sri Rangaraya built a temple and its compound walls, made a series of grants towards the daily rituals to God Chennakeshava, established the village of Dharmavaram, and built a tank called Dharmasamudram. He also built a temple for Lord Hanuman in Gandi (GoAP 2003: 112–17]. This activity also indicates the remarkable 'business-as-usual' situation even 100 years after the Kakatiya collapse in a region under alien Muslim rule.

Sherwani (1973) also comments on the importance of the contribution of Ramaraj. He was a powerful Telangana feudatory *nayaka*, who eventually left the service of the Golkonda sultan and moved over to Vijayanagar. There he married the emperor's daughter and eventually succeeded as a Regent. Such a relationship between the Hindu feudal order and its personalities and the Muslim central power is a curious one, but its stability seems to indicate a *quid pro quo* between the two elements, which otherwise had no common identity.

The Hindus were commanders of fortresses, treasury, units of the Golkonda army, governors of districts, and even confidential advisors to the sultans. In crucial situations, Hindu *nayakas* played a decisive role in determining the succession to the Golkonda sultanate, as in the case of the succession to Jamshid, the second of the Golkonda sultans, elaborated in the following excerpt:

> Of one thing we are certain, and that is the increasing part which Hindus begin to play in the affairs of the state. We have already seen how Ramaraj was appointed to the important charge of a newly conquered frontier district by the founder of the dynasty, and how 'he gained firsthand knowledge of the internal conditions of the Qutub Shahi kingdom which enabled him later to wage a successful war against Golkonda (Sherwani 1973: 97).

The account further continues:

> Then we have the power of the *Naikwaris* [who were small Hindu aristocrats], which was evident as early as the reign of Sultan Quli Qutub-ul Mulk and which was again to its best advantage during the small but crucial role of Jamshid's son, Subhan. Jagadeva Rao, 'the most trustworthy of all the sardars', still continued to pull the strings, and we further hear of Jagapat Rao and others who are second to none in the power they yield (ibid.).

Formal submission and oaths of loyalty to the sultan from Hindus, along with Muslims, were recorded. After the death of his brother, Sultan Jamshid, Ibrahim Qutub Shah returned to Telangana after 10 years of exile in the Hindu kingdom of Vijayanagar, where he was a state guest. The inscription at Koilkonda records the following:

> The *arkuns*, officers, *Naiakwaris*, the army stationed there, blacksmiths, *odders*, well-diggers, guards, load bearers, bandsmen, tenants and many other Hindus and Muslims of the locality, who waited on him and swore on their honour and their wives honour that they would have nothing to do [with his opposition] (GoAP 2003: 167–72; Sherwani 1973: 103).

Further, an inscription in the Recharla stronghold of Rachakonda records that 'all *mannes*, subordinates and eighteen sects of people united made a pledge that they would remain only under the command of Malik Ibrahim Shah Vodayalu and none else' (GoAP 1992: 313–14).

Towards the end of his rule, Ibrahim, the most successful and famous of the Golkonda sultans, acknowledged the importance of Hindu cooperation and support, even going to the extent of appointing a Hindu Prime Minister, Marahari Rao, a Brahmin. Wielding new power,

> Rao became highhanded and tyrannical in his behaviour and even took upon himself to sack the famous temple of Adoni and remove the idol which is made of gold and silver and studded with rubies. It is said that when he brought the idol before Ibrahim, the Sultan was seized by violent type of typhoid and never recovered (Sherwani 1973: 176).

An inscription of 1584 AD at Chinna Ahobalim states that in 1579 AD, Ibrahim, along with his Hindu chiefs, captured Ahobalim and held it for five to six years. This refers to the raid that Maurahari Rao carried out on Adoni in 1579 AD. After the Vijayanagar defeat in 1565 AD at Talikota, Ibrahim's death in 1580 AD must have constituted the Golkonda push across River Krishna into the Vijayanagar territory. Ahobalim was recaptured by Kondaraju Venkatraju, leading the Vijayanagar forces during the rule of Sri Rangadeva Maharaja I, and it was restored to its past glory and established rituals (GoAP 2013: 327–30).

Sherwani's (1973) account suggests that Telangana was still very much under the control of local Hindu feudal *nayakas*, who switched their loyalties between the king of Orissa, the emperor of Vijayanagar and the Golkonda sultan, depending on the circumstances.

The data on the Qutub Shahi public works is sparse. However, there exists an inscription of 1554 AD, which states that a 'well-wisher' of Sultan Ibrahim Qutub Shah reconstructed a damaged dam across the Musi river and canal system to provide irrigation water to fill tanks, reservoirs and irrigate land. The tax was settled at 'the King's share one, people's share one and half, and one each for the *Turkas* [Muslims] and Brahmanas' (GoAP 1994b: 218–20).

Thus, after the restoration or construction of a tank, its crop output of irrigated land was to be distributed, where 33 per cent would be given to the farmers, and 67 per cent would be given to the state, of which the king retained 22 per cent and allocated 22 per cent each to Muslim and Hindu divines. This division seems rather ungenerous, to say the least, to the hardworking farmers.

The detailed inscriptional evidence that exists is that of the construction of the great tank of Sanigaram in Karimnagar, which states that 'according to the *firman* of the Sultan, his officer, named Syed Mazaffar Sarkhan has granted a sum of 540 *honnus* gold coins to the Havaldar Meenavi Beg for constructing the big tank' (GoAP 2016a: 126). This measure is perhaps one of the few instances of the construction of a major irrigation tank by the Qutub Shahi dynasty under Abdullah Qutub Shah (1626–72 AD). An inscription dated 1602 AD at Mangalapalli records the following details:

> ... [W]hile Mohamed Quli Padashah was ruling the kingdom and Narasan *nayaka* of Panugallu was administering Nalgonda *Faujdar* Mokhasa, the latter's servant Chama Venkatayya, son of Sarvaya, caused the well to be dug near the Siva-Kesava temple, and installed the Vinayaka pillar and garden. The garden was exempted from tax and *koru* (GoAP 1992: 314–16).

This inscription is full of implication. First, there is the recognition of the Qutub Shahi rule; second, the fact that a Hindu *nayaka* from the critical strategic town of Pangal was also ruling the Nalgonda military sector on behalf of the Golkonda sultan; third, that the temple was dedicated to both Siva and Vishnu, thus indicating a lack of hostility between the two major sectarian divisions of Hinduism. At Vallaturu in Nalgonda, in 1658 AD, additional deities were installed, stating that 'religious merit can be acquired by worshipping the deities and denying the duality of the Gods Vishnu and Siva' (GoAP 1992: 357–58).

It seems from all these inscriptions that local control rested with the Hindu *nayakas*, who continued their traditions of temple construction and devotion despite the presence of a Muslim ruler. It would seem evident that apart from their formal submission, and sometimes, participation along with their Muslim suzerain's armies, these local chiefs were in full control of their areas.

Furthermore, Hindu revenue officials regularly gathered and transmitted tax revenues, depending on the strength of the central authorities. These tax revenues were huge and rested oppressively on the Hindu farming community. In this regard, Richards (1975) provides the following account:

> Thus, as in previous regimes, Brahmin clerks and accountants appear to have filled most of the lower ranking positions in the Golkonda central administration. Brahmins were especially strong in the Telugu branch of the central secretariat which issued orders and edicts in the indigenous language. Telugu Brahmins also practised their traditional skills in the central fiscal office. Brahmins frequently rose to the highest positions in these state departments (1975: 17–18).

It continues:

> But by far the greater strength of this caste lay beyond the capital in its control of the revenue system. In every type of tax collection, the agents who actually made the collection were virtually all Brahmins. Brahmins also served as ubiquitous agents [*vakils*] for virtually all great men, whether Muslim nobles or Hindu, Armenian, or European merchants. In this capacity Brahmins often achieved substantial wealth and real (*sic.*) if delegated power (ibid.).

Without the aid and abetment of the Hindu *nayakas* and Brahmin revenue officials, the Muslim state could not have existed as a political and financial entity. It also required the Muslim state to avoid explicit and apparent opposition of local religious, cultural and political sensitivities.

A 1670 AD inscription in Kurnool district indicates the restoration of Qutub Shahi rule and refers to a donation by Timma Reddi, who installed the image of Hanumantaraya in his *mirasi* (land by hereditary right) village, while Sarfaraz Khan, having been crowned, was ruling in the city of Kandanavole (GoAP 2013: 370–72). The 1679 AD inscription at Orkal in Kurnool district, which records the grant of land by '*Maha nayamkachary Raja* Sri Mandla Chinna Timma Nayadu', however, does not acknowledge the Qutub Shah or Vijayanagar king. In 1697 AD, at Bollavaram in Kurnool district, Goparaju Prasanayya was said to have donated land, while 'Avaramga Padasha Sahab [Aurangzeb] was ruling at Amudanagaram, another name for Hastinapuram [Delhi]' (ibid.: 76–77). A 1706 AD inscription in Velpunur in Kurnool district records the grant of land by the village Reddis and *Karnams*, but it does not refer to any sovereign (ibid.: 377–78). The changes in the political situation, as evident from these inscription seem quick and sudden.

As for the administrative capacity of the Qutub Shahi state, it rested mainly on a Hindu local governance structure, which combined the *nayakas* and the Brahmins in a collaborative relationship with the central Muslim power. It seems somewhat strange that despite an onerous and discriminatory Muslim land tax of 50 per cent of crop output on Hindu farmers who would have paid only 16 per cent to Hindu rulers, there was no civil war, and a relative peace seems to have existed. The accommodation between Muslim rulers and Hindu farmers seems to be one of taxes paid in exchange of non-interference in local religious, social and political traditions and sensitivities.

The absence of any religious bigotry on the part of the Muslim Qutub Shahi rulers prevented the provocation of the Hindu population. During their rule, temple construction by local Hindu notables continued to take place, as evidenced by many inscriptions:

Richards (1975) concludes that the Muslim state depended heavily on the dominance of the the Hindu *nayakas* in military and political functions and on Brahmin revenue officials in tax collection. The *nayakas* and their followers provided troops available for active service at any time and remained as garrison troops. Telugu *nayakas* manned the great fortress of eastern Deccan, which was, however, now under Muslim control (Richards 1975: 18). In political terms, the *nayakas* were important parts of the Muslim state:

> *Nayaks* possessed political importance much greater than the purely military function. Members of the great Telugu warrior/cultivator castes, they had direct links of both kinship and interest with the regional aristocracy of Golkonda: the *zamindars* who dominated the traditional agrarian system of the kingdom. Involvement in the central political system, coupled with considerable autonomy in the agrarian sector, served as partial compensation for the loss of independent Hindu political power. The result was a substantial measure of support for the Qutub Shah regime (Richards 1975: 19).

They even assisted in campaigns against neighbouring Hindu rulers and states:

> For example, three Telugu chiefs mustered 30,000 spearmen to reinforce the Golkonda horsemen which invaded the southern Karnatik under the general Mir Jumla in the mid-1640s. These Golkonda *nayaks* willingly joined the campaign to extend Muslim domination over their fellow Telugu *nayaks* still loyal to the Vijayanagar successor state at Chandragiri (ibid.).

As for the Brahmins, the following excerpt talks about their roles and influence:

> The Neogies [members of the Brahmin Smartha caste] are engaged as writers and village accountants .... the *Arwelu* sub caste forms the bulk of the Neogies in this State. The word *Arwelu* means 6000, and it is said that the primary ancestors of the *Arwelus* were invested in one day with the *patwarigirship* of 6000 villages by Abul Hasan, the last of the Qutub Shahi Kings of Golkonda [1672–1687], through the influence of his Hindu [Brahmin] ministers, Akkanna and Madanna ... (Satyanarayana 2007: 36).

Towards the end, the last Sultan Abul Hasan Tana Shah had appointed a Hindu Brahmin, Madanna, as his Prime Minister and he, in turn, appointed his close relatives to important posts such as the minister in charge of the army, Qutub Shahi ambassador at Bijapur, Governor of Karnataka, and so on. (Sherwani 1973: 627–29).

All of this, with the alliance with Shivaji, the Maratha chief, inevitably led to discontent among the Muslim ruling elite that saw its power being taken away by the Brahmin bureaucracy, much to the distaste, anger and reaction of Aurangzeb, the Mughal emperor, who was nominally overlord of Golkonda. In 1687 AD, Golkonda became a Mughal province under the direct administration of the emperor, thus putting an end to the last of the great Deccan sultanates.

The relationship between the central Muslim authority and the Hindu feudal aristocracy and Brahmin bureaucracy in Golkonda always had to be kept in balance; and when this balance was upset, the state collapsed. Despite all of Aurangzeb's radical policy, the basic structure of governance in Golkonda, even after it became a Mughal province, rested firmly on the willingness and cooperation of the Hindu feudal order to collect and remit taxes in exchange for local control and governance.

Telangana Elite in the Mughal Interregnum

Both the Mughal emperors, Jahangir and Shah Jahan, had been content by dominating the Deccan sultanates and by extracting tribute and recognition of their suzerainty over them. Aurangzeb, the new Viceroy of the Deccan, had his own ideas on how to handle matters, but was always superseded by the central Mughal court. After various attempts at negotiation, and following horrific fratricidal battles and the executions of his brothers, the issue was finally settled in 1687 AD. After the bloody succession war and the establishment of Aurangzeb's sole and absolute power, he returned to the issue of Golkonda. However, even after a problematic conquest, the problems of governance of the now Mughal province of Golkonda were far more severe, and were in no small extent insoluble, given the attempt to impose the Mughal mode of governance. The leading scholar on the Mughal administration of Golkonda, John Richards, states that after Aurangzeb conquered Golkonda, his administration failed to realise its full economic potential. Golkonda experienced a sharp decline in both population and productivity. State revenues never recovered to their pre-conquest levels. He attributes part of the cause to the fact that by 1711 AD, the previously strong bond between the Hindu *nayaks* and the Muslim State of Hyderabad had withered away. This seems to have led to a failure of public order and security in Golkonda (Richards 1975: 306).

The previous accommodation between the Muslim state and Hindu local powers had ceased to operate under Aurangzeb's rule.

Aurangzeb ordered the imposition of *jizya* on Hindus, and this created turbulence, as the tax had never been imposed by the Qutub Shahs or by the Bahmanis. In the end, this amount was added to the land tax, which already appropriated 50 per cent of the crop output. Collection of taxes was vigorously pursued and it created dissatisfaction. In addition to this, Aurangzeb also divided the kingdom of Golkonda between the Hyderabad (Telangana) region and the Karnatik (Andhra) region to make governance manageable and to prevent the concentration of power by his governors.

The early years of the Mughal conquest, despite Aurangzeb's direct intervention, required collaboration as well as force to ensure governance and tax collection. Richards feels that collection of taxes was 'precariously dependent on the goodwill, loyalty, and efficiency of the Reddi, Velama and Kamma *deshmukhs*, and to a lesser extent on the largely Brahmin *deshpands*' (1975: 142).

After the conquest was consolidated, Mughal administration became more effective in rural Golkonda (now renamed Hyderabad) by adopting the Qutub Shahi system of working with the Hindu rural potentates. As Richards points out,

> The usual pattern appears in this process: in Telangana, the older core area of Muslim domination, the Mughals dealt with Reddi, Velama or other zamindars who were powerful in one of two *parganas* but rarely more. In Andhra, they negotiated with a handful of Velama, Razu and Brahmin leaders who were prepared to act as *deshmukhs* and *muniwars* over complete districts (1975: 132).

However, unlike in the Qutub Shahi system, Aurangzeb excluded Hindu feudal elements from the military structures:

> After 1687 no channel for personal contact existed between the Muslim ruler of the eastern Deccan and the Telugu warrior aristocracy of that region ... Diminished personal loyalties, coupled with widespread resentment of the newly imposed discriminatory taxation, encouraged a generally sullen attitude among the former *nayaks* of Golkonda. Each of the various Telugu rajas in Hyderabad was still operating more or less within the boundaries of a single district. When engaged in rebellions or plundering activities, these tended to have a specific focus in or near his own territories and had a limited existence (ibid.).

However, the Muslim rulers could neither ignore the *nayakas*' role, nor could the role of the Brahmin revenue officials be avoided. The *nayakas* became *deshmukhs*, and the Brahmin revenue higher officials were called *deshpands*. All the *deshmukhs* belonged to the traditional ruling castes: 'the majority of *deshmukhs* were from the dominant military/agricultural castes: Reddi [*Kapus*], Velamas and Kammas. The Reddis held *deshmukh* positions in 41 of the total 103 *parganas* listed' (Richards 1975: 139). The transformation of the *nayakas* into revenue administrators ensured the loyalty of the Hindu feudal military elements. In the appointment of these *deshmukhs*, the most important consideration was 'political and military power at the local level. The *deshmukhs* received a percentage of the taxes collected, which could vary without fear of reprisal' (ibid.: 141). The Mughal system survived largely due to the continuation in content rather than form of the political structure of Golkonda. As late as 1700 AD, the Telugu warriors of the region continued to see all their political relationships in the pre-Mughal perspective and were likely to rebel if their rights were threatened (ibid.: 134).

The available documentation of a spectacular revolt—and that, too, by a non-dominant caste person—illustrates the rapid collapse of the Mughal system after Aurangzeb's departure from the region. The revolt of Papa Rai, the toddy tapper, broke through the traditional feudal caste domination of physical power, also defying Mughal rule. Richards provides in his work a detailed account of Papa Rai (Richards 1975: 245–52). Papa Rai rose rapidly from service under a Hindu *zamindar* (landowner) to setting up a fortress in Shahpur and Tarikonda. Mughal records indicate that he was also adept at kidnapping wealthy and beautiful women. Despite direct orders from Aurangzeb to his governor, Papa Rai continued his activities (ibid.: 247).

However, in 1798 AD, his night raid on Warangal and its fort, and the consequent sack and massacre, was a major setback to the Mughals. The fact that it was during the Muharram holiday added to his advantage and made the raid successful. The Mughal record describes the attack in these words:

> Throughout that night and the next day an estimated 12,000 to 15,000 persons lost their lives, while those who survived—especially the local gentry—had little honour or wealth left. Between 2000 and 3000-foot soldiers and 400 and 500 horsemen had mustered under the bandit chief's banner for the assault on Warangal (Richards 1975: 247–48).

Two months later, he looted Bhongir town and carried off 2,000–3,000 prisoners (Richards 1975: 249). The Mughal solution was to co-opt Papa Rai into their system. As Richards describes:

> During [Emperor] Bahadur Shah's stay in Hyderabad [1709] Pap Rai had won recognition and legitimation of his power at a personal audience in which the emperor bestowed robe of honour on him. In return for acceptance as *zamindar* within the imperial system, the chieftain made a large tribute payment [reportedly 1,400,000 rupees]. He also supplied quantities of provisions for the imperial army as well (1975: 245).

This suited the Mughal administration; but it was opposed by the local Hindu aristocracy and the Muslim gentry of Bhongir and Warangal districts, and the accommodation was reversed. Issues of caste, status and religion, apart from the vengefulness of his victims and their families, were too great to sustain his position within the Mughal administration. In the end, of course, this opposition stimulated a temporary alliance among the Mughal army, Muslim *ulema* and the Hindu *nayakas*, and he and his followers were crushed (Richards 1975: 248). The Mughal army launched a massive attack, with 10,000–12,000 cavalry, and 20,000 foot soldiers at Papa Rai's fortress at Tarikonda. When this direct attack failed, Papa Rai and his followers were besieged for nine months. Many, including Papa Rai, deserted the fortress as supplies were running short. Later, Papa Rai was captured and met a very grisly end at the hands of Mughals (ibid.: 249).

As Richards comments: 'To understand the fierce enmities aroused by Pap[a] (*sic.*) Rai one must comprehend the manner in which he violated the most jealously protected areas of status, caste, and religion. Simultaneously he threatened the stability of the social and political system of that area' (1975: 247). The entire episode illustrates what a forceful personality could get away with in troubled times. As long as opposition to his activities was partial and muted, his existence was assured; but due to various factors, the opposition consolidated and resulted in his end. Currently, he is a hero for the toddy-tapping community in Telangana, and his resurrection as a fighter against the Mughals is celebrated. What he did not have in his lifetime—honour and glory—are now assured (Richards and Rao 2015).

Telangana Elite under the Nizamate

As the Mughal empire collapsed under multiple strains of lack of internal cohesion, Maratha expansion, Persian invasion and weak rulers, the Deccan became a plaything between Mughal governors and the dominant Maratha power. Only after the victory of British power over the Mughals, French, Hyder and Tippu, Marathas, Sikhs and the Nizam by 1830, came a sort of peace that may be called Pax Britannica. By the 1850s, this induced Sir Salar Jung I, the Regent and Prime Minister of successive Nizams, to carry out reforms in Hyderabad, of which Telangana was a major part. Sir Salar was a member of a family that had provided leadership to Hyderabad and service to the Nizams for over nearly a century, starting with Mir Alam (he was Diwan from 1804–08), his son-in-law, Munir ul Mulk (1809–32), Munir ul Mulk's son, Siraj ul Mulk (1846; 1851–53), to finally, in 1853, Munir ul Mulk's younger son, Salar Jung (1853–83).

By 1718 AD, the Mughal emperor, much decreased in power and wealth, handed over the Deccan to the Maratha *durbar* (court) at Poona by appointing it to the *sirdeshmukhi* (title for a revenue administrator; head of a set of *deshmukhs*) of the Deccan, with the power to collect both the 10 per cent due to the *sirdeshmukh*, in addition to the *chauth* (a regular tax imposed by the Marathas on Mughal provinces)[5] of 25 per cent levied by the Marathas on local state revenues. This burden meant that the Poona *durbar* captured nearly 35 per cent of the revenues of the Deccan. Failure to pay meant that the Maratha armies descended upon the region for direct collection, and other expected damage and depredation followed as a consequence. The governors of Golkonda, appointed by the Mughal emperor, and later, by the Nizams were helpless and tried as far as possible to keep the Marathas at bay through the payment of tribute and the occasional military resistance.

The Nizamate of Hyderabad was therefore dependent on several forces that were concentrated upon it. The situation was not ideal; the Mughal emperor could contest the legitimacy of the Nizamate; the Marathas exercised taxation rights and collected their dues physically; the Telugu *nayakas* and *deshmukhs* (revenue administrators) exercised total power at the local level, and the Brahmin bureaucracy was responsible for revenue collection. A further complexity arose from the active presence of French and English forces, as their respective East India companies began to participate directly and indirectly in the governance of the region.

The Nizam progressively surrendered the Northern *circars* (north-eastern Andhra) first to the French and then to the English. He then gave away the Guntur *circar* to the English and acquired the Karnatik districts after the defeat of Tippu Sultan by the allied English, Maratha and Hyderabad armies. Finally, he acquired Marathwada after the defeat of the Maratha armies by the combined English and Hyderabad alliance.

In the end, however, the Nizam had to surrender the Karnatik and much of what became Madras Province to the English.

Much of this sad state was caused due to military incompetence, strategic failure, the lack of collaboration by the Hindu population and its natural leaders, as well as financial mismanagement and lack of adequate tax collections. The Nizamate borrowed continuously and surrendered territory or territorial tax revenues in place of the repayment of loans, or even for military protection and assistance during the succession of the Nizams. The Nizamate was never an independent entity, and it existed mainly at the mercy of the Marathas, French and English, in that order.

Under Salar Jung and his successors, the modernisation of the Hyderabad government proceeded in stages. The conversion of feudal rights and privileges of the local notables, *deshmukhs* and others were compensated by regular income from the Central Exchequer, which allowed the regime to increase its control over the rural countryside. Some great Velama and Reddi chiefs were recognised as *rajas* (kings), and their estates were called *samasthans*, where they exercised powers of taxation as well as civil and criminal justice. As in the Hindu *samasthans*, title-holders exercised powers of taxation and civil and criminal justice in the estates of the great Muslim notables (including Sir Salar Jung), the *paigahs* (former military leaders) and the Crown. Non-local Hindu prime ministers and other non-local Hindu high officials were also given *jagirs* (fixed tenures of large estates) and *zamindaris* (landownings) (Nayeem 2009, Volume 1: 191–205). As shall be observed later, nearly one-third of the state was controlled by these sub-state entities.

It is only after the reforms of Sir Salar Jung I that the Nizamate achieved some kind of internal cohesion, a certain degree of financial and military capacity, and clear-cut governance structures that were based on the collaboration between the Muslim rulers and the Hindu elite. Under Sir Salar Jung, and even later, the government imported personnel to manage the state. These personnel were generally Persian Shias (as was the case in the earlier Muslim rule); or were Shia Muslims, Hindu Kayasthas and Khetris from north India; from Bombay, Parsis, and from Madras Province, Brahmins. Moreover, the central governance structure was primarily based on a bureaucracy composed of imported Persian, Urdu and English-speaking officials.

The local Muslim elite, which formed the leading part of the governance structure, received estates in and around the capital city, Hyderabad. They received extensive estates, especially in the Marathwada region, which had been detached from the Poona *durbar*. There was considerable unrest between the Hyderabad-born Muslims and the imported Muslims and Hindus since they were competing for office. A sprinkling of British officers, seconded to the Nizam's state, completed the cocktail that constituted the Hyderabad urban elite. Till the twentieth century, the Hindu feudal elite avoided living in the capital and preferred the comfort, security and status that they had in their rural base. Their interest in state government employment began after they sent their sons and nephews to Hyderabad city for formal education in Persian, Urdu and English. New opportunities for Hindus expanded to the degree that the state modernised and secularised. This situation once again created an inevitable tension over competition for jobs and preferences.

The Hyderabad army was notoriously weak, leading to the decision to outsource the defence of the state and the protection of the dynasty to the British-organised and commanded Hyderabad Contingent. It was paid for by the Nizam through the allotment of specified districts and revenues to the British government.

The increasing modernisation and secularisation of the state led to rapid growth of the middle-class elite, which was dependent on state administration and allied institutions. The state also embarked on an ambitious policy of industrialisation and sponsored, or even started, industrial and infrastructure ventures. By 1948, there were at least 26 large-scale units, ranging from fertiliser, chemicals, paper, cement, textiles, railways and bus transport, airline to coal mines, construction, machine tools, engineering, asbestos, sugar, cigarettes, leather and other products. These units needed technical and managerial staff as well as entrepreneurs. Given the demand, the supply was forthcoming, both from local people as well as from the imported personnel.

The expansion of the school system and the creation of Osmania University generated the demand for teachers and scholars. The growth of the legal system generated the demand for lawyers and judges. Combined with the growth of print media, this generated a high degree of critical thinking and diversity in opinion. All of these elements, in turn, led to the creation of a middle class that was mostly independent of the rural economy and polity. Some of the younger elements of the rural elite moved to Hyderabad city and other large towns for education and found employment there.

As always, local power in the villages continued to rest with the traditional and natural elite, composed of mainly of the Reddis and Velamas, and some Brahmins. The three village officials, *patwari* (accountant), *mali patel* (tax collector) and police *patel* (law and order functionary), formed the basis for governance at the lowest level. The *patwaris* were generally Brahmins, while the *patels* were predominantly from the Velama or Reddi *jatis*. This system continued until it was abolished in 1985.

With the takeover of Hyderabad by the Indian army in 1948, the first set of moves resulted in the demobilisation of the Hyderabad state army consisting of 22,000 personnel, and the sacking of about 15,000 Muslim bureaucrats and officials. In 1950, the *jagirs* and *zamindaris* were abolished, and nominal compensation in bonds and cash instalments of cash was made to those who lost their primary income as well as status. All these traumatic changes affected both Muslim and Hindu *jagirdars* (title-holders of *jagirs*). The Hyderabad Land Tenancy Act, 1950, arbitrarily conveyed property rights to tenant farmers, and dispossessed the entire upper section of the Hindu landed aristocracy as well as feudal families. Telangana was unsure of its future and was unable to assert itself, primarily due to the absence of a representative, strong and robust elite. In 1951, state elections on the basis of the unrestricted adult franchise were held for the first time, and this electoral process has continued to this day (see Table 2.1).

The elections resulted in a confused polity with the four Marathwada districts seeking to join the state of Bombay, the three Karnatik districts choosing to join Mysore state, leaving the 10 Telangana districts unsure of their future and unable to assert themselves, primarily due to the absence of an influential elite class. In 1956, Telangana reluctantly chose to merge with the newly-created state of Andhra to form the Andhra Pradesh state.

The new method of elite creation through electoral process permitted the old elite castes to assert themselves. The results of successive elections indicate the resilience of the dominant caste of the rural Reddis to sustain themselves. It is interesting to recall that in 1687 AD, 41 out of 103 *deshmukhis* were held by 74 Reddys (Richards 1974: 139). The balance would have been held mainly by the Velamas and the Brahmins. In the whole process of democratisation, the Velama and the Reddy castes have capitalised on their rural strengths and networks while a complete disappearance of Brahmin electoral representation by 2014 has been observed. Muslim electoral representation was confined to the old city of Hyderabad to less than 7 per cent of the general electoral segment. Moreover, the Muslim ruling elite, which had ruled in Telangana for 700 years, has now been extinguished in political, economic and electoral terms.

Table 2.1: Reddy Members of Legislative Assembly (MLAs) in Telangana

Election Year	*Total*	*Reserved*	*General Seats*	*Reddy MLAs*	*Indian National Congress (INC)*	*People's Democratic Front (PDF)/Communist Party of India (CPI)/Communist Party (Marxist) (CPM)*	*Telugu Desam Party (TDP)*	*Telangana Rashtra Samithi (TRS)*	*Other*	*Reddy MLAs as Percentage of General Seats*
1951	100	24	76	24	9	10			5	31.6
1957	85	22	63	24	15	6			3	38.1
1962	104	20	84	36	19	6			11	42.9
1967	100	20	80	33	18	2			13	41.3
1972	100	20	80	25	19	1			5	31.3
1978	106	23	83	30	19	9			4	36.1
1983	106	23	83	32	12	4	16			38.6
1985	106	23	83	31	3	1	17		10	37.3
1989	106	23	83	31	22	2	4		3	37.3
1994	106	23	83	33	4	1	19		9	39.8
1999	106	23	83	31	16		11		4	37.3
2004	106	23	83	41	21	2	4	11	3	49.4
2009	119	30	89	36	19	1	11	2	3	40.4
2014	119	30	89	41	13		5	19	4	46.1
2018	119	30	89	38	9			29		42.7

Source: Election Commission of India, various.

Notes

1. The 'working class' phrase (which is a modern notion) seems to be not quite the right interpretation. The inscription reads: '*samantha visti-vamsha sriman Kakatipur adhinatha Beta*'. The word '*visti*' is taken to mean 'serve' and a '*Samantha-visti-vamsha*' may also mean 'from a lineage of subordinate ruler serving [his sovereign]'. If so, it may have no allusion to caste whatsoever. Further, one account has it as *Samantha-visti-kula*! The word *visti*, according to Sastry (2016), may be a corruption of the term *Vrishni*, or a clan. Either way, Sastry comprehensively deals with the issue, and prefers to rely on the Bayyaram Tank and Bothpur inscriptions to conclude that the Kakatiyas are Sudras (2016: 20–29).
2. Manu says in the verses in Chapter 1:

   v. This [universe] existed in the shape of Darkness, unperceived, destitute of distinctive marks, unattainable by reasoning, unknowable, wholly immersed, as it were, in deep sleep.
   vi. Then the divine Self-existent [Svayambhu, himself] indiscernible, [but] making [all] this, the great elements and the rest, discernible, appeared with irresistible [creative] power, dispelling the darkness.
   vii. He who can be perceived by the internal organ [alone], who is subtle, indiscernible, and eternal, who contains all created beings and is inconceivable, shone forth of his own [will].
   viii. He, desiring to produce beings of many kinds from his own body, first with a thought created the waters, and placed his seed in them.
   ix. That [seed] became a golden egg, in brilliancy equal to the sun; in that [egg] he himself was born as Brahman, the progenitor of the whole world.
   x. The waters are called narah, [for] the waters are, indeed, the offspring of Nara; as they were his first residence [ayana], he thence is named Narayana.
   xi. From that [first] cause, which is indiscernible, eternal, and both real and unreal, was produced that male [Purusha], who is famed in this world [under the appellation of] Brahman.
   xxxi. But for the sake of the prosperity of the worlds, he caused the Brahmana, the Kshatriya, the Vaisya, and the Sudra to proceed from his mouth, his arms, his thighs, and his feet.

   Therefore, the confusion between Bramha and Vishnu as the creator of caste is understandable. However, Bramha originates from Vishnu's navel.
3. Mellacheruvu Inscription of Saka 1233 (1311 AD), reads ' . . . Bomi-raju Errya-Pregada vari-nayamkara Mamdu-(Na)gi-Radi-Bolayya Raddi-vari adhikarama . . . . Melacervu mula sthanamu sri-svayambhu devaraku ramga-bhojanaku *amdula Veluma-vegu* runu samsta prajanu a devu ni samnidhi dharalu vosi iccina kramamu deva-brahmana . . . (Sreenivasachari 1940: 88). Sreenivasachari renders it as 'Mahamandelesvara Prataparudra, Maharaju ruling . . . . On the authority of

Mamdu Nagi-Radu-Bollaya Reddi, the Nayamkara of Bomiraju Erraya-pregada, the Velamas and all the people of that place poured (gift) water and gave in the presences of that God for public enjoyment of the Mulasthanam God, svyambhudeva of Melacervu ...' (ibid.: 89). Sreenivasachari leaves out the 'Thousand' reference to the Velamas, which Talbot (2001) has spotted.

4. In the Vijayanagar successor state of Mysore, the following offices were hereditary, and established in all towns and villages, under the general name of *Ayagar* in Canarese and *Bara Baluti* in Hindustani: (1) *Shanbhog* (accountant), (2) *Gauda* (headman), (3) *Kammara* (ironsmith), (4) *Badgai* (carpenter), (5) *Agasa* (Washerman), (6) *Panchnagi* (calendar-keeper), (7) *Nayinda* (barber), (8) *Madiga* (shoemaker), (9) *Akasale* (goldsmith), (10) *Talari* (village watchman), (11) *Nirganti* (watchman of tanks) and (12) *Kumbara* (potmaker) (Rice 1896: 579). This system continued into the modern period (ibid.: 641). Three of the 12 *Ayagars*, the *Madiga*, *Talari* and *Nirganti*, were members of *jatis* considered 'untouchable' (Purushothaman and Kashyap 2017: 4), and are now classified as Scheduled Castes. A similar system existed in Telangana for a millennium, and has been the mainstay of village order and governance until recently. This seems to be an evolution of the *ashtadasapraja* system of the Kakatiya and Vijayanagar periods.
5. *Chauth* (from Sanskrit meaning one-fourth) was a regular tax or tribute imposed, from the early-eighteenth century, by the Marathas levied on Mughal provinces, as a payment for protection or non-interference.

References

Ferishta, Mohamed Kasim. 1989. *History of the Rise of Mahommedan Power in India*, Volume 2, trans. John Briggs. New Delhi: Allied Publishers.

Ganapathi, Racharla. 2000. *Subordinate Rulers of the Medieval Deccan*. New Delhi: Bharatiya Kala Prakashan.

Ganguli, K. M. 2003. *The Mahabharata of Krishna-Dwaipanyana Vyasa*, Volume VIII.

GoAP. 1956. *Corpus of Inscriptions in the Telangana Districts*, Part III, *Hyderabad Archaeological Series*, No. 19. Hyderabad: GoAP.

——. 1973. *Corpus of Inscriptions in the Telangana Districts*, Part IV, *Archaeological Series*, No. 32. Hyderabad: Ajanta Printers for GoAP.

——. 1977. *Inscriptions of Andhra Pradesh: Cuddapah District*, Part I, *Epigraphical Series*, No. 12, ed. P. V. Parabrahma Sastry. Hyderabad: Department of Archaeology and Museums.

——. 1992. *Inscriptions of Andhra Pradesh–Nalgonda District*, Volume I, *Epigraphical Series*, No. 21, ed. Sastry. Hyderabad: GoAP.

——. 1994a. *Inscriptions of Andhra Pradesh–Nalgonda District*, Volume II, *Epigraphical Series*, No. 23, ed. N. Venkatramanayya. Hyderabad: GoAP.

——. 1994b. *Epigraphica Andhrica*, Volume VI, *Epigraphical Series*, No. 22, ed. N. R. V. Parasad. Hyderabad: GoAP.
——. 2001. *Inscriptions of Andhra Pradesh: Medak District, Epigraphical Series*, No. 24, eds N. Mukunda Rao and N. S. Ramachandra Murthy. Hyderabad: Department of Archaeology and Museums.
——. 2003. *Inscriptions of Andhra Pradesh: Mahbubnagar District*, Volume II, *Epigraphical Series*, No. 26, eds N. S. Ramachandra Murthy and P. Jogi Naidu. Hyderabad: Department of Archaeology and Museums.
——. 2013. *Inscriptions of Andhra Pradesh; Kurnool District*, Volume II, ed. G. Venkatratnam. Hyderabad: Department of Archaeology and Museums.
——. 2016a. *Inscriptions of Karimnagar District*, Volume II, *Epigraphical Series*, No. 8, ed. Sastry. Hyderabad: Department of Archaeology and Museums.
——. 2016b. *Inscriptions of Warangal District, Epigraphical Series*, No. 6, ed. N. Venkatramanayya. Hyderabad: Department of Archaeology and Museums.
Gune, V. T. 1974. 'Land Laws', in *History of Medieval Deccan [1295–1724]*, Volume II, eds H. K. Sherwani and P. M. Joshi. Hyderabad: Director of Printing, GoAP.
Hanumantha Rao, B. S. L. 1987. *The Boyas in Medieval Andhra History*, in *Journal of the Andhra Historical Society*, eds Dr N. Venkatramanayya Commemoration Volume, R. Subramanyam, and V. V. Krishna Sastry, Volume XXXVIII, Part IV. Hyderabad: Government of Andhra Pradesh (GoAP).
HEH the Nizam's Government. 1940. *Corpus of Inscriptions in the Telangana Districts*, Part II, *Hyderabad Archaeological Series*, No. 13, Calcutta: Baptist Press for HEH the Nizam's Government.
Hultzsch, E. 1902. *Epigraphica Indica*, Volume VI, Archaeological Survey of India. Calcutta: Government Printing Press.
Joshi, P. M. 1973. 'Historical Geography of the Deccan', in *History of the Medieval Deccan [1295–1724]*, Volume I, eds Sherwani and Joshi.
Manu. 1886. *The Laws*, in *Sacred Books of the East*, Volume 25, trans. George Bühler. Available at https://www.sacred-texts.com/hin/manu.htm.
Nayeem, M. A. 2009. 'Administrative Structure of Hyderabad State', in *History of the Modern Deccan [1720/24 to 1948]*, Volume 1, eds Kulkarni, Nayeem and Seshan. Hyderabad: Abul Kalam Azad Oriental Research Institute.
Pramila. 2002. *Economic and Social Conditions of Andhra Desa:* AD *1000 to 1323* AD'. New Delhi: Bharatiya Kala Prakashan.
Purshothaman, Seema and Sham Kashyap. 2017. 'A Historical Analysis of Land Ownership and Agroecology in the erstwhile Mysore Region of South India', Paper Presented at BICAS 2017, Moscow. Available at https://www.iss.nl/sites/corporate/files/2017-11/BICAS%20CP%205-60%20Purushothaman.pdf.
Ramayya Pantulu, J., and N. Lakshminarayan Rao (eds). 1948. 'Telugu Inscriptions from the Madras Presidency', *South Indian Inscriptions*, Volume X. Director [Epigraphy], Mysore.
Ramesan, N. 1973. 'The Reddi Kingdoms and Other Minor States', in *History of Medieval Deccan [1295–1724]*, Volume 1, eds Sherwani and Joshi. Hyderabad: GoAP.

Rao, M. Rama. 1947. 'The Fall of Warangal and After', *Proceedings of the Indian History Congress* 10: 292–97. Available at www.jstor.org/stable/44137150.

Richards, J. F. 1975. *Mughal Administration in Golkonda*. Oxford: Clarendon Press.

Richards, J. F., and V. Narayana Rao. 2015. 'Banditry in Mughal India: Historical and Folk Perceptions', in *The Mughal State, 1526–1750*, eds M. Alam and S. Subrahmanyam. New Delhi: Oxford University Press.

Rizvi, S. A. A. 2005. *The Wonder that was India*, Volume II. New Delhi: Picador.

Sarma, Somasekhara M. 1948. *History of the Reddi Kingdoms [1325–1488]*. Waltair: Andhra University.

Sastri, Hiranand. 1932. *Shitab Khan of Warangal, Hyderabad Archaeological Series*, No. 9, Calcutta: Baptist Mission Press for HEH the Nizam's Government.

Sastry, Alladi Jagannath. 1922. *A Family History of the Venkatagiri Rajas*. Madras: Addison Press.

Sastry, P. V. Parabrahma. 2016. *The Kakatiyas*. Hyderabad: Department of Archaeology and Museums, Government of Telangana.

Satyanarayana, A. 2007. *Society, Economy and Polity in Modern Andhra*. New Delhi: Kanishka Publishers.

Sherwani, H. K. 1973. 'The Bahmanis', in *History of the Medieval Deccan [1295–1724]*, Volume 1, eds Sherwani and Joshi. Hyderabad: GoAP.

Sircar, Dineschandra. 1966. *Indian Epigraphical Glossary*. New Delhi: Motilal Banarsidass Publishers. Available at https://archive.org/details/indianepigraphic00sircuoft.

Sreenivasachari, P. 1940. *Corpus of Inscriptions in Telingana Districts of HEH The Nizam's Dominions*, Part II, *Hyderabad Archaeological Series*, No. 13. Calcutta: Baptist Mission Press for HEH the Nizam's Government.

Talbot, Cynthia. 1995. 'Inscribing the Other, Inscribing the Self: Hindu-Muslim Identities in Pre-Colonial India', *Comparative Studies in Society and History* 37(4): 692–72. Cambridge: Cambridge University Press.

——. 2001. *Pre-colonial India in Practice: Society, Region and Identity in Medieval Andhra*. New Delhi: Oxford University Press.

Venkatramanayya, N., and M. Somasekhara Sarma. 1960. 'The Kakatiyas of Warangal', in *Early History of the Deccan*, 2 Volumes, ed. G. Yazdani. London: Oxford University Press for GoAP.

——. 1962. 'Vilasa Grant of Prolaya Nayaka', *Epigraphica Indica*, Volume XXXII, pp. 239–68, eds D. C. Sircar and D. C. H. Chabra. New Delhi: Republished by the Manager of Publications, Government of India.

Wagoner, Phillip B. 1993. *Rayavachakamu [Tidings of the King]*. Honolulu: University of Hawaii Press.

3

Semi-Feudal Tenure in Telangana and Andhra

Origins

In India, the subject of 'feudalism' is much written about and debated. The concept itself originates in Western Europe and has been adopted, mostly due to intellectual laziness, by the nationalist, secular and Marxist scholars, and then by politicians of all persuasions. Thus, when and why did the 'feudal' set-up come into being in India? The origins are ambiguous and the answer must be speculated upon. However, Marc Bloch, a renowned scholar on the subject, provides clues on the matter when he attributes the origins of West European feudalism to the collapse of the centralised rule of the Western Roman Empire and the recovery of civilisation after the Dark Ages that followed it. The definitive text, Bloch's (2011) seminal work on European feudalism, is worth a close reading. It casts much essential light on the similarities and differences between 'feudalism' in India and feudalism of the classical European model.

Bloch locates the development of feudalism in the West to the need to confront external enemies and protect the peripheral regions where central authority was weak. From the middle of the ninth to the early-thirteenth centuries, Western and Central Europe faced raids, attacks and invasions in the south by Arabs and other Muslims, in the north by Scandinavians, and in the east by Hungarians (Bloch 2011, Volume 1: xxv, 4–5, 84–85).

Bloch (2011) considered the evolution of feudalism to be a response to the alien invasions of Europe on all the three sides, that is, north, east and south. The centralised armed response was not quick enough to counter raids and invasions at the periphery. The solution was to empower local warriors to defend the empire or kingdom and to grant them the capacity to mobilise financial, human and other resources to be able to meet the challenge successfully. This solution also required the granting of status, legitimacy and permanence to these local notables who were part of the land and people. A graduated series of privileges, honours, marital alliances ensured the strengthening of ties between the feudal nobility and the sovereign. Feudal nobles also had an obligation to protect the Church and ensure the application of both secular and religious law. Rivalries between the feudal nobility as well as an occasional revolt against the sovereign were problems that arose from this type of decentralised governance and power. Over time, the Christian Church conferred legitimacy, and the assembly of feudal nobles yielded power to the king on his coronation. To that extent, the Christian Church arbitrated over these differences, strengthened the Crown, and expeditiously resolved matters. More relevant to our problem, of tracing the origins of Indian feudalism, Bloch writes, citing this as a subject of interest:

> It is a question of the deepest interest whether there have been other societies, in other times and in other parts of the world, whose social structures in their fundamental characteristics have sufficiently resembled that of our Western feudalism to justify us in applying the term "feudal" to them as well . . . the feudalism which we shall attempt to analyze here is that to which the name was first applied (Bloch 2011, Volume 1: xxv).

In the narrative which follows, we will use the expressions 'feudal' and 'feudalism' with circumspection and in its historical context. Much of the discussion about feudalism in Indian scholarship has been focused on the extractive elements in taxation and other privileges exercised by the feudal class, without balancing their political, military and financial roles in the society and the nation. At the extreme, these terms are used as epithets and are applied to elements in the contemporary capitalist and democratic system.

A reading of ancient Hindu texts—the Mahabharata, as well as travellers such as Hsian Tsang seem to indicate a system of central administration which collected taxes through officials and not through intermediaries (Ashoka 289 BC; Ganguli 2003; Kautilya 1915; Manu 1886; Mookerji 2007). A few millennia later, however, in the Kakatiya and Vijayanagara Empires, we find the presence of *nayaka*s with military functions. However, there is no evidence of the *nayaka*s collecting and remitting taxes to the central power, but there is evidence of only them paying homage and contributing armed men. This function of the *nayaka*s would have been a response to the threat of invasion and conquest by Muslim powers. In this sense, the role of these Hindu traditional elites would be similar to the classical European model of feudalism, both in terms of motivations and functions.

There is considerable historical evidence on the origins of feudalism in Telangana and Andhra. The model that evolved during the Kakatiya and Vijayanagar empires was that of decentralised governance by warrior chieftains. This system developed gradually in order to ensure quick military response to alien threats, maintain law and order, grant civil and criminal justice, and assure a source of revenue and military support to their sovereign when required. However, the collapse of these two empires, their conquest by Muslim power, and later, British rule over them, introduced a hybrid structure that involved both classical feudal elements and tax farming and tax collection roles.

The period from the 1700s to the early-nineteenth century is one of chaos, involving the depopulation and abandonment of cultivation because Telangana had become a war zone and was subject to random attacks and regular extraction of onerous taxes by the Mughals, Marathas, Nizams and as well as by local Hindu chieftains. The reforms of Sir Salar Jung in the 1860s attempted to centralise taxation, empower the state, and create order in the rural areas to ensure stable cultivation and predictable tax revenues. In this process, Sir Salar confirmed the role, authority and benefits of the class of Hindu chieftains who had managed to survive the chaos of the past centuries. These Hindu *samasthans* and *jagirdars* were a class of regime supporters who originated from the land and its people, and were not alien interlopers. Besides these groups, Muslim generals and courtiers, as well as north Indian Hindu court functionaries were assigned *jagirs* or were confirmed in earlier grants with new conditions and less responsibility for actual military support to the state. This system naturally did not extend to the Andhra region, which had been handed over to the British by the Nizam in the late-eighteenth and early-nineteenth centuries. In Andhra, feudal land tenure took a slightly different trajectory.

However, there seems to be an asymmetry in the approach to the feudal question when scholars deal with Telangana, as opposed to Andhra, with much of the available evidence confined to footnotes. Scholars argue that the nature of Telangana feudalism is an important subject that must be explored, especially owing to the ambiguity and lack of scholarship on it; for instance, can feudalism in Telangana be studied primarily by looking at the roles of *jagirdars* and *deshmukhs*? What kind of power did they command?

> Most studies on Telangana have inadequately discussed the complex nature of feudal society and domination exercised by the landlords over the peasantry

> at the grassroots .... How the *Deshmukhs* were able to sustain and strengthen their domination was left unexplained .... Nevertheless, the question is not how the feudal system collapsed but more important is to why and how the feudal order based on *Jagirdars* and *Deshmukhs* survived and lasted so long .... In the existing literature, the internal dynamics of feudalism in Telangana has been inadequately explained (Satyanarayana 2007: 9–10).

Interestingly, Satyanarayana attributes the formation of a landlord class in Andhra to a transition of a warrior class into the landed gentry (2007: 1–8). Both Telangana and Coastal Andhra were part of the Kakatiya empire, and after that, part of its successors, the Vijayanagar empire, the Sultanate of Golkonda and the Nizamate of Hyderabad. Consequently, the analysis of the origins of the ancient feudal structure in Andhra should also apply to Telangana.

The *jagir* system is somewhat similar to the classic feudal structures found in Europe and in the Kakatiya kingdom (Mahdi Ali 1879a: 3). The divergence between the two regions takes place mainly with the advent of British rule in Coastal Andhra after the area was given away by the Nizam of Hyderabad, while Telangana remained under his direct rule. The Nizam and, later, the British accepted the status of ancient feudal entities and their conversion into a class of landholders with the civil and criminal powers and revenue collection authority, but without a military role. The ancient Hindu 'little kingdoms' were distinguished from the minor feudal entities in both regions by the central authorities in a similar manner. Thus, the origins of feudalism in Telangana would undoubtedly be the same as its origins in Andhra. There is no mystery regarding this matter.

Feudalism in Telangana

Much of the taxation of agricultural output was carried out by the central state in areas that it directly administered. However, a substantial portion of the land and the population depending on it was under the ownership and control of *jagirdars* and *samasthans* (in Telangana) and *zamindars* and estates (in Andhra). These entities dealt directly with the central state authorities and the farmers on their territories, and acted as intermediaries between the state and the subjects. Their historical origins date back to periods much earlier than the mid-nineteenth century. The *samasthans* of Telangana and the estates of Andhra had the most ancient origins, while the others belonged to later periods. The Nizams established *jagirs* in Telangana for various functions and gave them differential rights and privileges. The British established the *zamindars* in Andhra as a way of collecting fixed and predictable taxes in what is called a 'permanent settlement' during the nineteenth century. What was common to both regions was that this group of state actors who administered not only decentralised governance, but were also loyal supporters of their effective rulers. From the very beginning of their appointments, they had responsibilities of paying a fixed tribute as well as providing military support.

The modern state waived the latter as it began to provide a standing armed force for itself. Despite this lack of a defining role, this group is usually called 'feudal', with the implication that they closely approximate the feudal class known in Europe. The *samasthans* and estates were ancient and classical feudal entities, which undoubtedly had different characteristics from the other 'feudal' tenures. However, apart from their origins, functions and characteristics, there are significant differences in taxation of land between these entities and the state (see Essay 4). In this essay, I propose to compare the 'feudal' tenure in Hyderabad/Telangana and Andhra in relation to the roles of the state actors as collectors of land tax.

In the Nizamate state of Hyderabad, out of the 5,30,00,000 acres of land, 60 per cent was under *diwani* or *khalsa*, 30 per cent was under the *jagirdari* system, while 10 per cent fell under the category of *sarf-i-khas* (the Nizam's crown estates) (Vaikuntum 2002: 26). Vaikuntum further states that 1,128 out of a total of 21,875 villages fell under *jagirs*, while one-third of the state population resided in the *jagir* areas; moreover, 3,335 villages fell under *sarf-i-khas* (ibid.).

It is important to point out here that there is some problem with the data. While Vaikuntum (2002) is aware of Khusro's (1958) work on this subject, Khusro's figures are substantially different. According to Khusro, in 1949, only 7,430 villages were under *jagir* and other similar tenures. Out of a total of 21,875 villages in the state of Hyderabad, 3,598 (which is 48 per cent) were in Telangana, 1,821 (which is 25 per cent) were in Marathwada, and 2,011 (which is 27 per cent) were in Karnatik.[1] Unfortunately, we do not have the data for the acreage under *jagirdari* in the three Hyderabad regions, but the 1901 Census indicates that 6,235 villages out of a total of 20,012 villages were under the *jagir* tenure.

While Telangana contained 50 per cent of the total *jagir* land, the concentration of *jagirs* was most substantial in the smaller Karnatik region of Hyderabad, which was acquired in 1800 from Mysore after the final defeat of Tippu Sultan. In Telangana, *jagirs* and *samasthans*, notably in Mahboobnagar, Medak and Nizamabad, were held mostly by Hindu feudal entities, many predating Muslim rule. Hyderabad district was called *Atraf-e-Balda* (area surrounding the city) and also the Crown District. The *Atraf-i-Balda* was a 'cordon sanitaire' and a protective zone for the capital city of Hyderabad, as well as the seat of the Nizam and his Court and government. This district was owned almost entirely by the Nizam as Crown property, and the remaining part was owned by loyal Muslim and Hindu courtiers.[2]

By 1949, the area covered by *jagirdari* tenure (*jagirs*, *paigahs* [military *jagirs*], *ilaquas* [whole districts conferred upon important nobles], *samasthans*, *sarf-i-khas*) in Hyderabad (including Telangana) amounted to 35.7 per cent of the total area of the state, covering 34 per cent of all the villages and 29.4 per cent of the total population (Khusro 1958: 2). It seems, however, that over the previous 50 years, the proportions between feudal and *ryotwari* (small holder) tenure fluctuated, but the number of villages grew, indicating increased cultivation and population, as highlighted by the following excerpt and the data presented in Table 3.1 below.

> In 1901, the villages were 13,039 *ryotwari*; 2,094 *Jagir*; 664 *akta* or *sarbasta*; 681 *peshkash*; 415 *ijara*; 309 *agrahar*; and 1006 deserted, and the revenue derived from the *ryotwari, makta and peshkash* villages was rupees 191 lakhs, 6.7 lakhs and 139 lakhs respectively. In the next four decades, by 1947, the *ryotwari* villages increased to 21,875; and *jagir* villages to 7,430 (Nayeem 2009: 73).[3]

Table 3.1: *Jagir* to Total (in Per cent)

District	*Extent*	*Villages*	*Population*
Atraf-i-balda	39.5	46.6	37.1
Indur-Nizamabad	25.9	35.0	36.0
Medak-Gulshanbad	42.7	41.2	33.6
Mahboobnagar	45.2	45.8	38.3
Nalgonda	21.0	21.2	23.7
Warangal	35.0	18.0	15.8
Elgandal-Karimnagar	18.1	18.7	20.1
Sirpur-Tandur-Adilabad	3.7	11.0	9.8
Total Telangana	28.4	28.4	26.1
Aurangabad	24.2	23.7	22.4
Parbhani	19.5	16.0	15.9
Nanded	24.0	23.5	27.0

(*Contd.*)

Table 3.1 (*Contd.*)

District	*Extent*	*Villages*	*Population*
Bhir	12.0	14.3	14.9
Gulbarga	40.7	46.2	51.2
Total Marathwada	20.1	19.9	20.0
Lingasur	39.2	50.5	46.1
Osmanabad	34.5	34.4	28.1
Raichur	35.7	36.5	29.4
Bidar	50.9	57.0	60.6
Total Karnatik	40.3	46.6	45.1
Total Hyderabad	29.5	31.2	30.5

Source: Government of India (GoI) 1909: various.

The revenue-paying villages were assessed differently for annual taxation, that is, Rs 1,465 per *ryotwari* village (villages where the ownership of land and payment of revenue are by individual cultivators), Rs 320 per *makta* village (a grant of a village on specific concessional terms), and Rs 2,041 per *peshkash* village (villages granted to nobles on the condition that they pay tribute). The above data seems to indicate that in the first half of the twentieth century, the proportion of *ryotwari* villages in Telangana remained constant at around 72 per cent of the total. However, what is remarkable is the 72 per cent increase in the number of villages inhabited and cultivated.

The *jagirdari, paigah* and *samasthan* villages did not pay revenues to the state apart from a nominal 'tribute'. Out of these, the 1,089 *paigah* villages had an annual income of Rs 76 lakhs, 1,123 *ilaquas* and exempted villages (those of Salar Jung and other high officials, including former prime ministers) Rs 76 lakhs, 457 *samasthan* villages Rs 55 lakhs, and other 3,122 minor *jagir* villages Rs 143 lakhs (Khusro 1958: 9). From this, it is clear that in the 1940s, the income of the landed aristocracy (Rs 3.50 crores) equalled the state revenue from the cultivating classes (Rs 3.30 crores). However, the share of land revenue in the entire state revenues declined from 85 per cent in 1854 to 20 per cent in 1944 (Nayeem 2009: 73; Vaikuntum 2002: 72).

The *paigah* or military *jagirs*, and to a lesser extent, the *samasthan* estates had an obligation to provide armed horsemen and soldiers to the Nizam. Vaikuntum comments in this context:

> *Paigah* was a grant to a nobleman of the state for the purpose of maintaining the Nizam's troops. After the Subsidiary Alliance [1800], the relevance

> of this was lost, but noblemen continued to maintain [retain?] *paigah* lands. The maintenance of the troops remained symbolic. They not only controlled the revenue administration, but also the judiciary, education, health, public works, survey and settlement etc. The 1927 Reilly Commission recommended the disbanding of *paigah* troops as they were not serving any useful purpose. The Nizam did not favour these recommendations (Vaikuntum 2002: 33).

If so, the nature of the original tenure ended when the state organised its own standing army and ceased to rely on feudal levies. With the lack of reciprocal military obligation of this class, the classic feudal pattern in Telangana ended by the turn of the century. At the minimum, as agents of the state, this class exercised and ensured law and order, and a certain degree of civil administration within their jurisdiction. Following this, the possessors of estates under such tenure seemed to constitute only an aristocracy privileged by birth and antecedents without rendering any particular service to the state, rather than play the role of a classic feudal class.

Apart from the 'feudal' groups described in this essay, in Telangana there existed a group of *deshmukhs* and *sirdeshmukhs*, an institution borrowed from the Maratha system of tax collection. The Mughal emperor granted the *sirdeshmukhi* of the entire Deccan, including that of Golkonda/Telangana in 1719 AD to the Marathas. This change seems to be the origin of the Telangana *deshmukhs* and *sirdeshmukhs*. As part of the reforms of Sir Salar Jung, their responsibilities of tax collection were taken over by the state, which compensated them with annual payments and confirmed their status.

The *deshmukhs* were confined mainly to the *diwani* areas (a territory where the state collects taxes directly from landowners), as their original function was to collect government land revenue from the *ryots*, which, of course, was not due by feudal entities. Salar Jung removed them from the position of tax collectors. However, they continued to hold a high status and extensive lands, as indicated above; these holdings, however, have nothing to do with the traditional role of the *deshmukhs*.

In comparison to the Marathwada region, Telangana was a region of mostly small landholders. Within Telangana, Warangal *suba* (sub-region) (Warangal, Khammam, Karinagar and Adilabad) accounted for most of the small landholders. Stating this fact, Reddy thinks it is directly responsible for the peasant revolt of 1946–51 which broke out in parts of Warangal *suba* (2009, Volume 2: 2). Reddy attributes the impetus for the revolt as coming from small landholders wanting to expand their holdings at the expense of the larger ones. However, as the figures are for land holders not tenant farmers, the latter have been seen as the important elements in the revolt.

From such details, it is difficult to conclude, as Reddy (2009) does, that the peasant movement, ostensibly against 'feudal' exploitation, had a 'direct relation' in areas with extensive peasant landownership. Admittedly, there was no agitation or movement of peasants in the feudal *jagirdari* areas in Marathwada, Karnatik, or even in other feudal areas of Telangana, other than Warangal and Nalgonda. The question regarding the causes of the peasant movement in Warangal and Nalgonda districts, therefore, may still be considered open. Curiously, the *samasthans*, or the classic feudal entities, seem to have been left out of this literature: it is because there was no exploitation there or was there no peasant movement? The link between the two is rather tenuous in Telangana generally as exploitation did not necessarily generate the peasant movement. The figures for the villages under different tenures are given below in Table 3.2, which reinforce the points made above:

Table 3.2: Villages under Tenure

District	*Diwani*	*Jagir*	*Total*
Nalgonda	1,002	254	1,256
Warangal	1,177	259	1,436

Source: Report of the Royal Commission on Jagir Administration and Reform, Bangalore 1947, p. 37 quoted in Thirumali 1994: 223.

What seems clear from the documents and known history is this: the *samasthans* were classical feudal entities, with ruling family lineages going far back into the past; the *paigahs* and *ilaquas* were also feudal, although imposed on the land and the people by alien rule; the other *jagirs* were basically grants for services rendered or to be rendered, and were of a lesser feudal quality in as much as they had diminished responsibility and power. The *sarf-i-khas* were part of the royal prerogative, and as such would be outside any feudal classification. The *deshmukhs* occupied an intermediate position due to their transformation from tax collectors to their status as landed gentry. The *ijaras and inams* were conditional grants and cannot be seen as feudal. The fact that all these entities exercised power in their jurisdiction to a varying degree is not doubted, nor is their status as 'pillars of the regime' questioned. This subject, however, needs much more serious attention than is possible in the scope of this essay.

Feudalism in Andhra

The British introduced what was called a 'permanent settlement' in the Madras Presidency and they assigned large tracts of land to a class of people called *zamindar* against the fixed annual of payment. Quoting data on the entire Madras Presidency, Raghavaiyengar indicates that the land tax in the *zamindari* areas works out to Rs 0.73 per acre, while for the *inam* lands, it is Re 0.10 per acre (1988: 106–08). The *zamindari* rates indicate the element of financial support for a class of the landed elite that was created by the British Raj for its supporters. This tenure also covered 35 per cent of the overall in Madras Province (of which Andhra was a part). In the Andhra region, there was a high concentration of *zamindari* areas in the coastal districts of Ganjam, Visakhapatnam, Godavari, Kistna, Nellore and Chittoor. Districts of Guntur, Cuddapah, Anantapur, Bellary and Kurnool had a minimal concentration of *zamindari* tenure (Rao 1963: 1).

Thus, the proportion of feudal tenure in the Andhra districts varies widely, with higher proportions in the districts acquired from the Nizam in the late-eighteenth century to lower ones in the districts acquired from the Nizam in the early-nineteenth century. Further, many of the districts dominated by feudal tenure also seem to have high proportions of irrigated land (Satyanarayana 1990: 11, 13).

As for the difference between the tax collected by the government and the equivalent rent collected by the *zamindars*, these are large and significant, with *zamindari* rent per acre more than government tax in *ryotwari*, varying between 40–85 per cent more, depending on the district concerned. Overall, the per acre average of Andhra for *zamindari* rent exceeded the average tax on *ryotwari* land by 60 per cent (Rao 1963: 10). In contrast, some scholars have a peculiar and unsubstantiated view of feudal extraction of taxes and revenue from the land in Telangana. In this regard, Rao writes:

> Here some of the biggest landlords, whether *jagirdars* or *deshmukhs*, owned thousands of acres of land. Such concentration of land ownership was more pronounced up in Nalgonda, Mahboobnagar and Warangal *than elsewhere*. The exactions from the peasants in these areas were quite high in the *Jagir* areas. The peasants had to pay land taxes on irrigated land *ten times more than*

> *those collected in that the Diwani areas*, the tax amounting to Rs 150 per acre or 20-30 maunds of paddy per acre (1986: 153–54) (emphasis added).

First of all, there is confusion regarding the concentration of 'feudal' as opposed to *ryotwari* tenure in Warangal and Nalgonda. Reddy states that the number of these small holders was more in Warangal *suba* (a set of districts with a Viceroy at the helm) than elsewhere in the Marathwada region, like the Gulbarga and Medak *subas*, except the Nalgonda district of Medak *suba* (2009: 2). Mahboobnagar was dominated by four or five large Hindu *samasthans*, which do not seem to have attracted violent action by the Communist Party on behalf of peasants, unlike Warangal and Nalgonda. There exist contradictory views on the matter, with the largely Communist narrative claiming that widespread 'feudal' tenure existed in Warangal and Nalgonda, while the data indicates otherwise. In areas with a high concentration of feudal tenure, there seems to have been little agitation, or at least, no Communist intervention.

Further, as can be observed, the very notion that anyone, let alone a peasant, was paying Rs 150 per acre as tax is absurd. Rao (1986) refers to Someshwara Rao (1980), who does not provide any source for his claim. Moreover, the idea that this was equivalent to the value of 20–30 *maunds* (weight equivalent to 37 kilograms) per acre is even more absurd, as the entire paddy crop would not amount to that figure. The paddy estimates range from a low estimate of 11–32 *maunds* per acre for Nalgonda to 9.5–27 *maunds* per acre for Warangal, the low estimates being that of Statistical Abstract (1955–66) and the high estimates were of the settlement officers interviewed (GoAP 1959, Part I, Volume ii: 296, 314).

Khusro (1958) carried out a sample survey of the *jagir* and *diwani* areas and presented interesting data. He was confronted with differences in the weights of *maunds* in different areas and different types of land and crops grown on them. In order to achieve comparability, he reduced the physical weights and physical acres to 'standard' *maunds* and 'standard' acres by giving weights to the different crops and to different types of land–irrigated and un-irrigated (1958: 64–65, 85). His 'standardisation' is not sound methodologically, but there seems to have been no alternative if a comparison had to be made (see Table 3.3).[4]

Fortunately, Khusro also gives us substantial evidence of the differences between taxation and rent in the *jagir* and the *diwani* areas (see Table 3.4). After the abolishment of the *jagirs* in 1948, the land revenue payable by their farmers was reduced by 12 per cent. Rents, of course, were payable to the owner of the land.

Table 3.3: Productivity (Standard *Maunds* Per Standard Acre)

	Owner		*Tenant*	
Feudal Tenure	*1948–49*	*1953–54*	*1948–49*	*1953–54*
Sarf-i-khas	2.83	2.59	2.59	2.23
Paigahs	3.25	2.84	2.98	3.42
Ilaquas	3.15	2.77	2.66	2.89
Samasthans	2.35	2.08	1.88	1.33
Other *jagirs*	3.35	3.34	2.37	2.71
Sub-*jagirs*	3.17	2.72	3.68	3.16
Total	3.07	2.85	2.62	2.64

Source: Khusro 1958: 158.

Table 3.4: *Jagir* and *Diwani* Taxes and Rents

	Rupees Per Standard Acre			*Difference (in Per cent)*	
	Jagir		*Diwani*		
Exactions	*Pre-1948*	*1948–49*	*1948–49*	*Pre-1948*	*1948–49*
Land revenue	1.43	1.28	1.11	29.2	15.3
Rent	8.43	7.53	6.00	40.6	25.5
Total	9.87	8.81	7.11	38.8	23.9

Source: Khusro 1958: 101, 107.

The difference in Telangana of land revenue and taxes between *Jagir* and *Diwani* in the pre-abolition phase was much less than between *zamindari* and *ryotwari* in Andhra (40–85 per cent more than in *ryotwari* areas). Even among different 'feudal' tenures, there were significant variations, as seen in Table 3.5, which indicates that while land revenue went down, rent charged by the owners (except in *samasthans* and *ilaquas*) went up soon after *jagir* abolition!

The classic feudal entities, the Hindu *samasthans*, seem to have taxed and charged significantly lower rates (the lowest) than the Crown (*sarf-i-khas*) property, and those of *paigah*, *ilaquas* or other 'feudal' entities.

ON '*DORAS*'

A traditional nomenclature adopted by the Communist Party, and later, by scholars repeatedly refers to '*dora*' without much effort at defining it, but rather placing it in the feudal category. This nomenclature continues into the modern period, and it may be useful to attempt to define the term.

Table 3.5: Land Revenue and Rent in *Jagirs*

	Rupees Per Standard Acre					
	Revenue		*Rent*		*Total*	
Feudal Tenure	*1948–49*	*1953–54*	*1948–49*	*1953–54*	*1948–49*	*1953–54*
Sarf-i-khas	1.53	1.44	6.79	8.14	8.32	9.58
Paigahs	1.66	1.21	9.00	10.32	10.66	11.53
Ilaquas	1.15	1.14	18.43	13.72	19.58	14.86
Samasthans	1.04	0.86	3.81	2.53	4.85	3.39
Other *jagirs*	1.09	1.10	6.55	7.27	7.64	8.37
Sub-*jagirs*	1.37	1.35	5.77	12.43	7.14	13.78
Total	1.27	1.17	7.53	8.96	8.8	10.13

Source: Khusro 1958: 103.

Thirumali (1992; 1994) adds to the confusion by introducing a class of '*doras*' in the *diwani* areas as 'exploiters' and ascribes the genesis of the peasant movement to exploitation by this class of landowners/landlords, which he labels 'feudal'. In fact, the lack of distinction of the terms feudal, *deshmukhs* and landowners/landlords from the term '*doras*' is equally confusing. Rao combines all the categories thus:

> In the local idiom, these powerful *jagirdars* and *deshmukhs* were called *durra* (also spelled *dora*) meaning 'sir', 'master' or 'lord of the village'. A *durra, often a combination of landlord, moneylender and village official,* traditionally enjoyed several privileges, including the services of occupational castes in return for some payment in cash or kind, but more often than not exacted without payment owing to his power and position (1986: 153).

It seems clear from the above excerpt that there is a tendency to club together as 'feudal', those entities that have been of a feudal nature before their transformation into extraordinary landowners. Gray (1968) provides a more nuanced and realistic picture.

The Crisis of Zamindari

The viability of land taxation is critically dependent on the supply and demand of both land and farmers. The increasing availability of land and fewer farmers both act to prevent the upward revision of land taxes and rent. Conversely, less land and more farmers have the opposite effect. In Telangana, land was abundant and farmers were few, while in Coastal

Andhra, land was relatively scarce, except in the tribal region, and farmers were many. With official encouragement, the former region saw colonisation and the latter, emigration.

In Coastal Andhra, the high population densities in some districts resulted in cultivators abandoning *zamindari* areas and migrating to far off places such as Assam and Burma.[5] This was so extensive in some areas that the Maharaja of Jeypore communicated to the Labour Commission that he would have no tenants left to cultivate his lands, and he would be unable to pay the tax unless he imported labour at higher wages from other parts of India (Satyanarayana 2007: 132).

In fact, 'The Crisis in *Zamindaris* in Andhra, 1900–39' is eloquently described by Satyanarayana (2007: 55–89). It is clear from this discussion that as economic entities, *zamindaris* were rapidly becoming defunct, although playing an active political role in the government of the Madras Province. In Telangana, on the other hand, as stated earlier, the situation was moving towards colonisation, leading to a different kind of crisis from that of Andhra:

> The migration of Coastal Andhra peasants into Telangana commenced in response to the invitation by the Nizam's Government in the 1920s. The Government advertised the scheme of 'colonisation' in order to bring about nearly 40 lakh acres of new land under cultivation. It envisaged the distribution of cultivable wastelands to outside settlers and provided certain incentives (Satyanarayana 2007: 41).

This scheme encouraged the landlords of Telangana as well as the farmers to move to the frontier areas in Adilabad and Warangal. Coastal Andhra farmers also moved to Nizamabad, Warangal and Khammam, where black cotton soils and irrigation were available. In Telangana itself, significant tracts of land, especially forests and uncultivated land, were given on favourable terms, such as a waiver of land revenue for fixed periods, to the existing landed gentry. This scheme also took care of the growing number of their adult male family members and problems of subdivision of their existing holdings due to partitions of their Hindu joint family and its land assets. The sale proceeds of timber felled on these lands supplied them with capital to carry out and undertake the construction of tanks and to settle farmers in the newly established villages.

Once again, this would have had the effect of channelling towards the new settlements the increasing number of those peasant farmers who were hard-pressed to maintain their families on their limited holdings.

All in all, the colonisation scheme served to re-populate the periphery of the state and divert the land hunger of both the landed class as well as the peasantry. This scheme was a feature of the *diwani* areas, that is, the directly administered state areas, and did not apply to the *jagirdari* or *samasthan* areas, except in as much as peasants from these areas might have moved out to the newly colonised regions.[6]

As for other feudal obligations, the situation in Telangana reflects the general pattern associated with feudal tenure elsewhere. In Andhra, for example, *vetti* (unpaid labour from tenants as part of their obligations) was exacted in the Ganjam and Vizagapatnam districts. Debt slavery and bonded labour existed in the Jeypore area of the Ganjam district. Satyanarayana found that 'apart from the *zamindars*, the government also practised *vetti*. They normally granted or permitted the tribal population to freely cultivate in unreserved forest areas for which they had to render labour whenever required' (1990: 131).

In Telangana, such a situation was not unfamiliar, although we have only anecdotal evidence here when compared to the official data of the Royal Commission on Labour for Andhra. As observed, the *zamindari* tenure and the similar *jagirdari* dispensation provided the regimes of the British and Nizam, respectively, with a class of landed elites, who performed similar roles and exercised similar powers. In this sense, then, the appellation of 'feudal' tenure applies to Andhra as well as Telangana to the extent indicated, especially at the rural base of the economy, polity and society. Despite having a strong base in Coastal Andhra, the Communist Party, which sponsored and led the violent anti-feudal revolt in Eastern Telangana, seemed to have ignored the situation in its own base areas.[7]

As far as their history through documentation is known, the feudal order in Andhra was composed of the estates, basically comprising the *samasthans*, who faced much greater supervision and monitoring by the ruling (British) power than the Telangana *samasthans* had to face from the Nizam. The *zamindari* estates, which were part of the 'permanent settlement', were tax entities with limited power within their jurisdictions, and the *inams* (tax-free grants of land) and *agraharas* (tax-free villages) were traditional grants to officials of the old order or to Brahmins, which the British confirmed. This was a stronger legal position and protection for the feudal order in Andhra than the Telangana *samasthans* and *jagirs* had to face from the Nizam, who could take away their rights at will.

Concluding Remarks

The feudal epoch was not uncommon to medieval societies over the world. Its evolution was historically relevant, and its role in its national context was productive in terms of ensuring stability, peace and protection of the land and people. Needless to say, as in all systems, exaction of taxes and labour, as well as forms of oppression, were present to varying degrees. In these areas, there were hardly any checks on feudal power, but the monarch could and did intervene in case of breakdown. The religious leaders also played a role in mitigating feudal misdeeds. Feudal subjects, in desperation, could flee their overlord and find refuge either in other feudal territories or in towns and cities. Finally, the recourse to outright revolt was the last resort.

Also, as the central state became more powerful militarily and financially, feudal rights and roles were weakened by the monarch. With the rise of towns and cities and the growth of trade, commerce and industry, the urban population increased and the tax base of the state expanded. The evolution of urban capitalism was the death knell of feudalism. With the dominance of the central state and capitalist economic formations, the feudal epoch came to an end. As Karl Marx wrote in his Preface to *A Contribution to the Critique of Political Economy*,

> In broad outline, the Asiatic, ancient, feudal and modern bourgeois modes of production may be designated as epochs marking progress in the economic development of society .... No social order is ever destroyed before all the productive forces for which it is sufficient have been developed, and new superior relations of production never replace older ones before the material conditions for their existence have matured within the framework of the old society (Marx 1859).

Needless to say, even after the triumph of bourgeois capitalism, state socialism or popular democracy, feudal patterns of behaviour continue to exist and reveal themselves in individuals and social groups. Feudalism is a political, economic, social and cultural phenomenon. After its base in the economy and polity become redundant, its social and cultural aspects continue to exist and only fade away gradually. Analysing this historical process is essential to understanding the past and liberating ourselves from it in order to move forward.

Notes

1. In the 1901 Census, the total number of villages in the state was estimated to be 20,210; Telangana 8,942, Marathwada 5,490, and Karnataka 5,578

villages; the increase over 50 years of 1,665 villages may be attributable to the colonisation scheme of the Nizam's government in order to re-populate new areas (GoI 1909: 82).

2. His ownership may have been one of the reasons for the poor agricultural development of Hyderabad district, which was later bifurcated and the Ranga Reddy district was created. At the time as the settlement, the Nizam surrendered all his crown lands in exchange of a settlement from the government of Hyderabad. However, due to inertia, laxity and incapacity, these lands were not accurately surveyed and taken into the revenue records. This fact came in handy after the Andhra takeover, as it assisted the land grab movement of the Andhra settlers of this valuable government real estate.
3. For the 1901 figures, he is citing GoI (1909: 59).
4. This is so despite the fact that Rao is aware of Khusro (1958) definitive work on *jagirdari* abolition and quotes him (selectively). However, where hard data is available to him in Khusro, he seems to pass over it oblivious.
5. See 'Migration of Telugu Coolies to Colonial Burma 1871–1947' (Satyanarayana 2007: 294–311).
6. Further scholarly work on this subject may perhaps reveal exciting conclusions.
7. Thirumali (1992) provides an account of the agrarian situation that was affected by the Second World War, high agricultural prices, paddy levy and other related factors:

> However, the state's involvement in World War II and the imposition of a compulsory food grain levy pushed this stratum towards the 'fighting elements'. The government's policy of forcible extraction of land revenue and indiscriminate collection of food grain levy and coercion and high-handedness to contain the growing independence and social assertion of the peasantry was perceived by the peasantry as being in violation of village norms. With increasing state atrocities, these moral issues assumed importance for the villagers, and all peasant classes united, forgetting their sectional interests (1994: 237).

With 'moral' issues entering the picture, the lack of clarity in the matter of who the movement was aimed against and also the question as to why seems elusive.

References

Ashoka. 289 BC. *Lumbini Pillar Inscription*, trans. Venerable S. Dhammika. Available at http://www.cs.colostate.edu/~malaiya/ashoka.html (accessed 8 June 2015).

Bloch, Marc. 2011. *Feudal Society*, 2 Volumes, trans. L. A. Manyon. New Delhi: Gaur Publishers.

Ganguli, Kisari Mohan (trans.). 2003. 'Santi Parva', Part II, Volume IX, in *The Mahabharata of Krishna-Dwaipayana Vyasa*. New Delhi: Munishiram Manoharlal.

GoI. 1909. *Hyderabad State, Imperial Gazetteer (Provincial Series)*. Calcutta: Superintendent of Government Printing.

Government of Andhra Pradesh (GoAP). 1959. 'Report of the Land Revenue Reforms Committee', Part I, 2 Volumes; Part II, 4 Volumes. Hyderabad: Government Press.

Gray, Hugh. 1968. 'The Landed Gentry of Telangana, Andhra Pradesh', in *Elites in South India*, eds E. Leach and S. N. Mukherjee. Cambridge: Cambridge University Press.

Kautilya. 1915. *Arthasastra*, trans. R. Shamasastry. Bangalore: Government Printing Press.

Khusro, A. M. 1958. *Economic and Social Effects of Jagirdari Abolition and Land Reforms in Hyderabad*. Hyderabad: Osmania University Printing Press.

Mahdi Ali, Moulvi. 1879a. *Memorandum to the Famine Commission*. Bombay: Times of India Press.

Manu. 1886. *The Laws*, trans. George Bühler, *Sacred Books of the East*, Volume XXV. Oxford: Clarendon Press.

Marx, Karl. 1977 [1859]. *A Contribution to the Critique of Political Economy*. Moscow: Progress Publishers. Available at https://www.marxists.org/archive/marx/works/1859/critique-pol-economy/preface.htm (accessed on 16 October 2020).

Mookerji, Radhakumud. 2007. *Ashoka*. New Delhi: Motilal Banarsidass.

Nayeem, M. A. 2009. 'Administrative Structure of Hyderabad State', in *History of the Modern Deccan [1720/24 to 1948]*, eds A. K. Kulkarni, N. A. Nayeem and R. Seshan. Hyderabad: Abul Kalam Azad Oriental Research Institute.

Raghavaiyengar, S. Srinivasa. 1988. *Memorandum of the Progress on the Madras Presidency during the Last Forty Years of British Administration*. New Delhi: Asian Educational Services.

Rao, B. Sarveswara. 1963. *The Economic and Social Effects of Zamindari Abolition in Andhra*. New Delhi: Manager of Publications, GoI.

Rao, C. Siva Rama Krishna. 1986. *Agrarian Relations in India: A Study of Andhra Pradesh*. Hyderabad: MVR Foundation.

Reddy, V. Ramakrishna. 2009. 'Economic Development in Hyderabad State', in *History of the Modern Deccan [1720/24 to 1948]*, Volume 2, eds A. K. Kulkarni, N. A. Nayeem and R. Seshan. Hyderabad: Abul Kalam Azad Oriental Research Institute.

Satyanarayana, A. 1990. *Andhra Peasants under British Rule: Agrarian Relations and Rural Economy 1900–1940*. New Delhi: Manohar Publications.

——. 2007. *Society, Economy and Polity in Modern Andhra*. New Delhi: Kanishka Publishers.

Someshwara Rao, G. 1980. 'Peasant Movements and Organization in Telangana', in *Political Economy of India*, ed. B. A. V. Sarma. New Delhi: Light and Life Publishers.

Thirumali, I. 1992. 'Dora and Gadi: Manifestation of Landlord Domination in Telangana', *Economic and Political Weekly* 27(9): 477–82.

——. 1994. 'Peasant Class Assertions in Nalgonda and Warangal Districts of Telangana, 1930–1946', *Indian Economic and Social History Review* 31(2).

Vaikuntum, Y. 2002. *State, Economy and Social Transformation: Hyderabad State [1724–1948]*. New Delhi: Manohar Publishers.

4

History of Land Tax in South India

A Study of Telangana and Andhra

> '*In India, where the people have learned so well to govern themselves from the want of settled government, good or bad government* really depends almost altogether upon good or bad settlements of the land revenue. *Where the Government demand is imposed with moderation, and enforced with justice, there will the people be generally found happy and contented, and disposed to perform their duties to each other and to the state; except when they have the misfortune to suffer from drought, blight, and other calamities of season.*'
>
> —(Sleeman 2003: 86) (emphasis in original).

The issue of taxation is a vital and necessary part of sovereign functions, one which enables the state to fulfil its other sovereign functions. Whether it is to defend the realm, ensure law and order, or to provide civil and criminal justice, money is required. The manner and incidence of taxation is also a function of the ideology of the rulers, their governance methods, and the nature of the economy.

In India, the agricultural sector has, until recent times, constituted the major part of the economy. As such, agricultural taxation was a critical and major source of state revenues. Thus, the taxation of land meant that agriculturists had to pay direct taxes levied based on the extent and quality of land held and cultivated by them. The governance system also exempted or lightly-taxed agricultural landholdings of the ruling elite or religious and royal grantees, who, in their turn, collected the equivalent, or more, of the tax as rent or share of the product of land from their cultivator-tenants. Thus, the incidence of land tax fell mainly on the cultivator, even though he may not have been the owner of the land he cultivated. This system also provided a financial base for the landed elite.

The story of land taxation in India is a sad and torturous one, and this essay attempts to place it in the context of south India, covering a period of over 1,000 years, and also across ideological imperatives of the three ruling groups–Hindu, Muslim and British.

This essay also attempts to analyse the different trajectories of land taxation of the two Telugu regions–Andhra and Telangana. These regions were once united, although later, each came under different governance systems–the first, under the British, and the latter, under Muslim rule. This suggests that differential taxation in the two regions contributed to much of the difference between Andhra and Telangana in the context of agricultural and economic development, and the associated social and political development. This difference continued even after democratic dispensation, which followed the Indian Independence and the merger of the two regions into the state of Andhra Pradesh. Until the land tax was abolished in the 1980s, the divergence in land taxation existed. Other elements of exploitation continued as well till 2014, when Telangana broke away from Andhra Pradesh and became the twenty-ninth state of the Indian Union.

Data on Land Tax

In South India, there is an enormous number of inscriptional data[1] relating to royal grants to temples, village groups and individuals, with a sufficiently clear indication of the extent of land involved and the associated land tax in paddy granted by the royal authority. For the period from the tenth to the thirteenth century, there are 19,000 Tamil inscriptions and 9,000 inscriptions for the period from the fourteenth to the sixteenth century (Karashima 2011: Table 2). Subbarayalu (2012) reports that there are a total of 44,000 inscriptions relating to south India, with the dominant share in Tamil (28,000), with Kannada (11,000) and with Telugu (5,000) following closely. Only 15,000 of the Tamil inscriptions have been edited and published till now. Many of these deal with land grants and provide valuable information (2012: 18). The fact that nearly 30,000 or more inscriptions have yet to see the light of academic enquiry is a sad commentary on our lack of interest in our own history.

There are other documents and reports dating back to the Muslim and Maratha periods, which indicate the levels and methods of land taxation. However, it was only after the East India Company consolidated its hold over South India that reasonably accurate and representative data became available from the meticulous and elaborate land settlements conducted under the supervision of British military and civil officials. For the mid-to late-nineteenth century, the mass of data available is a treasure trove for historians. Being encouraged to follow the British pattern, even the Nizam's Hyderabad, of which Telangana was a significant part, developed a similar methodology of assessment of tax, which was, however, not based on the same low taxation levels. This data provides us with insight into the different trajectories that the two Telugu regions, despite their similarities in terms of religion, culture, and language, developed since the 1830s.

Canonical Sanction

Many pre-modern societies had their tax regimes legitimised by their holy books and by ancient precedent. The Bible, for instance, dictates that a tithe (tenth) is owed to the ruler as the obligation of all the believers. This tax share continues to recognise this canonical instruction. Hindu tradition similarly has its own cannon in this regard.

Hindu Canonical Rates

A reading of the Hindu texts suggests what the monarch can legitimately collect from the cultivators. In the *Mahabharata*, Bhishma instructs Yudhishthira that the 'king should fill his treasure' with '*a sixth part, upon fair calculation, of the yield of the soil as his tribute*' (Ganguli 2003, Volume VIII: 156). This becomes canonical for Hindu rulers. Manu leaves the scope for a variation in the quality of land and nature of crops: 'A fiftieth part of [the increments on] cattle and gold may be taken by the king, and *the eighth, sixth, or twelfth part of the crops*' (1886: Chapter VII, Verse 130). Manu also allows for crisis periods: 'A Kshatriya [king] who, in times of distress, takes even the fourth part [of the crops], is free from guilt, if he protects his subjects to the best of his ability (ibid.: Chapter X, Verse 118).

Müller, however, is unambiguous and provides a single figure: 'He must take from his subjects as taxes a sixth part every year of the grain; and [a sixth part] of all [other] seeds' (1880: 22–23). Baudhayana, in his *Dharmasutra*, says, 'Let the king protect [his] subjects, receiving as his pay a sixth part [of their incomes or spiritual merit' (1882: Chapter 18, Verse 1). But as per Gautama, 'Cultivators [must] pay to the king a tax [amounting to] one-tenth, one-eighth, or one-sixth [of the produce]' (1879: Chapter X, Verse 24).

Kautilya, in his *Arthasastra*, says that '... whatever in the shape of agricultural produce is brought in by the superintendent of agriculture [of crown lands] is termed *sita*. The taxes that are fixed [*pindakara*], *taxes that are paid in the form of one-sixth of the produce* [*shadbhaga*]' (1915: 112) (emphasis added). However, in a later section, Kautilya allows for variation, depending on the nature of the irrigation and labour involved in cultivation:

> Fields that are left unsown may be brought under cultivation by employing those who cultivate for half share in the produce, or those who live by their own physical exertion may cultivate such fields for one-fourth or one-fifth of the produce grown.... Those who cultivate irrigating by manual labour shall pay one-fifth of the produce as water rate; by carrying water on shoulders, one-third of the produce; and by raising water from rivers, lakes, tanks and wells, one-third or one-fourth of the produce (Kautilya 1915: 144).

As can be observed from the Hindu texts cited above, the legitimate land tax that a Hindu monarch can extract varies around the canonical figure of one-sixth, as set in the *Mahabharata*. The monarch bears this in one of his titles—*shadabhagin*, that is, one who is entitled to collect the *shadbhaga* (one-sixth share).

While some scholars are prepared to accept one-sixth rate as the general canonical rate, the translator and editor, Shamasastry, adding confusion, says: 'The word "*shadbhaga*" includes one-fourth, one-third portions, etc. Some take it to mean an excess of the one-sixth portion over and above the prescribed amount of tax' (Kautilya 1915: 112). He therefore links the two separate references, as *shadabhaga* is a clear expression, and so is *Chaturtha-panch-bhagikah* (one who pays one-fourth or one-fifth share) that Kautilya uses in a later reference (Mookerji 2007: 205).

Ashoka (269 BC), in his Lumbini Pillar Inscription, states: 'Twenty years after his coronation, Beloved-of-the-Gods, King Piyadasi, visited this place and worshipped because here the Buddha, the Sage of the Sakyans, was born. He had a stone figure and a pillar set up, and *because the Lord was born here*, the village of Lumbini was *exempted from tax and required to pay only one-eighth of the produce*' (emphasis added). This reduction to one-eighth indicates perhaps that the standard rate was the canonical one-sixth, or least something higher than one-eighth.[2]

There also exist observations by foreign travellers who visited India many centuries later, confirming that the canonical rate was being observed and implemented by the monarchs. During 629–45 AD, the

Chinese Buddhist monk, Hiuen Tsang (also known as Hsuan Tsang or Xuangzang or Youang Chawang), travelled through India and commented: 'The king's tenants pay one-sixth of the produce as rent' (Watters 1904: 176). Around 1017–30 AD, nearly 400 years after Hiuen Tsang's visit, Alberuni (973 AD), writing about Hindu peasants. says:

> With regard to that which he earns by crops or from cattle, he is bound to first pay the ruler of the country the tax which attaches to the soil or pasture land. He pays him one-sixth of the income in recognition of the protection which he affords to the subjects, their property, and their families (Sachau 2010: 557).

During the fourteenth to sixteenth century, despite much of northern and central India under Muslim rule, the Vijayanagar rulers tried to conform to the canonical rate:

> The latter kingdom [Vijayanagara] was now rising to its zenith when it gave birth to the celebrated minister and lawgiver Vidyaranya. On the subject of land tenures, he observes that 'the king who shall take more than one-sixth of the produce of the land from the proprietor, shall be deemed infamous in this world and shall be cast into hell flames in the next' (Briggs 1830: 62).

The Vijayanagar settlement in Canara between 1334 and 1347 AD conformed to it, although later, they also added another set of state 'collections' in favour of temples and Brahmins, which took the total stake of the state to 25 per cent. Following Appadorai (1936), Gune writes:

> The demand of the early rulers, the Hoysalas, seems to have been limited to one-seventh of the gross produce .... Under the Vijayanagar empire, the incidence of government assessment seems to have varied from one-sixth to one-fourth. It was arrived at after measurement of dry soil, and it varied according to the fertility of the soil and irrigation facilities. It was called *Raya Rekha* or Royal Line (1974: 561).

Even the Mughal emperor, Akbar (r. 1556–1605) was aware of the Hindu canonical rate, as his Minister and chronicler, Allami, states: 'Throughout the whole extent of Hindustan where at all times so many enlightened monarchs have reigned, one-sixth of the produce was exacted ... ' (Allami 1891: 55). It would seem that in the eyes of the cultivators, the canonical rate remained the legitimate share that the state could take and whatever political dispensation that came into being later did nothing to obliterate this concept. A state that implemented it naturally received the support of the cultivators,[3] but above 45 per cent, much cultivation was abandoned.[4]

Chola Land Taxes

There is no reference in the Chola inscriptions to the proportion of land tax to gross output. Sen quotes Lewis Rice's 1925 work, *Mysore and Coorg from Inscriptions*:

> The assessment is said under the Cholas in 1046 to be one-sixth of the produce, and this was the recognised Hindu rate from earlier times. However, a quarter of a century later it is described in more detail as a fifth of the produce of forest tracts and of lands on which dry [un-irrigated] crops are raised and a third of the produce of lands below a tank on which paddy is grown (Quoted in Sen 1925: 527–28).

Subbarayulu (2012) cites an inscription of 1073 AD, stating that the state's share in paddy cultivation is one-third. He also quotes Nilakanta Sastri as 'hesitantly' suggesting the same (2012: 105, 108).

Kakatiya Land Taxes

The evidence of Kakatiya land taxes is scarce; one of the sources is Venkatramanayya and Sarma (1960), who, however, does not provide any epigraphical evidence but estimates the tax expressions used and their respective meanings to indicate rates. According to him, the tax called *pangamu*, according to the Telugu dictionaries, meant one-fourth, and that called *para* meant one-eighth. But he does not provide inscriptional evidence for his assumptions. Sastry, however, relying on epigraphical evidence, says:

> ... [W]e can generalize the system of the levy in kind at the rate of one *tumu* per *putti* (both volumetric measures) of gross produce analogous to the *putti-manika* (volumetric measures) and *putti-kunchamu* (volumetric measures) which occurs in the epigraphs as the levy towards *desavandha* (tax for worship in the temple) or maintenance charges of tanks. One *tumu* per *putti* means 1/20 of the gross produce. This amount is what is called *kolochu* (Sastry 2016: 216).

Of course, this depends on how many *tumus* makeup a *putti*. Even in modern times, this has differed from area to area. Thus, we are left with weak evidence. However, the single clear reference is in the inscription of the Vilasa Grant of Prolaya Nayaka of 1330 AD, translated by Venkatramnayya and Sarma (1962). It celebrates the re-conquest and expulsion of the Muslim invaders, generically referring to *Yavanas*, and by an epithet, *parasikas*:

> Having overcome the Yavanas in this fashion, he restored to the Brahmanas the ancient Agraharas confiscated by them, and revived the performance of the sacrifices, the smoke issuing from the fire pits of which spreading over the countryside cleaned the pollution caused by the movements of those evil doers. The agriculturists surrendered willingly one-sixth of the produce of the soil to the king, and he set his hand to the task of repairing the damages caused by the *parasikas* (Venkatramnayya and Sarma 1962, Volume 32: 242).

Thus, the inscription seems to suggest that the Hindu tax rate was re-established after the restoration of Hindu rule. Taking into account the different rates estimated (one-eighth, one-sixth or one-fourth), it would have been a tremendous relief for Hindus from the 50 per cent Islamic tax rate for non-Muslims.

Maratha Land Rates

The Maratha assumption of imperial power required a policy regarding the collection of land revenue in their directly-ruled territories, apart from their demand of *chauth* (one-fourth) from their 'protectorates'. Sen (1925), quoting T. B. Jervis's *Statistical Survey of the Konkan*, states that under Shivaji, the Maratha empire carried out an extensive land survey, measuring and classifying all land, for levying taxes based on 12 different classes of land. These taxes were collected half in kind and half in cash. Out of the tax rates, Sen quotes the *Sukraniti*, which tradition says guided the *Ashta Pradhan* Council of Shivaji: 'Similar classification for assessment purposes was also in vogue, when the *Sukraniti* was compiled, where we find that 'the king should realize one-third, one fourth, or one-half from places which are irrigated by tanks, canals, and wells, by rains and by rivers respectively' (1925: 527).

Sen also refers to the survey of Annaji Datto: 'Annaji Datto, *Sachiv*, entrusted with the survey of the Konkan, fixed the rent at 33% of the gross produce, but Shivaji afterwards demanded a consolidated rent of 40% when all the taxes and extra cesses had been abolished' (1925: 89). Obviously, by this time, even a Hindu monarchy was collecting land taxes well in excess of the canonical rate of one-sixth. The Maratha state was a war state in continuous conflict with Muslim power, and this factor could explain the lapse from the canonical rate.

The Marathas replaced the Bahmani empire and its successor sultanate offshoots in large areas of the Deccan. Both Sen (1925) and Gune (1974) agree that Shivaji (1627–80 AD) modified the rates, but adopted the system that had been introduced by Malik Amber (1549–1626 AD), the Ethiopian Muslim ruler of Ahmednagar. The Maratha rates were midway between the canonical Hindu rate (one-sixth), and the canonical Islamic rate for non-Muslims (one-half) was a convenient expedient for those times.

Islamic Canonical Rates

Al-Qadrawi (2011) is the leading ideologue of the Muslim Brotherhood. He relies on the *Hadiths* ('traditions' of the Prophet many generations after his death, complied into six books, of which *Sahih al-Bukhari* and *Sahih Muslim* generally have the highest status). He stated the Islamic case:

> Al-Bukhari reports from Ibn al-Umar that the Prophet said: 'A one-tenth due is obligatory on that which is watered by the sky or springs or that which is not watered at all, and a half-tenth is obligatory on that which is watered by carried water.' Muslim reports from Jabir that the Prophet said: 'On that which rivers and clouds water, there is one-tenth due, and that which is watered by water carried by camels, there is a one-half tenth' (2011: 252).

The account further continues:

> Yahaya Ibn Adam reports from Anas, 'The Messenger of Allah imposed as one-tenth due on that which the sky waters, and a half-tenth on what is watered by animals and men carrying water in containers.' Ibn Majah reports from Mu'adh, 'The Messenger of Allah sent me to Yemen and commanded me to collect one-tenth from that which the sky waters, or draws [underground] water through its roots, and half a tenth from that which is watered by pails' (ibid.).

The above excerpt from the *hadith* traditions indicates unanimity on the issue, but the tax varies for unirrigated crops and crops watered manually. In the absence of any significant flow irrigation in Arabia, this is understandable. However, these principles of Islamic fiscal jurisprudence did not apply for non-Muslim populations in conquered territories. There the land tax (*kharaj*) and *jizya* (poll tax) was explicitly levied only on non-Muslims. This variation began during the time of the Prophet Mohammed after he conquered Khaybar, when he allowed the Jews there to retain their lands on the condition that they pay half of the produce as tax.

Katbi, referring to Ibn Shitab al-Zuhri (d. AH 124/747 CE), writes: 'The Prophet settled the [Jewish] people of Khaybar on their land, provided they spared the Muslims the work; and half of the fruits—or half of the crops—were for them, whereas the other half was to be distributed according to the Muslim's share' (2010: 7). She further adds: 'Therefore, in principle, the general direction was to divide Khaybar, on the consideration of it as *ghanimah* gained through battle. However, for practical purposes, the process of division was halted, and the land given to the Jews for them to farm in exchange for half the produce' (Katbi 2010: 8).

This event and the Prophet's decision to not distribute *ghanimah* (or booty taken in battle in the form of weapons, horses, prisoners and movable goods) of Khaybar, as earlier, became a critically important policy as Muslim conquests expanded to include territories of non-Muslims, who did not convert to the new Islamic faith. This enabled the Caliph, Umar ibn al-Khattab (r. 634–44) to extend this logic to the territories he conquered in Sawad (Iraq and Persia) despite pressure to divide the land as *fay* (the usual booty surrendered by the defeated) among the Muslims who participated directly in the conquest.[5] As Katbi concludes, Umar

> ... settled the people of the Sawad on their land and imposed the *jizyah* on their heads and the *kharaj* on their land.... The result of this decision was the emergence of a new understanding of the *fay*, namely that it was the lands conquered by force and because of this new understanding the lands became *fay*, endowed for the benefit of all Muslims. The application of the *ghanimah* was limited to movable property such as gold, silver, weapons and livestock (Katbi 2010: 9–10).

The logic of the Caliph was explicitly determined by the general aim of the Islamic objectives:

> In one of his narrations, Abu Yusuf also mentions Umar's fear that the troops and their sons would be isolated in the Sawad from the other Muslims, with the possibility this would stop the process of the conquests and consequently also halt the sources of funding for the army, and that would have an influence on future regiments.... This is in addition to the fear of the troops being preoccupied with agriculture and leaving the fighting (Katbi 2010: 11–12).

This policy continued under later Caliphs such as Harun al-Rashid (r. AH 170–93/783–808 CE), who even had the matter studied and implemented the tax. On his instructions, Abu Yusuf wrote a book on the *kharaj* and its rulings, the *kitab al kharaj*, a comprehensive financial document (Katbi 2010: 110–11). Later this issue was codified in the *Al-Hidayah*, the twelfth-century *Hanafi* manual of guidance, which established *kharaj* as canonical in Islamic law:

> The author of traditional Islamic *fiqh*, *Hidaya*, lays down that; if a prince conquers a country he is at liberty either to divide it amongst his soldiers in the manner prescribed by the Prophet or to leave it in the possession of the inhabitants on their agreement to pay the *jizya* and the *Kharaj* [land tax on non-Muslims], in the latter case the right of the property remains with the inhabitants. The *Kharaj* to be paid by the *Dhimmis* [non-Muslim subjects] amounted to one-half the produce of the land, while the Muslims were to pay a tenth called '*usher*' and '*zakat*' (Gune 1974: 559).

Thus, *usher* (or one-tenth) was paid by Muslims, while non-Muslim paid *kharaj*. This was further elaborated since even the source and use of irrigation water would determine whether the land was *ushri* or *Kharaji*. If water was supplied by the state to land cultivated by Muslims, they paid a tenth while non-Muslims paid *kharaj* of water supplied by earlier non-Muslim rulers (Qureshi 1944: 101).

As a disincentive for a non-Muslim to acquire land owned by a Muslim and an incentive to non-Muslims to convert to Islam, the policy laid down that if a *dhimmi* buys *ushri* land it becomes *kharaji*. But if the owner of a *Kharaji* land turns Muslim, his land still remains *kharaji*. All of the water carried in channels dug or controlled by the state is *kharaji*; so is water contained in reservoirs built with public money (Qureshi 1944: 102–03).

Land Taxes under the Delhi Sultanate

After the Muslim conquest of India and the initial random exploitation in terms of disorganised loot and other brutalities, the Muslim state settled down to rule the land and its people. Instead of following the Hindu practice in terms of land tax, they applied *Sharia* (Islamic law and practice) principles.[6]

> It is now being gradually recognized that the Sultanate was part of the greater word of Islam, that they possessed intimate sources of knowledge about the rest of the Muslim world, in particular of the eastern lands, and that the history and institutions of the empire of Delhi cannot be properly understood if they are divorced from the general background of Islamic history (Qureshi 1944: vi).

Sharia dictated the process and the rates, and the *ulema* decided any claims judicially and clarified issues for the monarch. The difference in land tax paid by Muslim and non-Muslims seems to have existed during the times of Muhammed bin Qasim, Sultan Qutb-uddin Aibak and Firuz Shah (Qureshi 1944: 101–02). As far as the Islamic canonical rate for non-Muslims, that is, almost all the peasants, were concerned:

> Allauddin Khalji claimed the land tax at the rate of half the produce .... Though no direct evidence about the Sultanates of the Deccan exists, similar assessment rates might have existed under them .... *After the conquest of the Deccan Allauddin Khalji levied one-half of the produce as land tax* (Gune 1974: 559, 561) (emphasis added).

As the religious scholar and priest, Qazi Mohammed A'la, stated:

> First, the established custom of kings, past and present, in most territories is that they take half the produce from the subjects [*Zimmis*], and by other cesses and imposts take [something] out of the other half as well. If we regard this as exaction of the [legal] tax [*kharaj*], the king will have to be held at fault for it is unlawful to take more than half the produce as we have mentioned (Quoted in Habib 2014: 18).

The standard textbook on India for this period put it thus:

> The Muslim owners paid one-tenth [*ushr*] of their produce in tax on land watered by rain .... The land left to its known Hindu owners and that allotted to Hindus was known as *kharaji or kharaj*-paying [land revenue paying] land. Other terms used for *kharaj*, especially of the Mughals, were *hasil* or *mal* .... The standard *kharaj* [revenue demand] was fixed at half the produce, and the tax was also imposed on pastures .... The new system of taxation was enforced in all of the areas easily accessible from Delhi, but these did not include Eastern Uttar Pradesh, Bihar, lower Punjab, and Gujarat (Rizvi 2005: 183–84).

Habib (1984), the key modern historian of the Muslim rule in India, sums up the situation during the early Muslim rule in northern India in the following words:

> ... [I]n the western Punjab, which had seen two centuries of Ghaznavid rule, the 'Islamic' taxation system was already in operation. By the end of the 13th century, it might have been imposed in the neighbourhood of Delhi. However, though such a process must have taken place, it is left entirely unrecorded. What is recorded is the seemingly sudden imposition of a uniform taxation system over a very large part of Northern India by Sultan Alauddin Khalji

[1296–1316]. The classic account of Alauddin Khalji's measures is given by Barani (1984: 61).

As for the areas where this Islamic tax of 50 per cent of crop output was collected, Barani stated that it was imposed over a very large region, extending from Dipalpur and Lahore in Punjab to Kara and Katehr (in Uttar Pradesh), and to Nagaur and Chha'in (in Rajasthan) (Habib 1984: 62). Also, under Muhammad Tughlaq (1325–1351 AD), the entire empire, including Gujarat, Malwa, the Deccan, South India and Bengal, were brought under the same rigorous system of taxation that prevailed in the villages of the Doab (ibid.: 63). The resultant effect of this imposition of the Islamic tax regime brought about an agrarian uprising of great intensity over a very large area near Delhi and in the Doab. As Habib (1984) quotes Barani's contemporary account:

> Such peasants as were weak and without resources were completely laid prostrate and the rich peasants, who had resources and means, turned rebels. Whole regions were devastated. Cultivation was totally abandoned. The peasants of distant regions, hearing of the ruin and the destruction of the peasantry in the Doab, fearful that the same orders might be issued for them as for the latter, turned away from obedience and fled to the jungles (Habib 1984: 64).

Worse was to follow:

> The two years that the Sultan was in Delhi [c. 1332–34], the country of the Doab, owing to the rigors of the revenue demand and the multiplicity of *awab* [additional cesses] was devastated. The Hindus set fire to the grain heaps and burned them, and drove away cattle from their homes. The Sultan ordered the *shiqqdars* and the *faujdars* [revenue collectors and commanders] to lay waste and plunder the country. They killed many *khots* and *muqaddams*, and many they blinded. Those who escaped gathered bands and fled into jungles; and the country became ruined (ibid.).

The chronicler's language leaves us little doubt that there was a massive peasant rebellion led by the upper village strata, the *khots* and *muqaddams*, or the headmen. The rebellion, in spite of the brutal methods of suppression, simmered on; and Ibn Batutta found much of the country around Kol (Aligarh) in the hands of rural rebels as late as 1342 AD (Habib 1984: 64). All of this disruption, massacres and revolt led to a collapse of the agricultural system, and shortages of grain and other produce brought about a 'famine which began in 1334–35 and lasted for about seven years.

Barani, as we have seen ascribes this calamity in its initial stages at least, to the heavy land tax' (ibid.).

The Muslim records indicate the basis, extent and results of the imposition of discriminative Islamic land taxation, based on the religion of the landowner. This was the hallmark of Muslim rule in India, and it casts light on the poor state of the agrarian economy, on which the vast majority of the people depended for their livelihood.

Land Taxes in the Deccan under Muslim Rule

As far as the Deccan is concerned, after the collapse of the Delhi sultanate, Muslim power consolidated under the Bahmani empire, which was assisted by Hindu kingdoms that had survived the fall of the Kakatiya empire. The Bahmani empire stretched across the peninsula along the River Krishna, confronting the older Hindu Vijayanagar empire, which stood as a guardian of South India for nearly 150 years. The Bahmani empire broke up into five Deccan sultanates, which combined in 1565 AD to defeat the Vijayanagar empire. Until then, Muslim rule had been confined north of River Krishna.

There exists one piece of inscriptional evidence of the taxation of land under the Bahmani rule. The inscription is on a stone set up near the *karnam*'s house at Malkapuram, Guntur *taluk*, Guntur district in present-day Andhra Pradesh, dated 1442 AD. It 'further states that the Kapus [Hindu cultivators] should pay the full assessment, Muhammadans half the assessment and Brahmins no assessment. Brahmins and Muhammadans are exempt from the grazing tax' (Ramayya Pantulu and Rao 1948: 385–86).

What is not clear is what the assessed rate was or its relation to the crop output, but what is definite is that Bahmani taxation was discriminative, based on religion and caste. Since almost all of the lower bureaucracy was Brahmin, they seem to have managed to get a total exemption, while the Bahmani rulers would have wanted to co-opt the revenue officials, on whose cooperation tax collection was critically dependent.

In the Bahmani successor state of Ahmednagar under the Nizam Shahi dynasty, the settlement had been made by Malik Amber (1549–1626 AD). Malik Amber organised the land taxation system in a rational manner, and seems to have demanded less than the Islamic canonical rate for non-Muslims: '... introduced a new system of revenue settlement. It was based on the correct knowledge of the fields cultivated and the money value of the crop produced. The state demand in kind was about two-fifths, and, in money, one-third of the total value of the crop' (Gune 1974: 562).

The data on the Qutb Shahi dynasty of Golkonda (modern-day Telangana) is sparse, but there exists an inscription of Ibrahim Qutub Shah from 1554 AD, whose increase/total, after the restoration/construction of a tank the product, is distributed in the following manner: 33 per cent to the farmers and 67 per cent to the state, of which the king retained 22 per cent and allocated 22 per cent each to Muslim and Hindu divines (Government of Andhra Pradesh [GoAP] 1994: 218–20). This indicates a higher than the canonical rate was extracted by the Islamic state in this case, which may be an exception.

This is the late period of Muslim rule in the Deccan, and the sultanates were under pressure from Vijayanagar in the early period, and from the Marathas in the later period. Certainly, Islamic canonical land taxation policy was undergoing marginal adjustments in the Deccan.

Land Taxes under the Mughal Empire

Evidence of Mughal taxation is, however, abundant and is recorded from the time of Emperor Akbar (r. 1556–1605). The authoritative text of Emperor Akbar's minister, Allami, cites how he

> ... says frankly that no moral limits could be set to the fiscal obligation owed by the subject to the ruler: the subject ought to be thankful even if he were made to part with all his possessions by the protector of his life and honour. If, then, the revenue imposed did not usually exceed the surplus produce, this was only because such a course, leading to a wholesale extermination of the revenue payers, would have reduced, not increased, the total revenues in the longer run and thus defeated its own purpose (Habib 2014: 231).

While Allami sounds a pragmatic note, the land tax rate does not seem to have changed, as Emperor Shah Jahan (r. 1627–58), after the annexation of the Nizam Shahi territories (of Ahmednagar), in 1637 AD, introduced the Mughal tax settlement where the state's share was about one-half of the produce (Gune 1974: 562).

Sir Jadunath Sarkar (1912) refers to the settlement of Murshid Quli Khan, Dewan of the Deccan (1708–09 AD), once Aurangzeb (r. 1658–1707) finally conquered the Deccan. This involved the following:

> ... Where the crop depended on rainfall, the State took one-half of it, [ii] where the crop depended on well-irrigation, the share of the State was one-third in the case of grain, and from one-ninth to one-fourth in the case of .... special and high priced crops requiring laborious watering and length of culture and [iii] where the fields was irrigated from canals the proportion of revenue to crop varied, being sometimes higher and sometimes lower than land irrigated by wells. *Under Murshid Quli, this became the prevalent system in*

> *the subahs of Mughal Deccan and was known for centuries afterwards as 'the dhara of Murshid Quli Khan'* (Sarkar 1912: 193–94) (emphasis added).

Another view of Murshid Quli's settlement links it with the lower Hindu canonical rates, as stated in the *Sukraniti*:

> Here, as regards the scale of assessment by Murshid Quli Khan, it may be curious for us to note what logicians call a chance coincidence of phenomena between it and the injunctions of *Sukra* about the share of revenue that is to be demanded by the State with regard to lands depending upon varying sources of nutrition. *Sukra* says; 'The king should realise one-third, one-fourth or one-half from places which are irrigated by tanks, canals, and wells, by rains and rivers respectively' (Sundaram 1929: 66).

Given below is another view:

> One half of the produce was taken as land revenue for lands in which rainfall assisted the ripening of crops. For crops which were irrigated from wells, one-third of the produce was fixed as the share of the State and two-thirds as the share of the peasants .... For crops such as sugarcane and grapes, the rates varied from one-ninth to one fourth. Whereas the most productive lands which required little labour and capital were assessed at the rate of one-half of the produce, those which needed some capital and considerable labour were assessed at lower rates (Siddiqi 1989: 46).

To sum up, the Islamic taxation of Hindus of one-half of the produce was drastic in comparison to the Hindu canonical rate of one-sixth. Akbar's minister and chronicler, Allami, was aware of the Hindu canonical rate: 'Throughout the whole extent of Hindustan where at all times so many enlightened monarchs have reigned, one-sixth of the produce was exacted' (Allami 1891: 55). But given that *Sharia* was incumbent on Islamic rulers and the temptation to extract the maximum was attractive,

> It seems that from the beginning that the demand was set so high that it could hardly have been increased any further. If we also take into account the other taxes imposed on the peasants and the regular and irregular exactions of officers and others, we can visualise what a heavy burden was borne by the peasantry (Habib 2014: 235).

This differential system of Islamic state policy, of a harsh and debilitating tax regime on Hindus, encouraged conversion to Islam with the objective of avoiding 50 per cent tax and substituting it with 10 per cent *ushr* (one-tenth share) instead. Of course, *jizya* ceased to be applicable once conversion to Islam took place. There is enough textual evidence provided by Muslim chroniclers of this policy, which, for India, was completely innovative and oppressive. Yet, the force of state power and the necessary accommodation by the subject population and its native elite ensured that the 50 per cent rate continued throughout Muslim rule in India. Its effect on nutrition, health and life-span of the population can be imagined. But, of course, this also affected the development of agriculture and capital formation.

However, with the establishment of a somewhat stable rule from the time of Mughal emperor Akbar onwards, there emerged detailed accounts of the revenue extraction, which we have at our disposal. But despite the more orderly extraction of taxation, the imposition was to the same degree as directed by Islamic law. Irfan Habib (2014) is a source of interesting, accurate and reliable accounts in this regard from contemporary Muslim chroniclers. According to his research of the historical record, Akbar collected two-thirds of the crop in Kashmir,[7] and in Sind, half of the product was the standard. In the desert areas of Ajmer, however, rates were lower at one-seventh or one-eighth of the crop. During Shahjahan's reign, the rate of one-half produce was adopted, for all crops of the *rabi* (winter) harvest wheat, the rate for which is put at one-third. Under crop-sharing, applied to *kharif* (monsoon) crops, the rate is uniformly one-third of the produce. In the Deccan, in the closing years of Shahjahan's reign, taxation was half of the produce from ordinary lands, but one-third from those irrigated by wells and still lower proportions (down to one-fourth) from high-grade crops. In terms of taxation of various crops, Moosvi (2010; 2015) has analysed the figures for Agra Province: ' … the total share of the produce claimed in revenue should have been around half; and one is therefore tempted to conclude that Akbar's administration …. flatly laid claim to one-half of the total produce' (Moosvi 2015: 111).

Evidence from Punjab indicates that Aurangzeb collected half of the produce. A contemporary foreign traveller, writing in 1629 AD, Geleynssen says that in Gujarat, three-fourths of the crop was extracted. Another foreign visitor, Fryer, found that the peasants near Surat were able to keep only one-fourth of the produce for themselves (Habib 2014: 232–34). Raychaudhuri (2015), providing his own broad interpretation of the possible consequences of the taxation policy, writes:

> If 50 per cent of the gross produce was actually extorted from the producers …. the peasant could hardly have been left with a subsistence income in any accepted sense of the term. Such a paradoxical situation may nevertheless be economically viable for a period of time, because the 'below subsistence income', implying very low calorie free content of food, may result in reduced longevity rather abandonment of cultivation, where the peasant has no alternative means of survival (Raychaudhuri 2015: 277).

With the decline in the central rule and power of the Mughal emperor additional factors became evident:

> As central Mughal authority waned, the state resorted increasingly to revenue farming, and the practice became even more widespread in the successor states. This served to raise the effective rent share to 50 per cent or more, greater than the 40 per cent maximum said to have been extracted by the Mughal state ... (Raychaudhuri 1983: 17)

Further, the Indian peasantry did not have much incentive to invest labour or capital since revenue assessment was geared to 50 per cent or more, in contrast to 5–6 per cent in China.

This is the most reliable evidence there is for the Mughal empire, and it establishes the rate of taxation close to the the approved Islamic tax rate of *kharaj* of 50 per cent of the crop output of Hindu cultivators.

As far as the *jama* (overall revenue demand) is concerned, there are detailed figures available from 1595–1720 AD. The question of *hasil* (the degree of collection) will be dealt with shortly. In this situation, one begins to get figures of revenue extraction from the time of Akbar to that of Aurangzeb, the last effective Mughal emperor. The figures that are gathered can be divided into the ones relevant to the core empire and the Deccan sultanates, which were conquered later. The differences in land taxes between the two regions are quite significant (Moosvi 2010: 215–16).

The differential in the rate of taxation per unit area between the empire and the Deccan seems significant, especially as the conquest and annexation of the Deccan was achieved during the last decades of the empire. Some of the Deccan sultanates provided tribute to the empire in the early period, until they were finally annexed by Aurangzeb from 1667 AD onwards. However, the area figures need to be treated with caution, as they are approximate geographical estimates derived from a map. They do not provide any but a vague estimate of the cultivated area (Moosvi 2010: 218). Moosvi's estimates vary marginally over time. Between 1601 and 1667 AD, the Deccan yielded 3–3.5 times more tax revenue per land area than the core empire.

A more robust analysis was made 120 years ago by Sir Jadunath Sarkar in 1901. He provided separate figures for each *subah*, thus allowing for differentiation between the core empire of 10 *subahs* and an additional six *subahs*, where data is missing or has gaps, which prevented comparison over the two periods, 1594 AD and 1720 AD. His figures for the four Deccan *subahs* can then be compared with those of the core empire. Taking *subahs* where comparable *bigha* data is available, his figures can be easily understood and tabulated in Table 4.1.

Table 4.1: Land, Land Revenue and Collection in Mughal India (Comparable *Subahs* in the Core Empire)

	Subah	*Area in Lakh (Daftari Bighas)*[8]		*Increase/ Decrease*	*Revenue in Rs Lakh*		*Increase/ Decrease*	*Rs/Bigha*		*Increase/ Decrease*
		1594 AD	*1720* AD	*In Per cent*	*1594* AD	*1720* AD	*In Per cent*	*1594* AD	*1720* AD	*In Per cent*
1	Delhi	311.32	693.57	123	150.40	264.66	76	0.48	0.38	-21
2	Agra	422.15	558.79	32	136.56	224.16	64	0.32	0.40	24
3	Allahabad	60.12	197.04	228	53.11	72.56	37	0.88	0.37	-58
4	Oudh	154.11	190.23	23	50.44	83.10	65	0.33	0.44	33
5	Bihar	37.03	131.53	255	55.48	94.60	71	1.50	0.72	-52
6	Malwa	64.64	129.65	101	60.17	90.05	50	0.93	0.69	-25
7	Ajmer	324.79	174.10	-46	72.10	175.30	143	0.22	1.01	354
8	Gujarat	256.61	127.49	-50	109.21	132.57	21	0.43	1.04	144
9	Multan	49.61	44.54	-10	50.42	45.91	-9	1.02	1.03	1
10	Punjab	244.78	243.20	-1	139.86	145.30	4	0.57	0.60	5
	Total 10 *Subahs*	1,925.16	2,490.13	29	877.76	1,328.20	51	0.46	0.53	17

Source: Sarkar 1901: xxviii, xxxii, 123–61.

It will be observed that for over more than 100 years (1594–1720 AD), there has been an expansion in the area subject to taxation in eight out of the 10 *subahs*. It is not clear whether this implies an increase in the cultivated area itself or an increase in the extension of the area under taxation, which was earlier left out of the tax accounts due to administrative inefficiency. Multan and Punjab saw a stagnation of both revenue and area cultivated. Ajmer has extraordinary figures, where its area declined by 46 per cent and revenue increased by 354 per cent. Gujarat's cultivated area declined by 50 per cent, while revenue increased by 144 per cent. Both Ajmer and Gujarat are curious exceptions. Overall in the core empire, the tax demand increased by 51 per cent, while area increased by 29 per cent, thereby resulting in the revenue per area growing by only 15 per cent over a period of 120 years. This would indicate a fiscal crisis of major proportions. Some core empire *subahs* have gaps in data. But for the sake of comparison, they are included here in Table 4.2.

Table 4.2: *Subahs* in the Core Empire with Data Gaps

	Area in Lakh Bighas		*Revenue in Rs Lakh*		*Revenue*	
Subah	*1594 AD*	*1720 AD*	*1594 AD*	*1720 AD*	*Increase/ Decrease*	*Rs/Bigha 1720 AD*
1 Bengal		3.35	118.18	140.73	19	
2 Orissa			31.43	43.21	37	
3 Thatha			16.56	17.33	5	
4 Berar		200.28	160.65	225.60	40	1.13
5 Khandesh		88.00	113.82	115.01	1	1.31
6 Kashmir			15.53	53.21	243	
Total six *subahs*		382.89	456.18	595.08	30	

Note: The figures for the Bengal area are mystifying.
Source: Sarkar 1901: xxviii, xxxii, 123–61.

Table 4.3: Deccan Under Mughal Rule (1720 AD)

Subah	*Area in Lakh Bighas*	*Revenue in Lakh Rupees*	*Rs/Bigha*
1 Aurangabad	255.71	295.00	1.15
2 Bijapur		336.85	
3 Haidarabad		273.21	
4 Bidar	78.72	155.14	1.97
Total four Deccan *subahs*	334.43	1060.19	

Source: Sarkar 1901: xxviii, xxxii, 123–61.

In 1594 AD, the Deccan was not a part of the core empire as it was ruled by Shia sultanates, the successors to the Bahmani empire. Some of them only paid tribute money to the Mughal treasury. The data for 1720 AD is comparable to that of the Core empire in this period, and is given in Table 4.3.

The comparative data for the three parts of the Mughal empire have now been put together in Table 4.4. The conclusion regarding total tax collections is clear enough. The Deccan *subahs* yielded nearly one-third of the total empire revenues. However, the data set used by Sarkar does not have area figures for all the six *subahs* and the Deccan *subahs*. As such, the calculation of tax yield per land area is not possible. The few credible figures in 1720 AD are for Berar and Khandesh, among the six *subahs* (Table 4.2), and for Aurangabad and Bidar, among the Deccan *subahs* (Table 4.3). When these are compared with the core 10 *subahs* (Table 4.1), they indicate substantially lower tax rates in the latter.

Moosvi (2010) has estimated the area of all the *subahs* by her 'map-area' methodology, and has concluded:

> In 1709 the revenues of the Deccan accounted for over 45 per cent of the *jama* (total tax), though it comprised only over 27 per cent of the entire area. Compared to 1667, the Deccan was enlarged (*sic.*) by an area equal to 16.2 per cent of the empire , and the jama increased by an amount equal to over 13 per cent of the *jama* of the Empire (Moosvi 2010: 218).

Table 4.4: Summary Table for the Mughal Empire

	Area in Lakh Bighas		*Increase/ Decrease*	*Revenue in Rs Lakh*		*Increase/ Decrease*	*Rs/Bigha*	
Subah	*1594 AD*	*1720 AD*	*In Per cent*	*1594 AD*	*1720 AD*	*In Per cent*	*1594 AD*	*1720 AD*
10 *subahs*	1925.16	2490.13	29	877.76	1328.20	51.32	0.46	0.53
Six *subahs*		382.89		456.18	595.08	30.45		
Four Deccan *subahs*		334.43			1060.19			
Total	1925.16	3207.46	60.39	1333.94	2983.48	55.29		

Notes: [1] In 1594 AD, some Deccan *subahs* paid a tribute of Rs 440 lakhs before annexation by 1720 AD; [2] In 1720 AD, the total excludes 2 *subahs*; the Kattha figure is not available and the Orissa figure is obviously wrong. Their revenue figures are of 1700 AD from *Dastur-ul-amal*. All other figures are taken from *Charar Gulshan*. Figures in the original, given in *dams*, were converted to rupees at the rate of 40 *dams* to the rupee.

Source: Sarkar 1901: xxviii, xxxii, 123–61.

Table 4.5: Deccan Collections

Year	*Jama in Rs Lakh*	*Hasil in Rs Lakh*	*Collection (in Per cent)*
1687–91 AD	1,500.55	839.68	56.0
1687–95 AD	1,467.50	919.48	62.7
1701–02 AD	1,625.55	1,126.20	69.3
1709 AD	1,509.33	1,087.20	72.0

Source: Habib 2014: 454–66.

The question of whether, in reality, the tax demands actually were realised by the Mughals, was raised. Moosvi (2010) suggests that the actual realisation (*hasil*) of the *jama* was below that which was intended. She suggests that in the empire, only 67 per cent of the *jama* was realised, while in the Deccan, it was much less, at 52 per cent. She relies on Habib in this regard (2014: 454–66). However, Habib is clear that the reliable figures for *hasil* are available for only four data sets (not all of these are used above) towards the end of the Mughal empire. Selecting the relevant data for the periods and regions, I have compiled in Tables 4.5 and 4.6.

It seems clear that the revenue collection from the core empire had reached stagnation, and collections had reached very near total. The only source left to keep the empire going were the revenues from the Deccan *subahs*. Here, the collections rates were much lower than in the core empire, as these were conquest territories and a war zone as well. Resistance to increasing Mughal tax demand would have been strong, as the tax demand by 1701–02 AD in the Deccan was close to the tax demand in the core empire, while Deccan collections were 41 per cent of the collections in the core empire. By 1709 AD, soon after the death of Aurangzeb, the Deccan demand was only 21 per cent, and the collections were only

Table 4.6: Empire Collections Excluding the Deccan

Year	*Jama in Rs Lakh*	*Hasil in Rs Lakh*	*Collection (in Per cent)*
1687–91 AD	1,950.05	1,484.3	76.1
1687–95 AD	1,550.48	1,494.5	96.4
1701–02 AD	1,689.48	1,587.8	94.6
1709 AD	1,825.68	1,529.8	83.8

Source: Habib 2014: 454–66.

Table 4.7: Mughal Revenue Collection, 1720 AD

	Subah	*Demand Rs Lakh*	*Collection Rs Lakh*	*Collection (in Per cent)*
1	Delhi	264.66	262.66	99.25
2	Agra	224.16	233.66	104.24
3	Allahabad	72.56	63.01	86.84
4	Oudh	83.10	83.11	100.01
5	Bihar	94.60	94.65	100.05
6	Bengal	140.73	140.73	100.00
7	Malwa	90.05	90.06	100.01
8	Ajmer	175.30	176.56	100.72
9	Gujarat	132.57	140.57	106.03
10	Multan	45.91	45.73	99.61
11	Punjab	145.30	145.30	100.00
12	Berar	225.60	229.80	101.86
13	Khandesh	115.01	115.00	99.99
14	Kashmir	53.21	53.21	100.00
15	Aurangabad	295.00	295.00	100.00
16	Bijapur	336.85	336.85	100.00
17	Haidarabad	273.21	299.01	109.44
18	Bidar	155.14	133.20	85.86
	Total	2,922.94	2,938.09	100.52

Source: Sarkar 1901: xxviii, xxxii, 123–61.

40 per cent of that of the core empire, and both totals were lower than the total in 1701–02 AD.

As far as the realisation of *jama* is concerned, Sarkar's translation of *Chahar Gulshan* (from which the 1720 AD figures are drawn) also provides the figures for collection of revenue in almost all of the *subahs*. Sarkar has not used the figures for Thatha and Orissa, as he had doubts about the figures being correct. So both *subahs* were excluded. These, as can be seen from Table 4.7, show almost 100 per cent realisation of the *jama*. The only exceptions are the collections for Allahabad and Bidar, the *hasil* for which are 87 per cent and 86 per cent, respectively. Some *subahs* have returned a marginally more revenue than the demand, which may be a carry-forward from the previous year. Overall for 18 out of 20 *subahs* of the empire, the collection is slightly above 100 per cent. Thus, the theory that the onerous tax demand of 50 per cent of the crop output was not actually realised seems false.

With regard to the Deccan, these were conquered territories annexed and brought into the empire, not only as a general *southern* expansion of the empire, and a sectarian conquest of *Shia* sultanates by the *Sunni* Aurangzeb, but also as a way of increasing imperial revenues. It is hardly likely that the collection of taxes were in some way mitigated; on the other hand, there was an increased incidence of taxation after the annexation of Golkonda by Aurangzeb. After the conquest, Aurangzeb increased the *jama* by 13 per cent, which included a *jizyah* of 4 per cent to the land tax. Collections of *jizyah* from individuals had resulted in revolts and had become impossible to collect (Richards 1975: 150–51).

Detailed figures are available for Golkonda after the Mughal conquest. The percentage of *hasil* to *jama* ranged from 55–117 per cent for the interior districts of Golkonda, averaging at about 76 per cent for the interior region. In the Golkonda coastal districts, it was 100 per cent for every district. Richards provides the *jama* and *hasil* figures for Golkonda (1689–90 AD) for each *subah* and the figures indicate a *hasil* collection of 83 per cent for the entire Mughal province of Haidarabad (1975: 152–53). This would indicate some weakness in collection in the interior districts of Golkonda (now Telangana), but not in the coastal districts (now part of Andhra Pradesh).

Incidentally, one needs to bear in mind that rupees signify the Mughal silver rupee of 11.5 gram, which were being imposed by Aurangzeb on the Deccan, as a substitute for the gold coins in circulation there. The figures are thus comparable over the 100-year period we are considering, up to modern times. Table 4.8 indicates the growth of these revenues of the empire from Rs 16.58 crores during Akbar's time to Rs 38.31 crores at the time of Aurangzeb, when the empire was its height. To sum up, therefore, Table 4.8 and Figure 4.1 below are illustrative of the Mughal empire's revenue extraction in India for over 100 odd years.

Combined with a reading of Mughal history, the above data makes it clear that the revenues rose from the time of the reign of Akbar, who initiated a grand compromise and accommodation between the Muslim rulers and the Hindu population. The height was reached under his grandson, Shahjahan, and fell precipitously during the succession wars, not recovering until his successor, Aurangzeb, attacked and annexed the

Table 4.8: Revenue Collection by the Mughal Empire (1594–1720 AD)

Year	*Jama in Rs Crores*	*Reign*
1594	16.58	Akbar
1628	17.5	Jehangir
1648	21.15	Shah Jehan
1654	26.35	Shah Jehan
1665	22.06	Aurangazeb
1695	20.12	Aurangazeb
1697	38.31	Aurangazeb
1700	33.68	Aurangazeb
1707	29.78	Aurangazeb
1720	29.38	Post Aurangazeb

Source: Sarkar 1901: xxxi.

Figure 4.1: Revenue Collection by the Mughal Empire (1594–1720 AD)

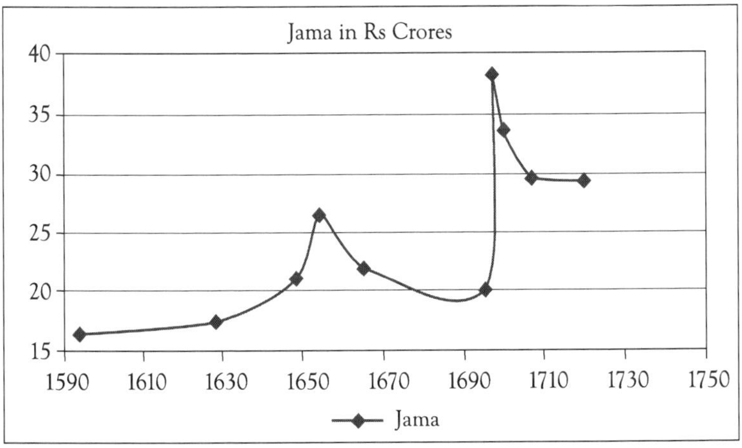

Source: Sarkar 1901: xxxi.

Deccan sultanates and accessed their revenue. Even prior to his death, Aurangzeb had exhausted his revenues, and the decline began during his last years. The post-Aurangzeb period saw extreme disruption. As shall be observed, stability was only achieved at around 1830 under the East India Company's rule.

The Effect of Muslim Rule on Land Taxes in South India

In South India, where the impact of Muslim conquest and rule was almost two centuries later than in north, west, and east India, the evidence relating to Hindu canonical land tax seems clearly established in practice. In modern-day Kerala and parts of Karnataka, taxation was 10 per cent of the gross produce of land. However, many categories of people, including Nambodri Brahmins and Muslim Moplahs, were exempt (Briggs 1830: 58–59). This situation was not just restricted to Travancore, Cochin and Coorg, but it also extended to the Tamil country, where the rate were one-sixth. This continued till the invasion by Hyder Ali (ibid.: 262). Remarkably,

> ... It is recorded that the ancient Hindu land tax did not exceed one-sixth: tradition even limits the demand to *one-tenth*; and experience shows us, in Ceylon, Travancore, Cochin, and the little principality of Coorg on the Malabar Coast, that *one-tenth only is still* exacted by those governments (Briggs 1830: 399) (emphasis in original).

Describing the situation in Coorg, Lewis Rice writes:

> It has been observed that the spirit of feudalism does not admit of the burthensome taxation, and the Kodagu [Coorg] would seem to justify the remark. The Coorgs held their lands on an average at an assessment of ten per cent of the gross produce .... Those inhabitants not of the ruling class of the country paid twelve per cent on the gross produce of their grounds (1878: 314).

But the advent of Muslim power in the South inevitably led to the imposition of Islamic canonical tax rates upon Hindu cultivators:

> ... However, after the Vijayanagar-Nayak period, the exactions in [Hindu] *poligar* [feudal] territory did not appear as oppressive as they were in the [Muslim] Circar [state] territory in the Deccan and Southern India. At times the oppressed *ryots* fled from the Circar country to the [Hindu] *palayams* [territories] in order to escape from the exactions. By the mid-eighteenth century, when Mohammed Ali, the Nawab of Arcot, annexed Ariyalur and Wodayapalayam, he found the taxes so small that he levied *four times* of what the *poligars* had collected (Nayeem 2009, Volume 2: 298) (emphasis added).

As a result, 'The economy of Ramanathapur appeared prosperous before the annexation of that territory by the Nawab, but it broke down in subsequent years. These facts established that the peasants of the *poligar* country were economically better placed than those in the Circar country of the Nawab' (ibid.).

If the Islamic canonical rate was 50 per cent that of non-Muslims, and the Nawab increased the Hindu rate by four times to achieve this rate, then the logical conclusion is that the existing rate was around 12 per cent, as compared to the Hindu canonical rate of 16.6 per cent.

However, the effect of Islamic jurisprudence [or state policy] can be observed when Tippu Sultan's regulations made a clear distinction based on the religion of the farmers/taxpayers: 'Every person who shall become a convert to the Mahommedan faith, if he be a *Reyut*, shall only pay half the usual assessment, and shall be exempted from the payment of house tax; if he is a dealer in merchandise, his goods shall pass duty-free' (Greville 1988, Volume 1: 44).

This phenomenon of the difference between the Hindu and Islamic canonical rates of land taxation may well explain the different trajectories that the subsequent development of the land and people of the south took, who escaped by 200 years Islamic land taxes.

The Company Period

As is well known, the English East India Company began to evolve into a territorial power in India in the second half of the eighteenth century. The Treaty of Allahabad of 1765 AD, was signed between the Mughal emperor, Shah Alam II, and Robert Clive of the East India Company, after the Company won the Battle of Buxar. Shah Alam granted the Company *diwani* rights, that is, the right to collect taxes on behalf of the emperor from Bengal-Bihar-Orissa. In return, the Company paid an annual tribute of 26 lakhs. Thus, the East India Company was appointed as the imperial tax collector.

After the disastrous famine of 1769–72 AD, in which nearly one-third of the population of Bengal died of hunger, the East India Company revised its stand and emerged as a territorial power. It also led to the intervention of the British Parliament when the Company applied for a loan (Berriedale 1936: 68–73). This was confined to Greater Bengal and evolved gradually and systematically to cover the entire country by 1856. During this period, the Company not only continued its trading operations, but also became increasingly dependent on territorial revenues since 1817, which were largely revenues from land. In the initial stages, the Company adopted the existing tax rates fixed by the Muslim powers it displaced. However, Company officials felt that these rates were excessively high and counterproductive in terms of expansion of cultivation, peace, and law and order. Over a period of time, these rates were reduced.

The position of the Company was altered by the British Parliament by the East India Company Act, 1793 (Charter Act 1793). This act legitimised the Company's rule over the British territories in India. The Act also established that the 'acquisition of sovereignty by the subjects of the Crown is on behalf of the Crown and not in its own right', which clearly reveals that the Company's political functions were performed on behalf of the British government. After all expenses, the Company would have to pay the British government 500,000 pounds annually from its Indian revenue. The Governor-General, the Governors, and the Commander-in-Chief would be appointed only after approval (Berriedale 1936: 100–01).

From 1793 AD onwards, the Company began to treat the land as its own property and make changes in the settlement of land rights and titles. Lord Cornwallis's Permanent Settlement dates from the time of the passing of this Act. From 1793 AD onwards, the British Crown and the Parliament were the source of sovereignty to the Company in India, and not to the Mughal emperor in Delhi. As part of the overall requirement under the Act, figures for Company revenues had to be placed before the British government.

By 1830, when it had conquered most of South India, the East India Company not only tried to maximise its income from land tax, but also bore in mind the consequences of implementing extortionate tax levels set by their Muslim predecessors. Initially, the Company, having received *de jure* approval from the Mughal emperor for their management and governance of large parts of India, was bound by him to continue the established practice. The Company, however, was more robust in the collection of taxes, with the misguided notion that the rates were acceptable to the agriculturists and payments had been made willingly.

This change in governnance led to many unfortunate events, such as migration and even famine, namely the infamous 1770 AD famine in Bengal and Bihar. The Company was caught between the need to remit to the emperor his tribute, which was Rs 12.35 crores out of the total Mughal revenue of Rs 33 crores (Wink 1986: 306), to be paid based on territories that the British had conquered. There was the need to satisfy the Company's shareholders of dividends, for which they depended on revenues from India. However, as rural distress inevitably led to declining and abandoned cultivation, and therefore, revenues, the Company officers began to apply their minds to the issue and departed from the simplistic position of relying upon rights secured from the Muslim rulers.[9] Even these rights ceased to serve as a justification as the Company began to assume supreme power in the sub-continent and the Mughal emperor faded into the position of a pensioner rather than a collector of tribute.

An academic controversy raged over whether land revenue was a rent in the classical European sense of the term, payable to the ruler (considered to be the owner of the land), or a tax to be based on the ability to pay. Once the latter position was accepted, the issue of whether the rate was to be applied on gross income or net income was mainly resolved by application of the British sense of 'fairness' combined with practicality. The application of this method allowed the old rates to be reduced drastically in order to ensure a predictable, acceptable and regular stream of taxation based on an unpredictable agricultural sector. Further, the British wanted to rule in peace and to ensure the stability of their rule, while also ensuring regular revenues. The process of evaluating and fixing land taxes dependent on the quality of land, its potential yield, crop prices, and the cost of cultivation and irrigation sources was a significant effort by the British Raj. This revision was done once in every 30 years, thus ensuring predictable rates for an extended period in between settlements. The literature of the land tax issue is vast and has been dealt with adequately. I provide below an idea of the development of British policy and its implementation over 100 years.

In their research on past practices, Ravenshaw, the Collector of Canara, reported on 31 May 1800, referring to the settlement under Vijayanagar rule (1334–47 AD), that the '*circar*' (state) share was 25 per cent (Firminger 1985, Volume 3: 303). The Report for the Ceded Districts (Rayalaseema) cited a share of 33.75 per cent (ibid.: 43). For Tanjore and Trichinopoly, the rate varied from 33.75 per cent (unirrigated land and land irrigated by wells), 46.88 per cent (irrigated monsoon crop) and 25 per cent (garden land) (ibid.: 262).

Thomas Munro was an official whose influence, detailed application of mind, and balance made a significant impact on South India. He was responsible for the tax settlement of Salem, Canara, the districts ceded by the Nizam (now known as Rayalaseema) and Malabar. He later became Governor of Madras. In a Minute dated 31 May 1800, Munro reported that in Canara, he had made a full search of all the documents with the cultivators as well as the account books of the *curmuns* (or *karnams*, meaning village accountants).

He recorded that till the fourteenth century, all land was assessed in terms of rice, at a quantity equal to the quantity of paddy sown. Between 1334 and 1337 AD, the Vijayanagar emperor, Harihara, had a new assessment carried out in Canara, based on Hindu *Shastra* (cannon), and he fixed the state share at one-sixth of the gross produce (Munro 1881, Volume 1: 63–64). Additionally, the state collected another 8.33 per cent for grant to the temple and Brahmins. This took the collection rate to 25 per cent of the gross output, which was paid till 1618 AD, when it was revised upwards, following the collapse of Vijayanagar (ibid.: 65–66).

However, Munro, referring to the Vijayanagar empire's assessment on Canara province, 'which was a light one, having been a apparently considerably less than one-fourth of the gross produce, had rendered the district prosperous and had led to the formation of that which did not exist in any of the neighbouring countries, except Malabar, that is private property in land' (Munro 1881, Volume 1: 57).

Referring to the Vijayanagar assessment, he wrote: 'the ancient assessment is still written not only in all the general accounts of the districts, but in those of every individual land owner. It is alone considered as the due of the government. All subsequent additions are regarded as oppressive exactions. They are not called rent, but a stigmatised by the name of *chout*, imposts, fines etc and distinguished by the names of the *dewans* who first levied them … ' (Munro 1881, Volume 1: 57). The Vijayanagar assessment for Canara, introduced between the 1334 and 1347 AD, was based on the Hindu canonical rate of one-sixth, or 16.6 per cent: the *Raya Rekha*. The Vijayanagar successor state, Bednore government, raised the rate in 1601 AD to 19 per cent. After his conquest of Canara, Hyder Ali raised it to 31 per cent, while Tippu Sultan's rate was 51 per cent (exactly the Islamic canonical rate for non-Muslims). Munro reduced the rate to 27 per cent of the gross output.

Munro, (writing in 1807 about the ceded districts), summed up the issue for his superiors, concluding that according to him, the rent should be *one-third of the gross produce*, from the present rate of 45 per cent (emphasis mine):

> As one-third of the produce is, therefore, the highest point to which an assessment can, in general, be carried without destroying landed property, and it is also the point to which *it must be lowered* before persons who are not cultivators can occupy *Circar* lands without loss, it is obvious that *unless the assessment is reduced to this rate*, land can neither be occupied by all classes

> of inhabitants, nor ever become private property, nor can any Permanent Settlement be made calculated to improve the condition of the *Ryots* or the public revenue (Dutt 1960, Volume 1: 97) (emphasis added).

After the British conquest of the Punjab, however, John Lawrence was more radical in his analysis:

> To 'assess low' was John Lawrence's first principle in land administration; he soon perceived that the demand of one-third the gross produce, payable in money, was oppressive to the peasantry. Within a few years, the Punjab Administration corrected the mistake. *The Land Tax of the Punjab was reduced to one fourth, and then to one-sixth of the gross produce.* The wisdom of this measure was proved by the extension of cultivation, the rise in revenue and the increase in actual collections (Dutt 1960, Volume II: 68, quoting the First Administrative Report, 1852) (emphasis added).

Land taxes under the Sikh kingdom had been much higher, perhaps due to the war expenditures of Maharaja Ranjit Singh. According to Henry Lawrence, 'Two-fifths was the proportion nominally taken by the Sarkar' (Chopra 1928: 80). According to another source the state demand was one-half of the gross produce. The demand of the Sikh government may be said to have varied from two-fifth to one-third of the produce. However, the Punjab Administrative Report for the year 1875–76 stated that the Sikh government collected more than half of the gross output (Sharma 1985: 11–12).

Thus, finally, it took John Lawrence, and that, too, in Punjab, to restore the Hindu canonical land tax rate. The Madras government followed, after that, to reduce its demand, but did not set the tax rate as low as the Hindu canonical one-sixth that Lawrence's Punjab Government implemented. The progress of the Punjab agriculture seems to be largely linked to the low levels of taxation under the British Raj.

At the beginning of the twentieth century, eleven retired Indian Civil Service officers, all British except R. C. Dutt, presented a memorial to the British government, seeking to limit the land revenue collected to one-third of the gross product of the land. The Indian government was asked by the British government to consider this memorial as well as other documents and letters written by R. C. Dutt and report back. The result was the Parliamentary Paper of 1902, consisting of nearly 120 pages. The conclusions were unexpected. The Central Provinces reported that the revenue is only one-sixth to one-fourteenth of the gross rental. Bengal claimed that the government collected only 20 per cent of the gross produce directly from farmers, and it was a rate much lower than what the Permanently Settled estates collected from their tenants. Madras reported that its tax demand was 10 per cent of the gross output. Punjab claimed its tax demand was one-seventh or one-eighth of the gross output or even less. Similar conclusions were reported to the Famine Commission, with Central provinces reporting 4 per cent, Berar 7 per cent, Ajmer about 10 per cent, Hissar in Punjab 3.5 per cent. Delhi 10 per cent and Gujarat 20 per cent of the gross produce (His Majesty's Stationery Office [HMSO] 1902: 7–8).

This more or less ended the land revenue debate. What seems to have happened over time is that the increase in yields and in prices for the crops reduced the proportion that money tax had to the value of gross output. Money rates for land revenue were only revised every 30 years or so. There was always resistance to drastic increases by farmers, the budding popular movements and basic democratic institutions set up by the British.

There is some interesting field-level data collected by Buchanan-Hamiltonin 1988. Based on his extensive field observations, Buchanan-Hamilton concludes that under Tippu Sultan, the farmers had been forced to pay high taxes (Buchanan-Hamilton 1988, Volume II: 230). Near Calicut, he investigated the distribution of the crop output to various heads of expenditure (see Table 4.9)

The land tax in the case of poor soil land works out to 32 per cent, while for best soil, it is 22 per cent of gross output. If this was the general case, one would expect the poor soil land to be only cultivated after the best soil land was entirely taken up. On the Arcot possessions (the former Pandyan-Chola territories), the Fifth Report recorded the following:

Table 4.9: Share in Total Paddy Output

	WB Per Acre	
Head	*Poor Soil*	*Best Soil*
Land tax and charges	7.28	8.72
Seed	4.86	4.86
Cultivation expenses	4.86	4.86
Landlord	0.99	4.41
Interest on loan	0.55	0.55
Cultivator's profit	3.97	13.24
Total of two crops	22.5	39.65

Source: Buchanan-Hamilton 1985, Volume II: 475–76.

> The interest in the soil was generally found to be divided between the Government and the cultivator. The established or understood share of the former, in the crops, from paddy lands, or wet, designated by the term *nunjah*, was generally received in kind, at rates varying from 40 to 60 per cent of the gross produce; *subject to a deduction* of certain portions distributed mostly before, but sometimes after separation of the grain from the husk, among the servants belonging to each village community; and appropriated for charitable uses, the repairs of tanks, or the maintenance of pagodas (Firminger 1985, Volume 1: 223) (emphasis added).

This deduction could be a considerable share of the crop. Where the Mysore territories were concerned, the Fifth Report talks about the revision of the assessment rates on taxable products of the soil after the transfer of the province to the government of Fort St George:

> ... and it was then supposed that the land tax was less than one-third of the gross product. Those rates were, however, soon after superseded, *as being disagreeable to the inhabitants, from their inequality*, but particularly from the rates of exchange at which the produce was converted into money, and a recurrence was had to the principles of assessment, which were adopted by the Bombay Commissioners in 1800-01, and which still continues in force[10] (Firminger 1985, Volume 1: 258) (emphasis added).

Therefore, the land tax rates under early British rule lay between the canonical one-sixth (in Punjab) and one-third (in the South). The rates that we have been considering relate to irrigated land growing paddy or wheat (in Punjab. However, under British rule, the land settlement also covered the vast extent of unirrigated land. The procedure was similar, but the range of crops considered was diverse. Eventually, the tax was fixed for dry land as such without taking into account the nature of the crops grown (see Essay 5 on the elaborate process that the British adopted for fixing the land tax in order to ensure fairness and voluntary compliance).

The figures for collection of land revenue from 1792 AD till 1857 illustrate the increasing territorial control of the Company. This was despite the downward adjustment of the rates of taxes, especially in this south, Punjab and other areas. Except for the period 1827–1842, land revenue and total revenues increased consistently (see Table 4.10 and Figure 4.2).

It will be obvious from the figures that the revenue of the East India Company, even at its end in 1857, was half that of the Mughal empire under Aurangzeb 137 years earlier. It would seem that the Company's burden on agriculturists in terms of aggregate taxes was considerably lower, which may have ensured its acceptability by Indian farmers.

Table 4.10: Land Tax Collection by the East India Company

Five-Year Average from (with Start Date)	*Land Revenue (in Rs Crores)*	*Total Revenues (in Rs Crores)*	*LR /Total Revenue (in Per cent)*
1792	4.07	8.08	50.33
1797	4.13	9.82	42.02
1802	4.53	14.15	31.99
1807	5.08	16.03	31.68
1812	9.02	17.23	52.33
1817	13.26	20.04	66.17
1822	13.57	21.94	61.83
1827	13.11	21.53	60.90
1832	11.94	20.95	57.00
1837	12.38	20.97	59.05
1842	13.43	24.05	55.85
1847	14.95	26.66	56.06
1852	16.18	29.21	55.40
1857	17.11		

Source: Hendricks 1858: 278.

Figure 4.2: Land Revenue in Rs Crores (East India Company)

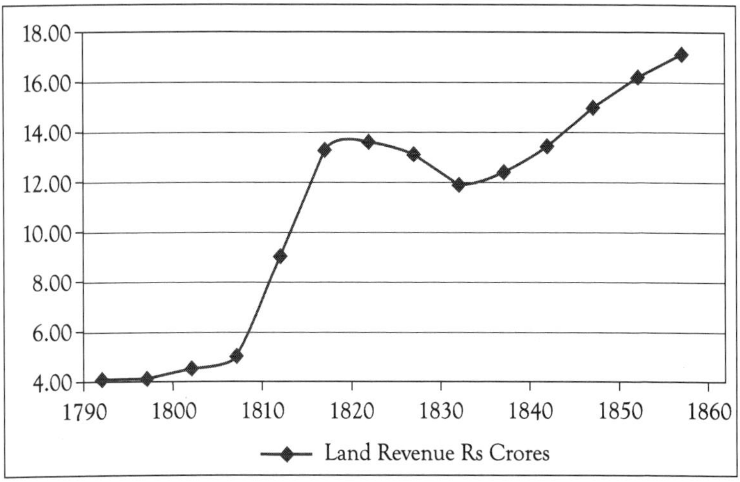

Source: Hendricks 1858: 278.

The British Indian Empire

The shock of the Revolt of 1857 resulted in a takeover of the Company by the British government and the establishment of the Indian empire. As far as land revenue was concerned, the empire continued to apply rational rules to the fixation of land revenue rates, based on productivity and costs of cultivation. Both peace and low rates seem to encourage increased cultivation, which was also spurred on by increased population due to the stability of governance and social order.

The official documents highlight the fact that as total revenues increased, the share of land revenue declined radically and secularly over time. For the British government in India, land revenue–once the mainstay of its budget–was declining over time as the non-agricultural sectors gained strength (Figure 4.3). The Famine Commission of 1878–80 made a rough calculation, which shows that the land revenues of the various provinces range from about 4–8 per cent of the gross product. The total land revenue of India was said to represent five-and-a-half per cent of the gross produce (Government of India [GoI] 1909, Volume 4: 216).

However, the burden on the farmers in the Permanently Settled estates created in the late-eighteenth century in vast areas of Bengal, Bihar, Orissa and Uttar Pradesh, as well as in Madras province was higher (GoI 1909,

Figure 4.3: Land Revenue as Percentage of Total Revenue

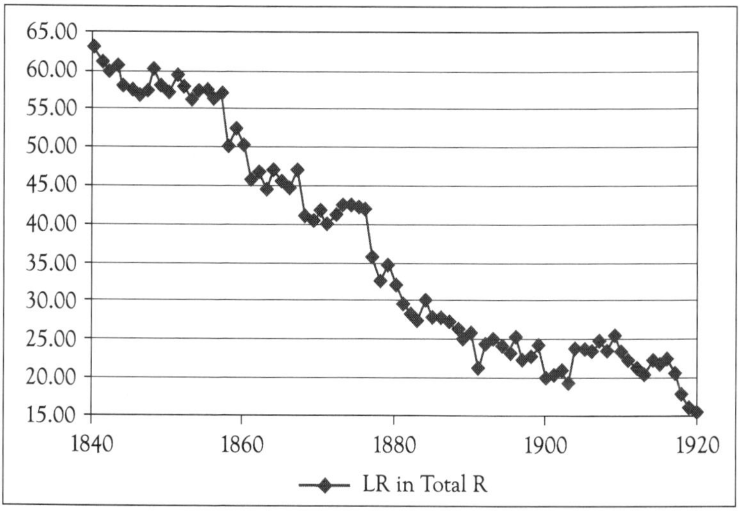

Source: HMSO 1915: various.

Volume 4: 231). These farmers had to pay rents, and the estate-owners had the power to set these as their right granted by the state. These rents were fixed in monetary terms at the time when the estate owners received the estates. The East India Company had assumed power from the Mughal rulers, and the same rates of Islamic land taxes seem to have been continued under the Permanent Settlement scheme. This is also one of the reasons why regions dominated by Permanently Settled estates were agriculturally backward. Progress here had to await Independence and abolition of these estates followed by subsequent land reforms.

It seems reasonably clear that over time, the share of land revenue and total revenues declined drastically and importantly, the share of land revenue in the gross output also declined to negligible amounts. The latter periods are largely a result of increased prices of agricultural output. It seems clear, however, that even towards the end of the British empire in India, its land revenue collections did not exceed the Mughal revenues at time of Aurangzeb's death in 1707 AD. While all alien rule is oppressive, as far as land taxation is concerned, it is clear that Pax Britannica was an extraordinary improvement over Muslim rule.

Land Taxes in the Two Telugu Regions

Telangana

After the collapse of the Kakatiya empire in 1324 AD, warfare between the Kakatiya *nayakas* and the Delhi sultanate governors and Bahmani rulers continued in Telangana for nearly 200 years. Thereafter, Telangana became a part of the Muslim state of Golkonda (1512–1686 AD), the Mughal province under Aurangzeb (1687–1712 AD), and then the Nizam's Dominions of Hyderabad (1712 AD–1948). There is no hard evidence of the land tax system, either before or after 1324 AD, up until the 1860s.

With the declining power of the Kakatiya monarch, the functioning of the system in force, during and after the conquest, was based on the *nayakas* and other Hindu chieftains. They were obliged to remit an annual tribute to the effective ruler or his representatives and provide armed men. Very little information is available as to how the Hindu chieftains, in their turn, collected taxes from the population, especially from the agriculturalists. But whatever evidence and reasoning there is based on canonical directions, they indicate the fact that the Kakatiyas adapted the Hindu canonical rate of one-sixth and the Muslim rulers enforced the 50 per cent Islamic canonical rate for non-Muslims on the Hindus.

After the conquest of the Kakatiya empire, Telangana was a war zone, with temporary accommodation between its Muslim rulers and Hindu subjects. Under the Bahmani and Qutub Shahi sultans, the collection of taxes, or rather, tribute were exacted either through Hindu chieftains who shielded their constituents from Muslim power at the cost of paying the tribute demanded, or directly by Muslim rulers by the use of force.

However, an accommodation was reached between the Qutub Shahi rulers and their Hindu chieftains through the means of a feudal settlement in terms of homage, loyalty, tribute and military support, on the one hand, and non-interference in local affairs, on the other. This accommodation eventually saw the Qutub Shahi Sultans appointing Hindus as prime ministers and relying on Hindu Brahmins to staff the state bureaucracy.

However, the conquest of Golkonda by Aurangzeb in the late-seventeenth century and the institution of much higher taxes more harshly exacted disturbed the Qutub Shahi equilibrium. Golkonda, of which Telangana was a significant part, contributed Rs 5.77 crores (17 per cent) to the total Mughal annual revenue of Rs 33.10 crores. Even in 1803, after the loss of the Andhra region to the French and later to the British, the contribution of the new ruler of Telangana, the Nizam of Hyderabad, was annually Rs 3.47 crores (10 per cent) to the nominal Mughal budget of Rs 33 crores (Wink 1986: 305–06).

Richards provides annual revenue figures for the 5,216 villages in Telangana and 3,648 villages in Coastal Andhra (1975: 154).[11] It appears that the average revenue collection per village in Telangana was Rs 2,543 and in Coastal Andhra Rs 1,510. Thus, the Telangana villages were taxed 1.7 times those in Coastal Andhra. Coastal Andhra *parganas* (districts) paid Rs 0.24 lakhs, while Telangana *parganas* paid Rs 0.88 lakhs, which is 3.6 times more (see Table 4.11).

Table 4.11: Revenues of Golkonda, 1685–86 AD

Sarkar	*Pargana*	*Rupees Lakhs*	*Rs Lakhs Per Pargana*
Mahummadnagar	22	15.38	0.70
Medak	16	35.16	2.20
Kaulas	5	7.42	1.48
Melangur	3	0.68	0.23
Elgandal	21	12.20	0.58
Warangal	16	7.48	0.47

(*Contd.*)

Table 4.11: *(Contd.)*

Sarkar	*Pargana*	*Rupees Lakhs*	*Rs Lakhs Per Pargana*
Khammammet	11	6.29	0.57
Dewarkonda	13	21.20	1.63
Pangal	5	4.55	0.91
Bhongir	11	1.48	0.13
Akarkara	6	5.18	0.86
Kovilkonda	13	10.52	0.81
Ghanapura	8	5.13	0.64
Telangana Total	150	132.68	0.88
Murtuzanagar	42	17.08	0.41
Mustfanagar	24	12.00	0.50
Machlipatnam	8	2.87	0.36
Nizampatnam	1	0.87	0.87
Ellore	12	6.90	0.58
Rajahmundri	24	6.28	0.26
Sikakol	118	9.09	0.08
Coastal Andhra Total	229	55.09	0.24
Golkonda Total	379	187.77	0.50

Source: Richards 1975: 153–54.

It is also evident from the data available that the Qutub Shahi rulers were unable to collect more than 74 per cent of the demand in Telangana but collected 100 per cent in Coastal Andhra. Aurangzeb managed to collect 76 per cent in Telangana (after the demand was increased by 46 per cent) and 100 per cent in Coastal Andhra (after an increase of 18 per cent). Lower rates seem to have helped with compliance (see Table 4.12).

With the collapse of the Mughal empire, came the exactions of the Marathas, who had been granted the right of *sirdeshmukhi* and *chouth* in the entire Deccan, including Telangana. The *sirdeshmukhi* right was to 10 per cent of the *subah* revenues and *chouth* to 25 per cent. Thus, the Marathas secured the right to collect 35 per cent of the revenues of the six Deccan *subahs*. No clear idea can be derived of the revenues of the six *subahs* in this period. However, James Grant Duff, a British official, examined the Maratha accounts and calculated the *sirdeshmukhi* and *chouth* revenues collected by the Maratha in the six Deccan *subahs*.

Table 4.12: Golkonda Revenue Collections (1689–90 AD in Lakhs Silver Rupees

District	*Golkonda Jama*	*Golkonda Revenue*	*Hasil (in Per cent)*	*Mughal Jama*	*Mughal Revenue*	*Hasil (in Per cent)*	*Increase in Jama (in Per cent)*	*Increase in Hasil (in Per cent)*
Bhongir	13.06	7.10	54.3	13.96	7.65	54.8	6.9	7.8
Deverkonda	14.09	9.33	66.2	14.28	10.04	70.3	1.3	7.5
Elgandal	11.07	10.71	96.8	11.30	10.86	96.0	2.2	1.4
Ghanpura	6.96	4.13	59.3	7.20	4.25	59.0	3.4	2.9
Kaulas	5.62	5.62	100.0	6.27	6.27	100.0	11.6	11.6
Khamammet	7.26	4.95	68.2	7.26	5.53	76.1	0.0	11.6
Malkanur	1.44	1.44	100.1	1.49	1.74	117.1	3.6	21.2
Medak	15.70	12.32	78.5	17.21	14.15	82.2	9.6	14.9
Muhammadanagar	18.50	13.09	70.8	21.39	14.62	68.4	15.6	11.7
Nalgonda	4.76	4.24	89.1	4.78	5.20	108.8	0.3	22.4
Pangal	5.28	3.39	64.2	6.73	4.40	65.4	27.3	29.6
Warangal	8.58	6.67	77.8	8.62	6.72	77.9	0.5	0.6
Total Telangana	112.33	82.99	73.9	120.48	91.41	75.9	7.3	10.1

(Contd.)

Table 4.12: (*Contd.*)

District	*Golkonda Jama*	*Golkonda Revenue*	*Hasil (in Per cent)*	*Mughal Jama*	*Mughal Revenue*	*Hasil (in Per cent)*	*Increase in Jama (in Per cent)*	*Increase in Hasil (in Per cent)*
Eluru	5.33	5.32	99.9	5.33	5.32	99.9	0.0	0.0
Machlipatnam	4.33	4.32	99.9	4.86	4.85	99.9	12.3	12.4
Murtuzanagar	9.42	9.42	100.0	11.68	11.68	100.0	23.9	23.9
Mustafanagar	8.28	8.28	100.0	11.87	11.86	99.9	43.4	43.3
Nizampatnam	2.46	2.46	100.0	2.46	2.46	100.0	0.0	0.0
Rajmundry	4.80	4.81	100.2	6.85	6.86	100.1	42.7	42.6
Sikakul	8.00	8.00	100.0	8.00	8.00	100.0	0.0	0.0
Total Coastal Andhra	42.61	42.60	100.0	51.04	51.03	100.0	19.8	19.8
Total Province	154.93	125.60	81.1	171.52	142.44	83.0	10.7	13.4

Source: Richards 1975: 153–54.

Grant Duff estimated the total Maratha revenues from these six *subahs* as Rs 1800 lakhs annually. The largest contributors were Hyderabad, which yielded Rs 649 lakhs, and Bijapur, yielding Rs 785 lakhs (Gribble 2002, Volume II: 7).

The figure for Hyderabad at Rs 649 lakhs is about 3.8 times the figure for the *jama* of Rs 171.5 lakhs in 1689–90 AD. This would mean that the Maratha annual claim of 35 per cent on this basis would be much in excess of the actual annual revenues of Hyderabad. Most likely, the Maratha policy was to deliberately not collect their claims regularly, but rather, allow them to accumulate so as to justify a raid or invasion to collect by force of arms more than their sanctioned share (Gribble 2002, Volume II: 7). If so, Grant Duff's figures are not annual claims, but rather, accumulated ones. If one relies on the annual *jama* figure for Hyderabad and calculates 35 per cent of it, the Maratha annual entitlement would be only Rs 60 lakhs. Following this logic, the Grant Duff figure of Rs 648 lakhs would imply that the Marathas allowed their claim to accumulate for 10 years.

Only after the victory of British power over the Mughals, French, Hyder and Tippu, Marathas, Sikhs and the Nizam by 1830, came a sort of peace that may be called Pax Britannica. By the 1850s, this induced Sir Salar Jung I, the Regent and Prime Minister of the Nizams, to undertake reforms in Hyderabad.

After the reforms of Sir Salar Jung, the process of collection of taxes was centralised, and the tax farmers were no longer required.[12] However, the land settlement came much later and followed the Bombay model in the procedure, although not in terms of the rates, as suggested by the following excerpt:

> The assessment was originally based on the quantity of grain sown in a field or its produce, of which a certain share was taken by the State as revenue. On 'dry' crops the share was one-fourth of the produce, and on 'wet' lands irrigated by tanks and wells, the State received half and two-fifths respectively of the produce (GoI 1909: 59).

With this policy, the arbitrary basis of tribute collection was converted into a rational basis of land taxation. There exists substantial data from the late-nineteenth century land revenue settlements made in Telangana, and later, from early-twentieth century settlements. The land settlement tried to follow the procedures laid down by the British for the provinces under their rule. Despite this, the execution of the procedure, as well as the high demand for revenue by the Nizam's government that was based on Islamic canon, led to higher taxation as compared to the rates of the British Provinces (Reddy 1967: 1280–81). Following the period of the reforms of Sir Salar Jung, there is credible data on the tenure and taxation of agricultural land in the Nizam's Hyderabad, of which Telangana was a significant part. These reforms had their effect on land tenure and agriculture.

This new system had its inevitable result, and together with general peace, it encouraged increased cultivation wherever cultivable waste was available. Table 4.13 below indicates that between 1874 and 1940, there was a growth of 300 per cent in the irrigated acreage, while cultivation on dry land increased by 440 per cent. It is clear that the reforms of Sir Salar, along with the peace that descended over the state, dramatically altered the situation by 1894, with land revenues increasing by 2.5 times between 1874 and 1927. Average land revenue rates, too, seemed to fall by one-third between 1874 and 1916, but they rose between 1927 and 1940 due to the revised revenue settlements, which succeeded the original nineteenth-century settlements as they expired.

The Nizam's government taxed agriculture (especially in the extensively irrigated Telangana region) at very high rates. However, once the share was commuted to money, the rates were fixed for decades (15–30 years); then if output and prices rose, they effectively reduced the real tax rate. The rates cited in Table 4.14 suggest, however, that though high, the Islamic rate of 50 per cent was not entirely achieved.

We have data available regarding the taxation of unirrigated land in Telangana as a part of the same settlement process. In the case of un-irrigated land, crop values per acre are lower by a high fraction than

Table 4.13: The Growth of Cultivation and Revenues

	Lakh Acres			*Rupees in Lakhs*	*Rupees/Acre*
Year	*Irrigated*	*Dry*	*Total Acres*	*Total Revenues*	*Tax 13*
1874	3.58	18.23	21.81	71.9	3.3
1894	6.09	33.98	40.07	112.94	2.82
1916	9.42	75.7	85.12	161.48	1.9
1927	9.8	80.28	90.08	181.98	2.02
1940	10.74	80.42	91.16	182	2.26

Source: Mahdi Ali 1879b: 57; Vaikuntum 2002: 60–61.

those in irrigated land and the tax rate equally low–except for Nalgonda where the estimate is not based on *jowar* crop as in other districts but on the *cholam* crop (see Table 4.15).

Overall, the Salar Jung reforms were a combination of many factors. First, there was general peace due to the alliance with the British and the complete cessation of the disruptive and damaging Maratha incursions. Second, the settlement and accommodation between the Nizam and the Hindu feudal chiefs guaranteed tranquility. Third, it restored general order for trade and transport to move freely. Fourth, the revenue settlement

Table 4.14: Taxation of Irrigated Paddy Land in Telangana

District	*Settlement Year*	*Gross Output in Rs/Acre*	*Tax in Rs/Acre*		*Tax on Gross Output (in Per cent)*	
			Max	*Min*	*Max*	*Min*
Medak	1890	64.29	24	10	37.3	15.6
Hyderabad	1891		24	8.57		
Warangal	1895	32.46	15.42	8.57	47.5	26.4
Nizamabad	1896	40.91	17.14	12	41.9	29.3
Khammam	1898		15.43	8.57		
Nalgonda	1902	31.57	18	6.85	32.3	16.2
Karimnagar	1903	53.01	17.14	8.57	42.6	21.3
Adilabad	1936	31.57	13.71	6.85	57	21.7

Source: GoAP 1959, Part I, Volume II: various.

Table 4.15: Taxation of Unirrigated Land in Telangana

District	*Settlement Year*	*Gross Output Rs/Acre*	*Tax in Rs/Acre*		*Tax on Gross Output (in Per cent)*	
			Max	*Min*	*Max*	*Min*
Medak	1890	18.6	2.56	1.25	17.77	6.72
Hyderabad	1891		3.42	0.85		
Warangal	1895	12.8	2.14	0.85	16.72	6.64
Nizamabad	1896		2.67	1.06		
Khammam	1898		2.46	1.06		
Nalgonda	1902	4.41	2.89	1.06	65.49	24.02
Karimnagar	1903	15.43	2.58	0.97	16.72	6.29
Adilabad	1936	10.49	2.57	0.85	24.5	8.1

Source: GoAP 1959, Part I, Volume II: various.

assured farmers of predictability in the tax demand. Fifth, state expenditure was rationalised and state debt reduced. Sixth, employment of competent officials from outside the state was initiated. Seventh, the rule of law was introduced. All these factors combined to lay the basis for peace, prosperity and development, which benefitted all classes.

Commercialisation of Agriculture

The growth of commercial agriculture began in 1876–77. During this period, out of the total commodity exports, Hyderabad exported cotton valued at Rs 132.38 lakhs and oilseeds at Rs 55.44 lakhs, both together constituting 38 per cent of the total. Food grains worth Rs 229.51 lakhs (46 per cent of the total) were also exported, but in the same year, Rs 167.07 lakhs (36 per cent of the total) were imported, resulting in a net export of Rs 62.4 lakhs. By 1931–32, commodity exports had risen to Rs 215 lakhs of cotton, Rs 194 lakhs of groundnut, Rs 94.9 lakhs of castor, Rs 51.8 lakhs of linseed, and Rs 139.5 lakhs of food grain, together constituting 60 per cent of the total exports. Moreover, import of food grains is not reported since 1915, except for 1929–32, when they were resumed (Vaikuntum 2002: 162–81).

By 1946–47, exports of oilseeds were Rs 601 lakhs, vegetable oils Rs 734 lakhs, and grains and pulses Rs 199 lakhs, making a total of Rs 1,534 lakhs (49 per cent of the total exports). In terms of the area under the cultivation of cash crops, in 1929–30, was nearly 50 per cent of the area was under food crops, and by 1942–43, it had reached 80 per cent.[14]

The above figures are for Hyderabad, of which Telangana was a major part. They illustrate the increasing commercialisation of Telangana's agricultural production, as well as a 28 per cent increase in the crop area over the period 1929–43 (Vaikuntum 2002: 69, 162, 167, 171]. Thus, despite high levels of taxation, Telangana's agricultural scenario, with all its 'feudal' features, had begun to show its dynamic potential and was seemingly in a position of 'takeoff' at the end of the Second World War, especially with the extraordinarily high wartime prices for paddy and other agricultural products.

Andhra

The Andhra data for 1870–71 indicates the extent of cultivation on irrigated land as well as unirrigated land. Nearly 10.48 lakh acres of irrigated land were cultivated together with 70.46 lakh acres of unirrigated land, making a total of Rs 80.94 lakh (Raghavaiyengar 1988: xcvii).[15] This indicates that 12.9 per cent of the total cultivated area was irrigated at least once, as there is no indication of whether this figure is for gross or net irrigated acres.[16]

Although somewhat late, the British developed a systematic approach to the issue. Initially they adopted the Islamic canonical rates in force. Later they realised that these had disastrous results, namely forced immigration, abandonment of cultivation, and famine. They therefore adopted a flexible approach, taking into account ground realities, and adjusted both the rate and the base of taxation. In the Andhra region of Madras province, the first systematic survey and settlement was made in 1802. By 1855, a new method of settlement was adopted as a reform measure. In the early phase, the rate of assessment of tax was 30 per cent of the gross output (GoAP 1959, Part I, Volume i: 62). It was estimated that the 'average rate of assessment for wetlands is Rs 5 per acre and for dry lands, 1 rupee per acre and these rates are between one-fourth and one-fifth and one-fourth and one-sixth, respectively, of the gross outturn according to the settlement calculations' (Raghavaiyengar 1988: 112). But as this was onerous for farmers cultivating less fertile land, and thus, the basis was changed in 1864 to net produce instead of gross produce [GoAP 1959, Part I, Volume I: 62). Rationalisation, reduction and predictability of land taxation were the main features of Pax Britannica in India

Moreover, the land settlement figures for nineteenth century are also available. The settlement in the former Madras Province under British rule was systematic and evolved. The British were conscious of the need to be seen to be fair on the one hand, and on the other, to ensure that the agriculturists were able to pay the land revenue on a regular and continuing basis voluntarily. The objective was to 'settle' the matter for at least 30 years till the next 'settlement'. This settlement allowed the agriculturists to take advantage of any increase in output that they may secure for themselves as well as an increase in the price of the product without having to pay any more than the fixed monetary value of the land tax (see Table 4.16).

In the districts of the Godavari and Krishna deltas, which had benefitted enormously from the massive canal irrigation systems built under British rule in the mid-nineteenth century on both rivers, their rich and well-watered soils produced paddy. It was estimated that between 1895–99 and 1919–24, the total irrigated area increased by 36 per cent in the Krishna and Godavari deltas. Overall, the cultivated area increased

Table 4.16: Growth of Cultivation

	Lakh Acres		
Year	*Irrigated*	*Dry*	*Total*
1853	6.8	53.16	59.96
1871	10.48	70.46	80.94
1881	10.37	58.29	68.66
1890	12.22	65.57	77.79

Note: This is for ryotwari areas only.
Source: Raghavaiyengar 1988: xcvii.

by 22 per cent in both Krishna district and west Godavari district, and 21 per cent in east Godavari district. Between 1891–92 and 1910–11, the cultivated area increased from 45 lakh acres to 97 lakhs acres in the entire coastal region. The area under food crops grew during this period from 37.6 lakh acres to 82.4 lakh acres (rice grew from 11.4 lakh acres to 12.5 lakh acres). The Resettlement Report, 1927, quoted in Satyanarayana (1990) discusses the role of these massive irrigation systems in facilitating rice cultivation; and this made the area of the two deltas the rice bowl of south India.

It is evident that the lighter land revenue exacted from irrigated land encouraged farmers in Andhra to take to rice cultivation, especially when national and international markets for rice and other crops were opening up.[17] Between 1901 and 1904, and 1917 and 1920, food grain exports from Andhra averaged 2.53 lakh tons per annum (Satyanarayana 1990: 25). The figures provided in Table 4.17 below combine both the land revenue tax as well as the water rate.

In comparison with Telangana, an additional factor, apart from the lower money tax and the consequent lower rate of land taxation of gross output, was a significant difference in the price of paddy between both the regions. Except for periods during and immediately following the First and the Second World Wars, paddy prices in Andhra were considerably higher than those in Telangana (Table 4.18). This divergence could be attributed mainly to the developed markets, better transportation system, and higher exports to other parts of the country from Andhra. The exceptional cases of the World War paddy prices being lower in Andhra than in Telangana were, no doubt, the result of firm wartime price control and levy operations by the British administration there.

As for the taxation of unirrigated land, the same procedures were followed, but the crops taken for the basis of the settlement were diverse,

Table 4.17: Taxation of Irrigated Paddy Land in Andhra

District	*Settlement Year*	*Gross Output Rs/Acre*	*Rs/Acre*		*Tax on Gross Output (in Per cent)*	
			Max	*Min*	*Max*	*Min*
Godavari	1860	31.63	10	1.25	31.62	3.95
Kurnool	1863	64.34	10	2.5	15.54	3.89
Krishna	1864	32.34	9	2	27.83	6.18
Cuddapah	1870	63.44	10	2	15.76	3.15
Guntur	1874	37.5	9.5	1.75	25.33	4.67
Nellore	1874	39.06	10.5	2	26.88	5.12
Srikakulum	1877	33.75	5.5	1.25	16.3	3.7
Chittor	1882	63	18.13	1.5	28.78	2.38
Ananthapur	1885	49.16	11	1	22.38	2.03
Visakhaptnam	1889	33.75	9.66	8.19	28.62	24.27

Source: GoAP 1959, Part I, Volume I: various.

with two districts (Srikakulam and Visakhapatnam) assessed based on Ragi, one on Sajja (Chittoor), and the rest of the seven districts being assessed on the basis of Cholam. The maximum rate for unirrigated land in Andhra is higher than the maximum rate for the same land in Telangana; but the reverse is true for the minimum rates (Table 4.19).

Commercialisation of Agriculture

In this matter, Andhra seems to have been way ahead of Telangana. This lead may have to do with the generally better infrastructure and transportation system in Andhra, including sea ports that Telangana did not have and also the *laissez-faire* policy of the British government in Madras Province, as opposed to the more autarkic policy of the Nizams. The available surplus with the peasantry in Andhra would also act as a spur to downstream activities and investment in trade. Satyanarayana (1990) elegantly describes the transition from peasants' self-sufficiency to full-blown capitalist agriculture over the period 1900–40.

Western rationality and calculus, not religious ideology, was the basis for the British taxation system in India. For 150 years, in the matter of land tax, Pax Britannica distinguished itself from its predecessor, Pax Islamica, which dominated India for some 700 years, and attempted to move towards the Hindu canonical prescription, which received wide acceptance by the mostly Hindu cultivators.

Table 4.18: Paddy Prices (Rs Per Quintal)

Year	*Andhra*	*Telangana*	*Variation (in Per cent)*	*Year*	*Andhra*	*Telangana*	*Variation (in Per cent)*
1890	5.39	5.02	6.83	1924	13.02	7.48	42.55
1891	6.2	6.26	-1.01	1925	12.15	7.15	41.17
1892	6.05	4.86	19.63	1926	12.24	6.95	43.26
1893	5.45	4.68	14.07	1927	12.21	7.05	42.29
1894	5.24	4.55	13.06	1928	11.4	6.59	42.22
1895	5.06	4.88	3.43	1929	10.27	6.67	35.07
1896	5.84	7.38	-26.41	1930	7.99	5.29	33.78
1897	7.21	6.64	7.95	1931	6.79	5.16	23.99
1898	5.69	5.78	-1.55	1932	6.29	4.55	27.55
1899	6.08	7.02	-15.57	1933	5.48	4.78	12.68
1900	7.06	6.41	9.24	1934	6.47	5.29	18.15
1901	6.38	5.78	9.41	1935	6.79	5.24	22.86
1902	5.48	5.11	6.64	1936	5.84		
1903	5.06	4.27	15.5	1937	5.84	5.8	0.62
1904	5.72	5.39	5.65	1938	5.87	5.78	1.56
1905	7.06	6.41	9.24	1939	6.67	6.84	-2.53
1906	7.63	6.51	14.67	1940	7.69	6.95	9.71
1907	8.23	7.43	9.75	1941	8.62	8.8	-2.12
1908	6.08	6.74	-10.96	1942	12.36		0
1909	7.84	6.41	18.24	1943	16.28	14.27	12.34
1910	7.15	6.23	12.87	1944	16.76	16.82	-0.33
1911	8.02	7.96	0.73	1945	17.12	18.19	-6.25
1912	9.28	8.22	11.44	1946	17.6	18.8	-6.83
1913	8.98	7.66	14.72	1947	20.08	26.94	-34.15
1914	8.5	5.93	30.26	1948	27	36.15	-33.91
1915	8.35	6.18	25.97	1949	27.03	33.91	-25.48
1916	8.59	7.61	11.45	1950	25.32	22.9	9.57
1917	8.8	9.34	-6.11	1951	26.25	28.11	-7.1
1918	12.39	13.41	-8.2	1952	28.11	28.24	-0.48
1919	15.86	13.05	17.73	1953	31.76	26.64	16.12
1920	13.71	9.57	30.22	1954	29.84	23.36	21.74
1921	12.66	7.56	40.32	1955	28.28	25.59	9.51
1922	11.94	7.56	36.73	1956	37.47	28.37	24.3
1923	12	7.68	35.99	1957	33.31		

Source: GoAP 1959 Part II Volume IV: 718–23.

Table 4.19: Taxation of Unirrigated Land in Andhra

District	Settlement Year	Gross Output in Rs/Acre	Tax in Rupees/ Acre		Tax on Gross Output (in Per cent)	
			Max	Min	Max	Min
Godavari	1860	25.25	5	0.25	19.8	0.99
Kurnool	1863	23.13	5	0.25	21.62	1.08
Krrishna	1864	15.44	3	0.25	19.43	1.62
Cuddapah	1870	25.47	4	0.25	15.71	0.98
Guntur	1874	19.6	4.5	0.25	22.96	1.28
Nellore	1874		5	0.25		
Srikakulum	1877	16.52	4	0.25	24.21	1.51
Chittoor	1882	19.22	2	0.13	18.21	1.3
Ananthapur	1885	16.15	2	0.13	12.38	0.77
Visakhapatnam	1889	16.52	4.94	3.46	29.9	20.94

Source: GoAP 1959, Part I, Volume I: various.

Andhra Pradesh

Since the original revenue settlements in Andhra and Telangana happened in the nineteenth and early-twentieth centuries, there have been revision settlements as and when the 15–30 year periods of the settlement expired.

Thus, the progress of enhancement of land revenue depended entirely on the price level of the output of crop production and would not generally disturb the relative differences established at the time of the original settlement. It is, therefore, reasonable to conclude that the differences between the two regions continued over the hundred years from 1850–1950, and even after that, as no substantive effort was made under a democratic dispensation to revise the basic structure of land revenue rates till 1962. This effort, as shall be observed, was struck down as unconstitutional by the High Court. This variation in the money land tax between Telangana and Andhra continued until the time of the merger of the two regions, as indicated below in Table 4.20.

However, in comparison with Telangana, the maximum rate for tax on unirrigated land in Andhra had been almost twice as much, while the minimum rate was three to five times lower. As the figures above illustrate, the higher taxation of land in Telangana, as compared to Andhra since the nineteenth century, continued despite the merger of

Table 4.20: Land Tax in Andhra Pradesh (1952–56) (in Rs/Acre)

REGION	*Irrigated*		*Dry*		*Max/Min Ratio*	
District	*Max*	*Min*	*Max*	*Min*	*Irrigated*	*Dry*
ANDHRA						
Srikakulam	13.37	1.31	4.06	0.19	10.21	21.37
Vishakapatnam	13.32	2.03	3.81	0.19	6.56	20.05
East Godavari	13.5	1.94	8.25	0.31	6.96	26.61
West Godavari	13.5	1.94	8.25	0.31	6.96	26.61
Krishna	13.5	3	5.94	0.31	4.5	19.16
Guntur	13.5	2.06	6.36	0.25	6.55	25.44
Nellore	13.5	2.06	5.12	0.25	6.55	20.48
Kurnool	13.5	1.12	4.5	0.25	12.05	18
Ananthapur	13.5	1.12	2.81	0.12	12.05	23.42
Cuddappah	13.5	2.06	4.5	0.25	6.55	18
Chittor	13.5	2.06	2.56	0.25	6.55	10.24
TELANGANA						
Adilabad	14.57	6.85	1.92	0.95	2.13	2.02
Hyderabad	20.57	10.28	2.78	0.85	2	3.27
Karimnagar	15.43	9.11	2.89	1.07	1.69	2.7
Khammam	16.39	10.28	2.77	1.06	1.59	2.61
Mahboobnagar	18.21	8.57	2.57	1.06	2.12	2.42
Medak	23.14	5.41	3.86	1	4.28	3.86
Nalgonda	18	9.11	2.88	1.34	1.98	2.15
Nizamabad	18.21	12.75	3	1.19	1.43	2.52
Warangal	17.14	9.11	2.64	0.96	1.88	2.75

Source: GoAP 1959, Part I, Volumes I and II: various.

the two areas into a composite state in 1956. The incidence of taxation varied, depending on the price of the crop as well as the rate of taxation. The tax on irrigated land in Telangana was substantially higher than in Andhra by more than 50 per cent for the maximum rates and several times more for the minimum rates. It is interesting to note the considerably lower ratio of maximum and minimum land tax for irrigated land in the heavily irrigated Krishna and Godavari delta districts, as compared to the much more lightly irrigated Telangana districts. Thus, it seems clear that throughout 100 years, the land revenue/tax system concerning irrigated land in Andhra had a substantially lower monetary level and incidence than it had in Telangana. The different paddy prices further accentuated this difference in both regions.

The rates of taxation of unirrigated land in Telangana, where the maximum rates were lower than in Andhra, while the minimum rates were higher, in the nineteenth century, seems to have been set to exact taxes from the newly introduced cash crops such as cotton, groundnut and castor, which were important export crops. Further, the ratio between maximum and minimum tax rates in Telangana was much smaller for both irrigated and unirrigated land than in Andhra, thus deterring the development of irrigation sources for dry lands. All of this would have had its inevitable effect on the differences in agricultural and economic prosperity in the two regions.

The variation and iniquity in the land revenue money rates, and their incidence between the Andhra and Telangana region was apparent when the two regions merged into the state of Andhra Pradesh in 1956. The Committee on Land Revenue Reforms stated clearly that the comparison of taxation of irrigated ('wet') land in Andhra and Telangana indicated that the tax rate was higher in Telangana. It also concluded that the efficacy and productivity of irrigation projects, especially in Coastal Andhra, were vastly superior to those in Telangana. This was made more extreme by the fact that crop yields in irrigated lands in Telangana were lower than those in Andhra. It therefore raised the issue of equity in taxation between the two regions as early as 1959 (GoAP 1959, Part III, Volume III: 590). This issue was not addressed at all, even in 1967, when the tax rates were enhanced; they were not adjusted between the two regions to give parity.

Instead of carrying out the recommendations of the Committee, the government enacted the Andhra Pradesh Land Revenue (Additional Assessment and Cess Revision) Act and an Amendment to the Act in 1962. This Act was challenged in the High Court of Andhra Pradesh in the landmark *Nalla Raja Reddy and Others Vs the State of Andhra Pradesh* case. Justice Pingle Jaganmohan Reddy and Justice Venketsam heard the case, and Justice Reddy wrote and pronounced the judgment. Dealing with the Report of the Land Revenue Reforms Committee, Justice Reddy commented on how the Committee's recommendation focused on the nature of the water source and land quality and important determining factors in the assessment of land revenue:

> These observations and findings of the Revenue Reforms Committee also justify the conclusion that the two principles upon which land revenue was fixed in the past were the grade of the soil and the nature of the water

> source, and the Committee recommended them to be maintained, but with this difference that the Committee's recommendation emphasized that the impact of the nature of the water source on the grade and quality of the land should properly reflect the fact in the levy of land revenue assessment (Reddy 1967: 1322).

Reviewing the action of the Legislature in setting land revenue rates, Justice Reddy stated:

> These provisions show that land revenue is assessed at a flat rate irrespective of the nature of the grade of the soil or the potential productivity of the land sought to be assessed or even on the actual income. We have already seen that throughout the centuries, an intelligible and systematic classification of soils was an essential preliminary in framing an assessment on land based on its productive powers and such justification to be correct and generally useful must be founded upon a consideration of the nature of the property and the composition of the several soils (ibid.: 1330).

Concluding by striking down the Act and the Amendment Act, Justice Reddy further held:

> The provisions of the impugned Act also are silent as to the machinery for making the assessment, and the requisite procedure is left to the Executive to evolve. Where the assessment is to be levied in the range of a fixed maximum and minimum, questions arise as to how the tax is to be levied, what the criterion is for imposing the tax within that range, what the rights of the assesses are to make representations, what the remedy is if their representations fail to impress the levying authority? The Act is silent on all of those aspects (ibid.).

Justice Reddy also ruled that the government is under an obligation to undertake a survey, which was a necessary *sine qua non* for the levy of land revenue and had been provided for in all previous land-related legislations, both in the state and in other states. Striking down the Act, after taking all these issues into consideration his decision was that '[t]he omission in the impugned Act to provide for machinery for making the assessment or for its levy and collection and for the requisite procedure would itself constitute the violations of Article 19 [1] [f] of the Constitution' (Reddy 1967: 1339–40).

It is clear from the above that there was no application of mind by the Legislature or the ruling elite of Andhra Pradesh in order to effectively ensure equity, not only between the regions in terms of the land taxation, but also between cultivators holding different kinds of land, both in terms of the quality of the soil and the availability or non-availability of different sources of irrigation. After 100 years of British land settlement, which was one of the essential benefits of Pax Britannica, a state in Independent India, legislating for the public interest, was unable or unwilling to follow the tradition of fair assessment and to ensure equity in taxation between different regions and different types of land.[18]

After the Supreme Court upheld the High Court's decision, the Legislature passed the Andhra Pradesh Land Revenue [Enhancement] Act, 1967, thus replacing the 1962 Act. This new Act simply enhanced the tax rates without affecting the structure of the rates concerning the land and its potential. In order to achieve 'the objective of bringing uniformity in the assessment of land revenue in the Telangana and Andhra areas of the State', an increase of 100 per cent was carried out on the existing land revenue rates in Andhra, and 30 per cent in Telangana areas. The purpose of tax rate equalisation as far as irrigated (wet) lands were concerned was not achieved. Thus also, a cess of 37 paisa per rupee (that is, 37 per cent) in the Andhra area, and 25 paisa per rupee (25 per cent) in Telangana would have to be paid. This move acknowledged that after 10 years of being part of one state, rates in Telangana were still higher by 65 per cent, as compared to the rates in Andhra. However, the position between the two regions where unirrigated land was concerned was, in fact, to the detriment of Andhra dry land owners.[19] The land revenue rates as per the 1967 Act in Andhra and Telangana are provided below in Table 4.21.

As can be seen from Table 4.21, the tax differential between the two regions was tilted in favour of Andhra where irrigated land was concerned, and in favour of Telangana where unirrigated land was concerned. In both cases, the idea of equity does not seem to have been considered necessary. Since no survey of the lands was made, the Act also made the unjustifiable assumption that there was a uniform fertility of land and efficiency of irrigation.

Over time, the share and importance of land revenue in the state budget reduced because land revenue rates had not been raised for many decades, although prices of agriculture products had risen considerably. Other sources of revenue, such as sales tax, excise duty on liquor, registration fees on the sale of land and property, and Central Government's devolution of All-India taxes overrode the need for land revenue (see Table 4.22).

As evident from Table 4.22, while land revenue contributed 13.9 per cent of the total state revenues in 1955–56, its share declined to

Table 4.21: Land Revenue Rates, 1967

	Andhra		*Telangana*	
Rs/Acre	*Minimum*	*Maximum*	*Minimum*	*Maximum*
Wet lands	2.24	28.5	4.62	32.4
Dry lands	0.21	14.44	0.1	6.78
With cess				
Wet lands	3.29	39.05	5.78	40.5
Dry lands	0.28	19.78	0.13	8.48

Source: Raman Rao 1993: 233.

Table 4.22: Andhra Pradesh Land Revenue

	Land Revenue	*Total State Revenues*	*Proportion*
Year	*In Rs Crores*		*(In Per cent)*
1955–56	8.6	62	13.9
1975–76	31.4	505	6.2
1986–87	12	3227	0.4

Source: Raman Rao 1993: 23, 468.

6.2 per cent in 1975–76, and by 1986–87, it was 0.4 per cent (Raman Rao 1993: 23, 46).

This decline in importance allowed for a degree of laxity, both in the collection as well as in carrying out new settlements when the old ones expired. Eventually, N. T. Rama Rao's Telugu Desam Party government, in 1987, abolished land revenue in Andhra Pradesh altogether. In 1987, land revenue was abolished, thus closing the 700-year long saga of oppression and mismanagement of land that had set agriculture back, and worse, had deprived farmers of their just returns. This radical move finally ended the issue of differential land revenue between the two regions.

Concluding Remarks

This essay has attempted to succinctly illustrate the vital importance of land taxes in south India. The development and change in the land tax regime from the Hindu canonical rates to the Islamic canonical rates, and following that, to more secular and rational British rates, suggests the impact of the ruling ideology, not just on the rates, but also consequently on the agricultural and economic well-being of the land and the people.[20]

In the case of Andhra and Telangana, the historical rates determined by British rule in Andhra and Muslim rule in Telangana over a 100 years (ultimately culminating in the merger of the two regions in 1956) had resulted in two different trajectories for the regions. In one trajectory, the agriculturists of Telangana paid a disproportionately heavy land tax, which led to the impoverishment of the people and the region, and stunted the growth of its society and economy, as compared to Andhra. In the second trajectory, the fiscal and revenue earning capacity of the state in Telangana was strengthened, whereas in Andhra, the state had a much narrower and restricted fiscal space and conceded larger economic space to the cultivators and to the people, generally. This economic growth in Andhra prepared the ground for concessions in the political space as well as in the development of society in terms of education and social change. Such a development was not apparent in the Nizam's Telangana, mainly due to the lack of a similar economic base.[21]

These two trajectories, in turn, later combined after the merger with the third, that is, the short term, ill-intentioned and narrow-minded attitude of the Andhra ruling elite, thereby resulting in continued exploitation in various ways of the established taxation capacity in Telangana and the diversion of those resources to fund the deficits in Andhra. This unstable and unfair situation eventually led to agitation in Telangana. After an extraordinary period of 58 years, it further resulted in the dismemberment of the state of Andhra Pradesh and the creation of the separate state of Telangana.

Notes

1. The state agencies mostly compile these and publish them in four series known as the *South Indian Inscriptions* (SII) and *Annual Report on Epigraphy* (ARE), *Epigraphia Indica* (EI) and *Epigraphia Carnataka* (EC).
2. Vincent Smith, however, speculates thus:

   > If Asoka was in the habit of taking one-fourth, the concession amounted to the remission of half the assessment. The proportion taken by the government varied at different times and places. One-sixth was the normal approved rate, but one-fourth was common .... Probably Ashoka ordinarily took one-fourth and in Lumbini remitted half of that. The *Arthasastra* interprets the word *athabhagiye* certain .... consequently, *ashta*

[atha] bhagya means 'one-eighth of the produce paid as land revenue' (2013: 222–23).

Also, Mookerji agrees and says, 'the usual king's share of the produce as land revenue which was one-fourth in Chandragupta's time according to Megasthenes, was reduced by half for this village as the birthplace of the Holy One' (2007: 204).

3. Five hundred years later, the British settlement under John Lawrence of the Punjab restricted the revenue to the Hindu canonical rate.
4. Thomas Munro, writing in 1820 to his superiors on Bellari district, taken over after the defeat of Tippu Sultan, says:

   > I once wished the reduction to be gradual, but the country was not then so impoverished as it is now. It must now be instant, or the country will be so exhausted that it will be almost impractical to restore it. Out of the 2,644 villages composing of the Collectorate, 1,788 have reverted to the Government, [not] yielding a revenue of about twenty laks of rupees. The revenue of the villages still in lease is only six and half lakhs .... It is, in fact, an insolvency of nearly 1800 villages .... In Raidurg half the *ryots* have emigrated. The state of many of the other districts is no better (Munro 1881, Volume 1: 111).

5. The narrations indicate the demand of the fighters in Syria to divide the land in the same manner as Khaybar. Habib Thabit (d. AH 119/734 CE or AH 122/739 CE) says: 'the companions of the Messenger and a group of the Muslims wanted Umar b.al-Khattab to divide up Syria, just as the Messenger had divided Khaybar'. Jarir b. Hazim (d. AH 170/786 CE) reports: 'The people in Syria were conquered. Among them was Bilal [b. Rabah] .... So they wrote to Umar that as for the booty [*fay*] which was obtained, "the fifth [*khums*] is for you and what is left is for us, there is nothing for anyone else. [This is] just as the Prophet acted at Khaybar]" ... but Umar said: "No, this is a source of wealth. I will hold it back as common property [*fay*] to provide for them [the fighters] and the Muslims ..."' (Katbi 2010: 8).
6. An exception seems to have occurred in Kashmir when the first Muslim ruler, who usurped the throne from the widow of the last Hindu king in 1326 AD, is said to have assumed the throne as Shams-ood-Deen and to have established Islam as the state religion. He 'fixed the assessment on land at seventeen per cent on gross produce' (Ferishta 1989, Volume IV: 263).
7. Ferishta records that the first Muslim king of Kashmir, Shamsudddin, who usurped the throne in 1326 AD by marrying the widowed Hindu queen, Rani Kowla Devi, fixed the assessment of taxes on land at 17 per cent (1989: 263). The translator, Briggs, writes in a footnote: ' ... would that Shamsoodin's assessment extended throughout India! It certainly seems to have been the case before Muslim conquest–a fact that Abu Fazl, Akbar's minister had also commented. However, the imposition of *sharia*-based taxation of land on non-Muslims was an Islamic mandate.

8. Sarkar's 1594 *illahi bighas* figures converted to *daftari bighas* of 1720 AD, which is two-third of the *Illahi bigha* (Habib 2014: 416).
9. See footnote 4 above.
10. This rate would be something below 30 per cent, around 25 per cent.
11. It is interesting that the number of villages is far greater in Telangana (by 43 per cent) than those in Andhra, even though the geographical extent of the two regions is somewhat similar, as Rayalaseema was not part of the Andhra region at that time.
12. This land revenue system is discussed by Fatheullah in the excerpt below:

    > On the abolition of the system of farming the revenue to private individuals, the administration of land revenue had been organised by the Raiatwari system. Payment of the Government demand in cash instead of in kind had been introduced, and the division of land into different classes for the purpose of assessment roughly effected. The accurate area of the different holdings and the real productive capacity of land being, however, unknown, it was impossible to fix a moderate and equitable assessment (Fatheullah 1935: 140–41).

    He further continues:

    > On the one side, the ryots complained from year to year of high and inequitable assessment, while on the other side the Revenue Collectors complained of misappropriation on the part of the Patels and Patwaris. It was, therefore, the unanimous opinion of the Revenue Officers that to remove the aforesaid defects in the administration, a Revenue Survey and Settlement Department should be organised. In the year 1294 AH, [1877 AD] this Department was accordingly created (ibid.).

13. Irrigated land was taxed at an average of Rs 12.79 per acre and unirrigated at Rs 1.44 per acre. The break-up for the rest of the years is not available.
14. By this time, Hyderabad cotton export had collapsed due to US subsidisation of exports of their massive cotton crop under FDR's New Deal Programe in 1935.
15. These figures are for the *ryotwari* areas only and they exclude the *zamindari* permanently settled areas.
16. Telangana therefore had an edge in terms of percentage of an irrigated area of 16.4 per cent.
17. The slow uptake by landowners of cultivation under irrigated conditions created by the major Nizamsagar project in Nizamabad district of Telangana in the early-twentieth century is probably due to the massive tax liability on such land, which needed heavy capital investment by the farmers. The uptake had to wait for increases in paddy prices and sugarcane cultivation after the establishment of the Nizam Sugar Company; the settlement of Coastal Andhra farmers was also encouraged by the Nizam's government.
18. It occurs to one that this is a watershed event and indicates the beginning of a general deterioration in the governance system.

19. Mostly, one suspects tax on the cash crops grown on unirrigated black cotton soils in Andhra, while Telangana farmers were raising coarse cereal crops such as sorghum and maize on similar land.
20. The above discussion has primarily focused on irrigated land, and the paddy crop grown on it, as the data on this subject is abundant. By the time of the British land settlements, the process of rational calculation meant that there is a considerable amount of data concerning irrigated and unirrigated land, qualities of land, irrigation season, irrigation sources, and output, prices and costs of cultivation. Much work can be done based on these large data sources. Apart from the published data of the settlement reports, there is undoubtedly original data of the villages and farmers, sampled in order to secure the data for enabling the settlement.
21. For a much more detailed account of the progress of commercialisation and agrarian capitalism in Andhra, especially Coastal Andhra, see Satyanarayana (1990).

References

Allami, Abul Fazl. 1891. *The Ain I Akbari*, Volume II, trans. H. S. Jarrett. Calcutta: Asiatic Society of Bengal.

Al-Qardawi, Yusuf. 2011. *Fiqh Al-Zakah: A Comprehensive Study of the Zakah Regulations and Philosophy in the Light of the Quran and Sunna*, trans. Monzer Khaf. Kuala Lumpur: Islamic Book Trust.

Appadorai, Angadipuram. 1936. *Economic Conditions in Southern India (1000–1500 AD)*, 2 Volumes. Madras: University of Madras Press.

Ashoka. 289 BC. *Lumbini Pillar Inscription*, trans. S. Dhammika. Available at https://www.cs.colostate.edu/~malaiya/ashoka.html (accessed 21 October 2020).

Baudhayana, Dharamasutra. 1882. *The Sacred Laws of the Âryas, Sacred Books of the East*, Volume 24, trans. Georg Bühler. Oxford: Clarendon Press.

Berriedale, Keith Arthur. 1936. *A Constitutional History of India 1600–1935*. London: Methuen and Company. Available at https://archive.org/details/constitutionalhi030959mbp/page/n6.

Briggs, John. 1830. *The Present Land-tax in India Considered as a Measure of Finance, in Order to Show Its Effects on the Government and the People of that Country, and on the Commerce of Great Britain*. London: Longmans, Green, Orme, Brown and Green.

Buchanan-Hamilton, Francis. 1988[1807]. *A Journey From Madras etc. ...* 3 Volumes. London: T. Cadell and W. Davies. New Delhi: Asian Educational Services.

Chopra, Gulshan Lall. 1928. *Punjab as a Sovereign State: 1799–1839*, Lahore: Uttar Chand Kapur and Sons.

Dutt, R. C. 1960[1882]. *The Economic History of India*, 2 Volumes. New Delhi: Publication Division, Government of India.

Fatheullah, M. 1935. *A History of Administrative Reforms In Hyderabad State*. Secunderabad, Deccan: New Hyderabad Press. Available at https://archive.org/stream/historyofadminis035274mbp/historyofadminis035274mbp_djvu.txt (accessed 26 March 2015).

Ferishta, Mahomed Kasim 1989[1829]. *History of the Rise of the Mahomedan Power in India*, 4 Volumes, trans. J. Briggs. New Delhi: Atlantic Publishers.

Firminger, W. K. (ed.). 1985. *Fifth Report of the Select Committee on the Affairs of the East India Company, 1812*, 3 Volumes. New Delhi: Neeraj Publishing House.

Ganguli, Kisari Mohan (trans.). 2003. *The Mahabharata of Krishna-Dwaipayana Vyasa*, Santi Parva, Part II, Volume IX. New Delhi: Munishiram Manoharlal.

Gautama. 1879. *Dharmasutra*, *Sacred Books of the East*, Volume II, trans. G. Bühler. Oxford: Clarendon Press. Available at http://www.sacred-texts.com/hin/sbe02/index.htm (accessed 13 June 2015).

GoAP. 1959. 'Report of the Land Revenue Reforms Committee', Part I, 2 Volumes; Part II, 4 Volumes. Hyderabad: Government Press.

——. 1994. *Inscriptions of Andhra Pradesh–Nalgonda District*, Volume II, *Epigraphical Series*, No. 23, ed. N. Venkataramanayya. Hyderabad: GoAP.

GoI. 1909. *Imperial Gazetteer of India*. Calcutta: Superintendent of Government Printing.

Grant Duff, James. 1826. *History of the Mahrattas*, 3 Volumes. London: Longman, Rees, Orme, Brown and Green.

Greville, Charles Francis. 1988[1795]. *British India Analyzed: The Provincial and Revenue Establishments of Tippoo Sultan and of Mahommedan and British Conquerors of Hindoostan Stated and Considered*, 3 Volumes. New Delhi: Crown Publications.

Gribble, J. D. B. 2002. *A History of the Deccan*, 2 Volumes. New Delhi: Rupa Publications.

Gune, V. T. 1974. 'Land Laws', in *History of Medieval Deccan [1295–1724]*, Volume II, eds H. K. Sherwani and P. M. Joshi. Hyderabad: Director of Printing, GoAP.

Habib, Irfan. 1984. 'Agrarian Economy', in *The Cambridge Economic History of India*, Volume 1: c.1200–c.1750, eds T. Raychaudhuri and I. Habib. New Delhi: Orient Longman.

——. 2014[1963]. *The Agrarian System of Mughal India 1556–1707*, Third Edition. New Delhi: Oxford University Press.

Hendricks, Frederick. 1858. 'On the Statistics of Indian Revenue and Taxation', *Journal of the Statistical Society of London* 21(3): 223–96. Available at https://www.jstor.org/stable/2338224 (accessed 29 July 2019).

HMSO. 1915. *Statistical Abstract Relating to British India (Various numbers)*. London: HMSO.

——. 2011. *Epigraphical Study of Ancient and Medieval Villages in the Tamil Country*, *Review of Agrarian Studies* 1(2). Available at http://ras.org.in/epigraphical_

study_of_ancient_and_medieval_villages_in_the_tamil_country (accessed 21 October 2020).

Katbi, Ghaida Khazna. 2010. *Islamic Land Tax–Al-Kharaj: From the Islamic Conquest to the Abbasid Period*, trans. R. Ali. London: I. B. Tauris.

Kautilya. 1915. *Arthasastra*, trans. R. Shamasastry. Bangalore: Government Printing Press.

Mahdi Ali, Moulvi. 1879. *Memorandum to the Famine Commission*. Bombay: Times of India Press.

Manu. 1886. *The Laws, Sacred Books of the East*, Volume XXV, trans. G. Bühler. Oxford: Clarendon Press.

Mookerji, Radhakumud. 2007. *Ashoka*. New Delhi: Motilal Banarsidass.

Moosvi, S. 2010. *People, Taxation and Trade in Mughal India*. New Delhi: Oxford University Press.

——. 2015. *The Economy of the Mughal Empire c. 1595: A Statistical Study*. New Delhi: Oxford University Press.

Müller, F. Max (ed.). 1880. *The Institutes of Vishnu*, Sacred Books of the East, Volume VII, trans. Julius Jolly. Oxford: Clarendon Press.

Munro, Thomas. 1881. *Selections from his Minutes and Other Official Writings*, 2 Volumes, ed. Alexander Arbuthnot. London: C. Kegan Paul and Co.

Nayeem, M. A. 2009. 'Administrative Structure of Hyderabad State', in *History of the Modern Deccan [1720/24 to 1948]*, eds Kulkarni, Nayeem and Seshan. Hyderabad: Abul Kalam Azad Oriental Research Institute.

Qureshi, Ishtiaq Husain. 1944[1942]. *The Administration of the Sultanate Of Delhi*, Second Edition. Lahore: S. H. Muhammad Ashraf.

Raghavaiyengar, S. Srinivasa. 1988[1893]. *Memorandum of the Progress on the Madras Presidency during the Last Forty Years of British Administration*. New Delhi: Asian Educational Services.

Raman Rao, A. V. 1993. *Andhra Pradesh Economy since Independence [1947–1992]*. New Delhi: Kalyani Publishers.

Ramayya Pantulu, J., and N. Lakshminarayan Rao (eds). 1948. 'Telugu Inscriptions from the Madras Presidency', *South Indian Inscriptions*, Volume X. Director [Epigraphy], Mysore.

Raychaudhuri, Tapan. 2015. 'The Agrarian System of Mughal India: A Review Essay', in *The Mughal State, 1526–1750*, eds M. Alam and S. Subrahmanyam. New Delhi: Oxford University Press.

Reddy, Justice Pingle Jaganmohan. 1967. 'Nalla Raja Reddy and Others Vs State of Andhra Pradesh', in *Indian Law Reports, Andhra Pradesh Series*, 1267–1341.

Rice, Benjamin Lewis. 1878. *Mysore and Coorg: Coorg*, Volume 3, Bangalore: Mysore Government Press.

Richards, J. F. 1975. *Mughal Administration of Golconda*. Oxford: Clarendon Press.

Rizvi, S. A. A. 2005. *The Wonder that was India*, Volume II, New Delhi: Picador-India.

Sachau, Edward C. 2010. *Alberuni's India*. New Delhi: Rupa Publications.

Sarkar, Sir Jadunath. 1901. *India of Aurangzib*. Calcutta: Sanyal And Company.

——. 1912. *History of Aurangzib: Mainly Based on Persian Sources*, Volume 1. Calcutta: M. C. Sarkar and Sons.

Sastry, P. V. Parabrahma. 2016. *The Kakatiyas*. Hyderabad: Department of Archaeology and Museums, Government of Telangana.

Satyanarayana, A. 1990. *Andhra Peasants under British Rule: Agrarian Relations and Rural Economy 1900–1940*. New Delhi: Manohar Publications.

Sen, Surendranath. 1925. *Administrative System of the Mahrattas*. Calcutta: University of Calcutta.

Sharma, Inderjit. 1985. *Land Revenue Administration in the Punjab [1849–1901]*. New Delhi: Atlantic Publishers.

Siddiqi, Noman Ahmed. 1989. *Land Revenue Administration under the Mughals*. New Delhi: Munshiram Manoharlal.

Sleeman, W. H. 2003. *Rambles and Recollections of an Indian Official*, ed. Vincent A. Smith. New Delhi: Rupa Publications.

Smith, Vincent. 2013[1909]. *Ashoka*. New Delhi: Low Price Publications.

Subbarayalu, Y. 2012. *South India under the Cholas*. New Delhi: Oxford University Press.

Sundaram, Lanka. 1929. *Mughal Land Revenue System*. London: The Basheer Muslim Library.

Vaikuntum, Y. 2002. *State, Economy and Social Transformation: Hyderabad State [1724–1948]*. New Delhi: Manohar Publishers.

Venkatramanayya, N., and M. Somasehkara Sarma. 1960. 'The Kakatiyas of Warangal', in *Early History of the Deccan*, 2 Volumes, ed. G. Yazdani. London: Oxford University Press for the GoAP.

——. 1962. 'Vilasa Grant of Prolaya Nayaka', in *Epigraphica Indica*, Volume XXXII, eds D. C. Sircar and D. C. H. Chabra. New Delhi: Manager of Publications, Government of India.

Wattters, Thomas. 1904. *On Youang Chawang's Travels in India [629–645 AD]*, eds T. W. Rhys Davids and S. W. Bushell. London: Royal Asiatic Society.

Wink, Andre. 1986. *Land and Sovereignty in India: Agrarian Society and Politics under Eighteenth Century Maratha Svrajya*. Bombay: Orient Longman, in association with the University of Cambridge.

5

Paddy Yields in Pre-Industrial South India

It has been established by Angus Maddison in his monumental 2007 work, *Contour of the World Economy, 1–2030 CE: Essays in Macroeconomic History*, that India was the world's largest economy from 1–1000 AD, constituting 28–32 per cent of the world's income during the period. Between 1000 and 1500 AD, that is, the Kakatiya-Vijayanagar period, Indian income continued to rise, but slower than earlier, and it saw a decline in India's share in global income, to 22–24 per cent. In 1600 AD, India's share had fallen to 22 per cent, and by 1700 AD, it rose to 24 per cent before beginning a secular decline onwards.

The question arises as to the basis of Indian income from 1–1700 AD, and the answer must surely be the high degree of agricultural development. This sector had been the major source of income, wealth and taxation during these periods. It produced the prosperity of the Kakatiya and Vijayanagar empires and partially offset the national figures due to the reverses encountered in north India due to the ravages of Muslim invasions from 1100 AD onwards.

Over time, scholars have been examining Indian traditional agrarian systems generally, but there is a need for more robust data on technology, yields and taxation. According to Stein, a recent historiographical view has emerged, which suggests that the 'pre-colonial eighteenth century rural economy was generally a robust one, partly so because the state regimes of this period were directly and *constructively* involved in the promotion of agrarian production and that this robustness continued well into the colonial age' (1992: 5–6) (emphasis in original). While the subject of the rural economy is vast, the dominance of the paddy/rice crop in South India is apparent.

This essay attempts to estimate the yields of the major crop, paddy, in pre-industrial south India, on which reasonable data exists. It may help scholars to examine the initial conditions of land productivity and paddy crop technology during that period.

High Level of Development of Pre-Industrial Indian Agriculture

Many British officials in the field recognised the sophistication and productivity of pre-industrial Indian agriculture. Alexander Walker (1780 AD–1810), during his travels in Malabar and Gujarat, identified more than 50 varieties of rice being cultivated. He also recorded the use of different kinds of ploughs (both with and without seed drills) by farmers, which were adapted to suit different seeds and soils: On agriculture in Gujarat, Walker commented:

> The whole world does not produce finer and more beautifully cultivated fields than those in Guzerat .... I have seen from Cape Comorin to the Gulf of Kutch details of the most laborious cultivation, of the collection of manure, of grains sown for fodder, of grains sown promiscuously for the same purpose, of an attention to the change of seed, of fallows and rotation of crops. In the Deccan, the cultivation is as good as that in Guzerat, and the people are in every respect as active and as intelligent as well as moral and independent as those of that country (Dharampal 2000: 188–89).

Captain Thos Halcott, in 1797 AD, recorded the practice of drill husbandry in present-day Andhra Pradesh, and acknowledged that 'although, it [i.e., drill husbandry] has been practised under the eyes of everybody in the Guntoor Circar, no one that I mentioned [it] to [had] ever observed it before, nor did I observe it myself till lately' (Dharampal 2000: 205). As these Guntur implements were far superior to the drills then in use in England, Halcott sent these various drills, etc., to the Board of Agriculture in London (ibid.).

Dharampal (1990) reports that John Hodgson, a senior member of the Madras Presidency Board of Revenue, in 1807, estimated the productivity of almost 60 quintals of paddy per hectare for the relatively better lands in Coimbatore. Further, that the *Edinburgh Review* around 1804 published reports that Indian agricultural productivity was about three times that in England while wages of the Indian agricultural labourer were also much more than his contemporary British counterpart. Again, William Thackeray, who in 1806 toured the Canara and Malabar districts ceded to the East India Company, stated in his report of 4 August 1807: 'The farmers of Europe seem to have been far less skilful, industrious and respectable, for many centuries, than those who have survived the calamities which have now for so many years, been heaped on these provinces' (Firminger 1985, Volume 3: 577). The observations and reports by British officials which were available contemporaneously indicate that the new rulers of India had a high opinion of the Indian agricultural sector.

In 1832, while testifying before a Committee of the House of Commons, Dr Wallick, the Superintendent of the Royal Botanical Gardens in India, was asked whether Indian agriculture was capable of any great improvement. He replied by stating that while it was certainly a possibility, it would not happen to the great extent as imagined. He further added about rice cultivation specifically: ' ... *the rice cultivation, I should, think, if we were to live for another thousand years, we should hardly see any improvement in that branch of cultivation*' (Dharampal 1982) (emphasis added). Dr John Augustus Voelcker, the Consulting Chemist to the Royal Agricultural Society of England, was deputed by the British government to make inquiries on the state of Indian agriculture. He toured the country extensively from December 1889 to January 1891, and his *Report on the Improvement of Indian Agriculture* is a mine of information on the subject.

According to Voelcker, the view that agriculture in India was 'primitive and backward', which was currently prevailing in England, and was also held by officials in India, was wrong. He was convinced that taking conditions under which crop cultivation is carried on,

> *At his best the Indian raiyat or cultivator is quite as good as, and in some respects, the superior of, the average British farmer*, whilst at his worst it can only be said that this state is brought about largely by the *absence of facilities for improvement which is probably unequalled in any other country* (Voelcker 1893: 10–11) (emphasis added).

All in all, the idea that pre-industrial agriculture was backward does not seem credible, in spite of observations by contemporary British officials in the field. Angus Maddison estimates that even in 1700 AD, India constituted 24 per cent of the global Gross Domestic Product (GDP) and 112 per cent of the 29 groups of countries in Western Europe; by 1820, however, these figures fell to 16 per cent and 70 per cent, respectively, and by 1870, to 12 per cent and 37 per cent, respectively (Maddison 2007: 261). It would seem that until full-blown industrialisation took place in Western Europe and the US, India had a substantial share of World GDP, and much of this would have come from its dominant agricultural sector.

It is therefore not surprising that due to the relative peace in south India from 1000 AD onwards, agriculture (and paddy crops) should indicate high productivity and relative prosperity.

We present here five data sets on paddy yields during the pre-industrial period for five regions of South India. The first and earliest is the inscriptional data from the tenth to thirteenth century in the Pandya-Chola region. The second is an extensive and impressive data set collected in the late-eighteenth century from the Madras (city) region, that is, the '*Jaghire*', the earliest acquisition by the East India Company in South India. The third is data collected by a reasonably systematic process based on field-level observations at the beginning of the nineteenth century in the Madras, Canara and Malabar territories that had been annexed by the East India Company after the defeat of Tippu Sultan. The fourth is an even more systematic data for the late-nineteenth century, based on crop-cutting experiments from the Madras Presidency, and the fifth is data from the Telangana region of the Nizam's dominions. All of these provide estimates of the highest and lowest paddy yields. These figures convey a strong impression of a combination of very high and not-so-low paddy yields over time and across South India.

Yields: Pandya-Chola Region (Tenth to Thirteenth Century)

There are an enormous number of inscriptions[1] relating to royal grants to temples, village groups, and individuals. Subbarayalu reports that there are a total of 44,000 inscriptions relating to South India. Many of these deal with land-grants and give valuable information about the land extent and associated tax in quantity of paddy (2012: 18). For our period (tenth to thirteenth century), there are 19,000 inscriptions and 9,000 inscriptions for the period fourteenth to sixteenth century (Karashima 2008: Table 2).

Land Tax in *Kallam* per *Veli* of Land

One of the earliest inscriptions mentioning land and taxes in grain is a grant by the Pandyan king, Varaguna II, which was made to the temple of Lord Subramanya at Tiruchendur. The approximate date of this grant is 874 AD, and it details the volumetric measures to be used and insists that the grain is measured as 'heaped' rather than 'struck'. Aiyer (1930–31), analysing the inscription, states that three measures of paddy yielded one measure of rice, although in other inscriptions it is given as five measures of paddy yielding two measure of rice.[2] Subbarayalu (2012) has made much effort of sorting the relevant inscriptions. From a corpus of 4,000 inscriptions, he selected 55 inscriptions (from 945–1300 AD), with references to paddy yields in *kallam* (a variable volumetric measure) per *veli* (a measure of land extent, about 6.6 acres or 2.64 hectares) (henceforth *k/v*). These 55 inscriptions provide 78 single data points after eliminating those for dry cropland (six inscriptions) and those with ranges of output (10 inscriptions). The data varies from 320–10 *k/v* (Subbarayalu 2012: 105–07). The reason for the variation seems to have been that the tax varied depending on the quality of the land granted. Table 5.1 below classifies these 78 data points: 31 per cent of the observations are for lands taxed above 90 *k/v*, and 50 per cent, for those between 30 and 89 *k/v*.

Table 5.1: Frequency of Land Tax from Inscriptional Data

The range of k/v	*Frequency*	*Average Tax in k/v*
> 120	6	176.02
90–120	18	104.87
60–89	16	74.67
30–59	23	44.32
15–29	12	20.19
<15	3	11.1
Total	78	67.8

Source: Constructed by the author (Subbrayalu 2012: 105–07).

Subbarayalu found that the average rate varied over time and thereby found that in the period from 850–985 AD, the standard was 125 *k/v*, while 'with the accession of Rajaraja I (r. 985–1014 AD), the standard of 100 *k/v* seems to have come into vogue .... Once established, the standard of 100 *k/v* had a long currency as it recurs as late as 1238 CE' (Subbarayalu 2012: 101). Almost all of the inscriptions and other data state the quantum of land tax, but they do not provide what the proportion is to the gross output.[3] Here, we have to rely on canonical and other statements in order to estimate what this proportion could have been.

Evidence of Tax Rates

The Hindu canonical taxation rate was one-sixth of the output of land, as stated in the *Mahabharata*. Ashoka (289 BC), in his Lumbini Pillar inscription, specified the reduction of taxes on Lumbini village (the birthplace of the Buddha) to one-eighth of the produce. This rate reduction indicates that the usual rate was the Hindu canonical one-sixth, or at least something higher than one-eighth. During his Indian travels (629–45 AD), the Chinese Buddhist monk, Hiuen Tsang, also confirmed that land taxes were one-sixth of the produce (Watters 1904: 176). Benjamin Lewis Rice suggested that in 1046 AD, under the Cholas, the tax rate was one-sixth of the produce; but he thought that 250 years later, the tax rate on irrigated paddy land had risen to one-third (1878: 527–28).

Subbarayulu cites an inscription of 1073 AD, stating that the state's share in paddy cultivation is one-third (2012: 105,108). Gune writes that the Hoysalas (1026–1343 AD) and Yadavas (850–1334 AD) collected one-seventh, and under the Vijayanagar empire (1336–1646 AD), land taxes seem to have varied from one-sixth to one-fourth (1974: 561). Alaev (1984) suggests one-fourth as a reasonable estimate for Chola taxes. Considering all the above, we assume a tax of 25 per cent share of output as a reasonable approximation for the Pandya-Chola period and the region.

After encountering stiff resistance to the continuation of Islamic taxes, the British experimented with other rates (Douie 1915; Dutt 1960, Volume 1: 97; Volume II: 236; Firminger 1985, Volume 1: 223, 258; Volume 3: 43, 262, 303; Munro 1881, Volume 1: 63–66, 111). By the early nineteenth century, John Lawrence restricted the Punjab land taxes entirely to the Hindu canonical rate of one-sixth (Dutt 1960, Volume II: 68).

Double Versus Single Crop Yields

Subbarayalu, while discussing the tax differential between double-crop and single-crop irrigated land, writes:

> During Period 1 [850–985 AD], the rate of 120 *k/v* seems to have been the normal rate for the 'standard' land. Under Rajaraja I, the rate seems to have been fixed at *100 k/v for the standard, that is river-irrigated double-crop lands.* But for the lands deviating from the standard norms, the rate fluctuated widely. An analysis of the land-rate inscriptions shows that for tank-irrigated lands or for river-irrigated lands *producing single crops the rates ranged between 20 to 60 k/v* and for dry crops between 1 and 20 *k/v* (Subbarayalu 2012: 97) (emphasis added).

With regard to crop intensity, Subbarayalu relies on Karashima (2001) to conclude that the rate of 100 *k/v* applies to the double-crop wetland

(Subbarayalu 2012: 101–02). If this is so and the state's share is one-quarter, then the gross output per single-crop per *veli* would be 200 *kallam*.[4] Based on these assumptions, we have a fairly reasonable set of figures by discounting for the double-crop, and we arrive at more reasonable estimates of single-crop paddy productivity (see Table 5.2).

Table 5.2: Crop Yield Per Hectare

Tax k/v	*Land Output (k/v) @ 25 Per cent Tax Rate*	*Single Crop Output (k/v)*	*Single Crop Output (k/hectare)*
100	400	200	75.8
112.5	450	225	85.2
120	480	240	90.9
125	500	250	94.7

Source: Compiled by the author (Alaev 1984: 232; Subbarayalu 2012: 105–07, 110).

The estimates of yield per hectare depend on several assumptions about [1] the share of land tax in total output; and [2] the weight of a *kallam* of paddy in kilograms. Here I have adopted an estimate of one-fourth as a reasonable estimate of the tax share for the region and the period. In this context, the second key question is: what is the weight of a *kallam* of paddy?

The Weight of a *Kallam* of Paddy

As a land measure, a *veli* is generally accepted to be equivalent to 6.6 acres or 2.64 hectares. On the other hand, it is equally clear that the estimate of the weight of paddy contained in a *kallam*, a volumetric measure, is highly variable. The *kallam* is generally fixed, as an aggregate of 12 *marakals* (a smaller volumetric measure). As the *marakal* varies, so does the *kallam*. The *marakal* itself certainly differs over regions (Parthasarathy 2019). A survey of the inscriptions reveal that there are at least 11 *marakals* named: [1] *Chalukya Narayana*, [2] *Uchchiyilninra Naryayana*, [3] Rajaraja, [4] *Poli Niraimadi Narayana*, [5] *Vira* Pandyan, [6] *Addavalan*, [7] *Tiruvidaimurdan*, [8] *Annalikkal*, [9] *Sulakkal*, [10] Tanjore, and [11] Kanchipuram. The first two standards are explicitly stated to have been 'preserved' at the temples at Tirupati and Tirumala, respectively. The *Addavalan marakal* was 'preserved' in the Rajarajeshwara Temple at Thanjavur.[5] However, all this ambiguity poses a severe problem when converting paddy, as measured by a variable volumetric unit, into its weight.

Alaev (1984) has estimates ranging from 21.5–100 kilograms per *kallam*, depending on the region. He uses 21.78 kilograms as the Tanjore *kallam*, while Yanagisawa (1996) cites an 1883 Manual of Tanjore district as stating that a *kallam* of paddy was taken to weigh 63.83 lbs (28.95 kilograms) (Alaev 1984: 232; Yanagisawa 1996: 290). Subbarayalu further says, 'In terms of modern units, a *kallam* of paddy is approximately 29 kilogram in weight' (2012: 100).

Arasaratnam (1968) converts the Tanjore paddy tax collections in the reigns of the kings of Tanjore (1675–1735 AD) from *callams* to tons, assuming a *callam* to be equivalent to 42.9 kilograms (1968: 210).[6] However, in the glossary to his work, Arasaratnam defines the *callam* as a Tamil measure of paddy and rice, which varied according to regions; it was equivalent to 63.69 lbs (28.9 kilograms) in Tanjore (1968: 389).[7]

Appadorai takes the *kallam* to weigh 170.5 kilograms, which is the highest ever estimate (1936, Volume 2: 762, 807). Maclean provides calculations of 800–840 cubic inches per *kallam*, which works out between 71.1–74.6 kilograms of paddy (1885, Volume 2: 474).[8] Relying on late-eighteenth century British data,[9] Bajaj and Srinivas calculate the *kallam* of paddy at 125 kilograms, taking it to refer to the Kanchipuram *kallam* (1996: 8). Koichi reports the *marakkal* still in use in Madurai district and says, 'According to our survey in June 2007 .... 1 *marakkal* equals 4.25–4.50 kg of paddy]... ' (2011: 11). That is, he assumes the weight of a *kallam* of paddy to range somewhere between 51 and 54 kilograms.

Parthasarathy (2019) has carried out a detailed study of this matter and bases his measure on the standard measure preserved in the Vardaraja Perumal temple in Kanchipuram. This measure, *ghalpadhi* (a volumetric measure, also measured as one-quarter *padhi*), provides estimates for the *kallam* (or in traditional expression, *ghalam*). His data indicates that the *kallam* holds 101 kilograms of year-old paddy and 120 of freshly harvested paddy. These current data are close to the higher estimates based on the historical data of 100 and 125 kilograms.

The figures provided in the first column of Table 5.3 are estimates of a simple average of *kharif* (monsoon crop season) and *rabi* (winter crop season) crop yield, which in my view are reliable and representative estimates. Depending on the different kilogram values assumed for a *kallam* of paddy, the highest yield range is near or over 10 tons per hectare; the middle range between 3 and 8 tons per hectare; and the lowest from 1.63–2.64 tons per hectare.

Table 5.3: Average Yields Per Hectare based on Different Weights for One *Kallam*

Kg/*Kallam*	21.5	29.0	42.9	54.0	71.1	74.6	100.0	125	170.5
Kallam/hectare	Tons Per Single Crop Per Hectare								
75.8	1.63	2.20	3.25	4.09	5.39	5.65	7.58	9.48	12.92
85.2	1.83	2.47	3.66	4.60	6.06	6.36	8.52	10.65	14.53
90.9	1.95	2.64	3.90	4.91	6.46	6.78	9.09	11.36	15.50
94.7	2.04	2.75	4.06	5.11	6.73	7.06	9.47	11.84	16.10

Source: Compiled by the author from Alaev 1984; Arasaratnam 1968; Appadorai 1936; Bajaj and Srinivas 1996; Koichi 2011; Maclean 1885; Subbarayalu 2012; Yanagisawa 1996.

The estimates for the weight of a *kallam* of paddy naturally affect the yield estimates radically. A more detailed study of the *kallam* itself needs to be done to assess the situation in tenth to thirteenth-century South India. Although these estimates provide a fair idea of the range of yields, one needs to be careful and parsimonious when it comes to drawing firm conclusions. Nonetheless, even if we adopt the lowest estimate for *kallam*, the Pandya-Chola period yields are significantly high.

Yields: The *Jaghire* (1774–76)

During the early British rule in South India, the process of data collection was more systematic, with a higher degree of accuracy. There is a study of data gathered from 800 villages by the East India Company when it acquired the '*Jaghire*' (region surrounding Fort St George, or the present-day Madras/Chennai city).[10] The analysis of this data by Bajaj and Srinivas is revealing. As they describe the original study: 'The survey was conducted by a British engineer, Thomas Barnard, on instructions from his superiors .... Mr. Barnard started work in February 1767 and took almost seven years to complete it in November 1774' (Bajaj and Srinivas 1994).

However, the Select Committee, in its Fifth Report, although appreciative, was more cautious, on the grounds that Barnard had no official status and could have been deceived by the village accountants and by the machinations of the Nawab, who was the titular ruler of the territory concerned (Firminger 1985, Volume 1: 192).

Following the logic of the Select Committee, we can assume that these figures, cited by Bajaj and Srinivas (1994) and Dharampal (1990), are underestimates. In the villages of Thirupporur and Vadakkuppattu, for the five years, that is, from 1762–66, Bajaj and Srinivas estimate an average yield of 11.8 *kallams* per *kani*[11] or about 3 tons per hectare (Thirupporur), and 15.6 *kallams* per *kani* or about 3.9 tons per hectare (Vadakkuppattu). After the cess of 10 per cent has been deducted, these yields represent the measured grain produced; therefore, actual yield figures are correspondingly higher, at 3.33 tons and 4.33 tons per hectare, respectively.

Further analysis by Dharampal (1990) indicates that for the entire set of 800 villages, where irrigated land formed 65 per cent of the total cultivated land, the average yield over the five years (1762–66)[12] was 3.026 tons per hectare, based on 34,136 hectares of cultivation. For 130 villages with high productivity (greater than 5 tons per hectare), the yield is 8.21 tons per hectare (based on 7,203 hectares of cultivation). For 18 villages with a similar high productivity (greater than 5 tons per hectare), but with more extensive cultivation (over 100 hectares of cultivation per village), it is 8.71 tons per hectare, based on 3,745 hectares of cultivation (Dharampal 1990: 6). Dharampal assumed a *kallam* to be 125 kilogram, as did Bajaj and Srinivas (1994), for making the volume conversion into paddy weight.

The figures presented by Dharampal (1990) also suggest that the cropping intensity of irrigated land was about 1.45 for the total set of 800 villages, and also for the subset of 130 high-yield villages. However, for the set of the highest-yield 18 villages, it was 2.0. The yields per hectare of land in the first two cases need to be divided by 1.45, and in the 18 highest-yielding villages, by a factor of 2, to get single crop yields per hectare. *Thus, there would be 2.5 tons, 5.66 tons and 4.36 tons per crop per hectare, respectively, for the three sets of villages* (Dharampal 1990). This data set is the most comprehensive one that is currently available for the period. Moreover, the data, unlike inscriptional data, seems to have been collected with the deliberate purpose of estimating the productivity of the land. As for three villages showing exceptional high yields, Dharampal states: 'Thus the village Kalakattur produces about 1,500 tons of paddy on 120 hectares of irrigated cultivation, Chinnumbedu produces about 4,700 tons on 435 hectares of irrigated land, Karasangal 885 tons on 83 hectares and Somangalam, 750 tons on 73 hectares' (Dharampal 1990: 1–2).

In these three villages, yields of 12.5 tons, 10.8 tons and 10.3 tons per hectare are presumably for two crops. However, even with a discount factor of 2, *they work out to 6.25 tons, 5.40 tons and 5.15 tons per single crop per hectare* (Dharampal 1990). These two sets of estimates indicate a very high crop productivity, averaged over a large area of cultivation (Dharampal 1982; 1990).

Yields: Madras, Mysore, Canara 1800–01

At the end of the Mysore wars, the East India Company acquired territories that were earlier controlled by Tippu Sultan. Dr Francis Buchanan-Hamilton, in 1800–01, assessed the economic and other aspects of the annexed territories. This led to a three-volume report (Buchanan-Hamilton 1988).

It is generally accepted that the *kharif* (monsoon) irrigated paddy crop has a higher yield than the *rabi* crop.[13] It is difficult to estimate this variability as the *kharif* crop usually involved the transplantation of seedlings, while in *rabi*, the seed ('sprouted' or otherwise) is broadcast. The latter process results in a lower yield. Buchanan-Hamilton reports nine comparable observations from different villages and sources, where the difference in favour of *kharif* (transplantation) over *rabi* (broadcast 'sprouted seed') ranges between 12 and 175 per cent (see Table 5.4).

Table 5.4: The Differential in Paddy Yields (*Kharif* and *Rabi*)

	WB per Acre		
Village/Source	*Kharif*	*Rabi*	*Average*
Halledy-pura	33.0	29.5	31.3
Kellamagalam	45.0	33.3	39.2
Priya-pattana	37.0	25.1	31.1
Nala-Rayan Pallyam	96.0	48.0	72.0
Nala Rayan Pallayam	88.0	32.0	60.0
Darapuram	47.4	39.5	43.5
Mr Drummond	25.0	17.0	21.0
Malabar	36.0	15.0	25.5
Malabar	48.0	35.0	41.5
Average	50.6	30.5	40.4

Source: Buchanan-Hamilton 1988: various.

Even an average of these nine observations yields a premium of 67 per cent for *kharif* over *rabi*. If this is taken into account, one would need to factor 25 per cent extra for the *kharif* crops over the average for both *kharif* and *rabi* crops.

Converting Winchester Bushels (WB) to Kilograms

The data collected by Buchanan-Hamilton relating to paddy yields is scattered across a vast region and is not as representative as the *Jaghire* data discussed earlier. However, Buchanan-Hamilton also provides details that may help us understand the causes for variation in yields. Crops, and sometimes land as well are classified into three categories: good, middling and poor. The yield is given in per acre terms of 'Winchester Bushels (WB)', a volumetric measure used in England. An analysis of Buchanan-Hamilton's 171 observations from 107 locales reveals that there are 106 for 'good', 47 for 'middling' and 18 for 'poor' yields. The average paddy yield for 'good' works out to 33.66 WB per acre, for 'middling' 32.20 WB per acre, and for 'Poor' 16.30 WB per acre (83, 80 and 40 WB per hectare, respectively).

When it comes to converting these yields to kilogram per hectare, we encounter similar, although a much less serious, problems with regard to *kallam* earlier. Buchanan-Hamilton estimates a WB of paddy to weigh 27.76 kilograms (1988, Volume II: 279). Sivramkrishna estimates a WB of paddy to weigh 29 kilograms (2015: 75). However, this figure of 29 kilograms is what Yanagirsawa cites from the 1883 Manual of Tanjore District as being the weight of one *kallam* of paddy (1996: 290). Subbarayalu says this is true of the modern *kallam* (2012: 100). Thus, there is the equivalent of the Winchester Bushel (WB), approximating the 1883 *kallam*, and the modern *kallam* in terms of the weight of paddy it holds, that is, 29 kilograms. The Sri Lanka Central Bank defines a bushel of paddy as weighing 46 lbs (20.87 kilograms). The bushel is still in vogue there and paddy cultivation in Sri Lankan conditions somewhat similar to those in South India, and this estimate of bushel weight may be taken into account when converting Buchanan-Hamilton's WB data.

The weight of a volume of grain depends on the density, dryness and type of the grain measured, and this introduces a degree of variability to the conversion. I have provided in Table 5.5 below the WB calculation converted as per the three rates for WB into tons per hectare.

Table 5.5: Paddy Yields on Varied Outcomes for Alternate Bushel Weight

		Tons/Hectare at the rate of WB =		
Crop	*WB/Hectare*	*29.0 kg*	*27.76 kg*	*20.87 kg*
Good	83	2.41	2.3	1.73
Middling	80	2.32	2.22	1.67
Poor	40	1.16	1.11	0.85

Source: Constructed by the author.

These are averages that have been taken over a highly variable data set of 171 observations. When we classify the observations by yield per hectare, we get the distribution, as provided in Table 5.6 below.

Table 5.6: Percentage Distribution of Observations of Paddy Yield in Tons/Hectare

Tons/Hectare	> 1	1–2	2–3	3–4	4–5	5–6	
WB=Kgs							
29.0	15.8	33.3	26.8	14.0	4.8	5.3	100
27.76	16.4	36.8	23.5	14.0	5.8	3.5	100
20.87	31.0	43.3	17.5	4.7	3.5	-	100

Source: Constructed by the author.

As can be observed from the above tables, not only does the average yield per hectare fall for different rates of kilograms per WB, but the percentage of highest yields of over 3 tons/hectare also falls from 24 to 8.2 per cent. In my subsequent calculations, I have used Buchanan-Hamilton's 27.76 kilograms as the weight of one WB of paddy.

Yield Variation at Village Level

Buchanan-Hamilton also provides specific village data for the yields by season, duration of crop, crop performance, as well as by the method of cultivation, that is, 'dry seed', 'sprouted seed' and 'transplanted'. In the specific village data, one gets an idea of the possible causes of yield variability in a particular village, for example, for Mundian village near Srirangapatam (see Table 5.7). The variability indicated here seems to have occurred mainly due to land quality and seed quantity. Duration of the crop, that is, months to maturity, does not seem to have affected crop output.

In the case of Madhugiri village, Buchanan-Hamilton has used the criteria of 'good' and 'indifferent' crop output (he also uses the expression 'poor' elsewhere). He indicates output variation for the same variety, crop duration and seed quantity (Table 5.8). The 'small'-sized grain, *Cari Sonabutta*, produced much higher yields, as suggested in his study.

As far as the crops raised without labour-intensive transplantation is concerned, Buchanan-Hamilton distinguished between 'dry seed' broadcast

Table 5.7: Paddy Yields in Mundian Village

			WB Per Acre		
Type of Rice	*Months to Maturity*	*Seed*	*First Quality Land*	*Second Quality Land*	*Third Quality Land*
Hottay Cimbuty	5	1.18	59.56	41.53	23.73
Doda/Bily Butta	5	1.18	59.56	41.53	23.73
Arsina Caimbuty	4.5	0.83	47.45	35.59	17.69
Puty Buta	4.5	0.83	47.45	35.59	17.69
Yalic Raja	4.5	0.83	47.45	35.59	17.69
Muargilly	6	0.83	47.45	35.59	17.69
Conawally	5	0.83	47.45	35.59	17.69
Sucadass	4.5	0.83	47.45	35.59	17.69

Source: Buchanan-Hamilton 1988, Volume I: 140.

Table 5.8: Paddy Yields in Madhugiri Village

			In WB Per Acre		
Crop	*Months*	*Size of Grain*	*Seed*	*'Good' Crop*	*'Indifferent' Crop*
Dodda Butta	4.5	Large	1.11	44.43	35.54
Cari Chaningy	4	Large	1.11	44.43	35.54
Caimbutti	4	Large	1.11	44.43	35.54
Gayurudu	5	Middle	1.06	48.87	33.32
Bily Sonabutta	4	Middle	1.06	28.88	15.55
Cari Sonabutta	5	Small	1.02	55.53	39.98
Cari Sonabutta	5.5	Small	1.02	66.63	44.43
Put Rajah	4	Small	1.02	33.32	22.21
Tripetty Sonabutta	3.5	Small	1.02	35.54	22.21

Source: Buchanan-Hamilton 1988, Volume I: 366.

and 'sprouted seed' (treated before broadcasting). Table 5.9 presents the data he gathered in Ani-Malaya village in Coimbatore district.

In the case of *Perum Sambu* crop, the 'dry seed' cultivation takes a month longer to harvest and yields 20 per cent more than 'sprouted seed' cultivation. The same applies to the *Molagy* crop. Buchanan-Hamilton is cautious about wholly accepting the figures provided by the farmers of Ani-Malaya village. The final figures he provided may therefore have been a combination of the cultivators' underestimates and Buchanan-

Table 5.9: Paddy Yields in Ani-Malaya Village

Crop	*Crop*	*WB Per Acre*	
Dry Seed	*Duration*	*Seed*	*Output*
Anacumba Sambu	6	3.645	32.8
Perum Sambu	7	3.645	32.8
Molagy	7	2.187	32.8
Sprouted Seed			
Perum Sambu	6	3.645	27.34
Molagy	6	2.187	27.34
Cutari	4	3.645	29.16
Shurinavalin	4.5	3.645	30.98
Cartic Sambu	5	3.645	30.98

Source: Buchanan-Hamilton 1988, Volume II: 334.

Hamilton's adjustment for compensation (Buchanan-Hamilton 1988, Volume II: 333).

The Highest Yield: Nala-Rayana-Pallyam

In the data collected at Nala-Rayana-Pallyam village in Coimbatore district, Buchanan-Hamilton records the highest yield he encountered. He also reports a great deal of scepticism in other villages when he later cross-checked the Nala-Rayana-Pallyam estimates, but he is convinced about the validity of those estimates. Under Tippu Sultan, the farmers had been forced to pay the Islamic land tax on non-Muslims of 50 per cent of the output, and as a result, they had to work harder and give up 'sprouted-seed' cultivation, which had low yields despite low labour requirement. They also gave up the cultivation of less fertile land. Owing to this pressure, the farmers produced yields that were almost double the previous ones (Buchanan-Hamilton 1988, Volume II: 230). The data from Nala-Rayana-Pallyam village, provided in Table 5.10 below, confirms the figures.

This high yield, as per Buchanan-Hamilton's estimation, is due to the methods of initiating the crop (seeding or transplanting) and crop duration. He stresses that these yields are only for the 'best soils', except for the *caru* crop, which is 'raised only on the very lowest rented fields' (1988, Volume II: 231–32]. Nala-Rayana-Pallyam has the highest yields, ranging from 6.88 tons to the lowest amount of 3.33 tons per hectare. Buchanan-Hamilton had cross-checked and encountered contradiction

Table 5.10: Paddy Yields in Nala-Rayana-Pallyam Village

Crop Type	*Initiation*	*Months*	*Grain Quality*	*Output in WB/Acre*
Pishanum	Transplanted	7	Coarse	96–88
Jeda Mulligy	Transplanted	6	Coarse	96–88
Deva Raya Sumbava	Transplanted	5.5	Small	80–72
Gundu Mulligy	Transplanted	5	Round/Small	80–72
Shitta Vogum	Transplanted	5	Small	56–48
Caru	Sprouted Seed	3.5	Coarse	48–32

Source: Buchanan-Hamilton 1985, Volume II: 232.

from farmers in other villages later (ibid.: 238, 253, 289, 312). He felt that only a more detailed survey over time could reveal the actual extent of yields, as he suspected that apart from the villagers of Nala-Rayana-Pallyam, other villages may have been giving him underestimates of yield (ibid.: 312). Even with Buchanan-Hamilton's professional training and extensive travelling, one is left sceptical enough to not to want to generalise. It is interesting to note that he did not. However, there is enough evidence to indicate that the level of yields achieved in the region during this period was well over 3 tons per hectare.

Yields: Madras Presidency (Mid- to Late-Nineteenth Century)

During the nineteenth century, the British government in Madras initiated a series of 'settlements' of land revenue demands for a 30-year period for each district, with an aim to identify the output of crops, their costs and net returns so as to be able to fix, that is, to 'settle' for 25–30 years, the land revenue (tax) payable by the cultivator or owner. These surveys were very detailed, exhaustive, and were conducted through crop-cutting experiments over an extensive area of cultivation.

In this context, Maclean (1885) provides paddy yields estimated through a large number of crop-cutting experiments for various districts of Madras Presidency. A maximum of 11 and a minimum of four soil types were used to classify the estimates, including a high/low estimate. Guha (1992), on the other hand, provides only single output figures for the same settlement surveys. His methodology implies an averaging or 'standardising' carried out by him. Some of Guha's estimates relate to earlier, and some to later, years than the Maclean Settlements.

Table 5.11 provides figures extracted from Maclean's study, where we have selected the high/low yields of the type of soil that provides the highest and lowest range of yields.[14] Still, a range of per hectare yields, even truncated, provides a more realistic picture of the complicated situation in the field.

Table 5.11: Madras Presidency: Yield of Paddy

			Tons Per Hectare			
		Number of	*'Best' Soil*		*'Poorest' Soil*	
District	*Period*	*Experiments*	*High*	*Low*	*High*	*Low*
Chinglepet	1886	1,756	3.69	1.70	1.70	1.02
North Arcot	1872–80	300	3.40	1.84	2.84	1.42
South Arcot	1853–58	3,184	2.72	1.91	1.23	1.02
Salem	1859–65	1,572	3.01	2.72	2.04	0.79
Coimbatore	1887	568	3.40	0.85	2.55	0.85
Trichinopoly	1859–61	1,349	3.06	2.72	1.57	0.89
Tinnevelly	1872	n.a	3.40	2.04	2.72	1.36
Godavari	1856	2,230	3.40	1.89	1.32	0.94
Kistna	1859	407	3.12	2.27	1.27	0.85
Nellore	1861	n.a	2.91	2.41	1.77	1.42
Cuddapah	1865	57	4.11	3.69	1.70	1.02
Kurnool	1859–61	256	3.12	2.27	1.27	0.85

Source: Maclean 1885, Volume II: 406–19.

Maclean's figures are in Madras Measures per acre, and we have converted them at 2.53 lbs (1.148 kilograms) per Madras Measure.[15] Yields on 'Best Soil' are high, but the range of outcomes is also wide; this is also the case for 'Poorest Soil'. Here 'Best' and 'Poorest' is our usage and not that of the Settlement Commissioners, who classify land by description, as black or red soil, and further classify it by its content, that is, clay, loam and sand. The soils are classified as 'exceptional' or 'inferior' in other cases. Although the range of yields is quite broad, the highest yields are impressive.

Yields: The Nizam's Territory of Telangana (Late-Nineteenth Century)

The Nizam's government, in its submission to the Famine Commission of 1881, provides some reasonably accurate figures for Telangana in 1875–76,

(Ali 1879: 24–26). These figures are based on crop-cutting experiments and are classified by season, that is, *abi* and *tabi*, or *kharif* and *rabi*, respectively, and also in terms of the three types of crop outcomes (see Table 5.12). Here the *rabi* yields are substantially higher than the *kharif* yields in all cases except in Warangal. This effect is an observed phenomenon in Telangana's dry and semi-arid climate and is the reverse of the situation in the semi-humid Tamil Nadu.

Table 5.12: Paddy Yields in Telangana (1875–76)

District	*Village*	*Season*	*Outcome*	*Maunds*[16] *Per Acre*	*Tons Per Hectare*
Medak	Kallabgur	Kharif	1st	65	5.99
			2nd	48	4.43
			3rd	32	2.95
		Rabi	1st	99	9.13
			2nd	65	5.99
			3rd	48	4.43
Nizamabad	Banswada	Kharif	1st	54	4.98
			2nd	43	3.96
			3rd	32	2.95
		Rabi	1st	75	6.91
			2nd	64	5.90
			3rd	55	5.07
	Yellareddy	Kharif	1st	44	4.06
			2nd	35	3.23
			3rd	26	2.40
		Rabi	1st	70	6.45
			2nd	52	4.79
			3rd	35	3.23
Khammam	Warangal	Kharif	1st	25	2.31
		Rabi	1st	21	1.94
N-kurnool	N-kurnool	Kharif	1st	27	2.49
		Rabi	1st	34	3.13
Hyderabad	Hyderabad	Kharif	1st	41	3.78
		Rabi	1st	54	4.98

Source: Ali 1879: 24–26.

Concluding Remarks

To summarise, Table 5.13 below sets out the high/low yield figures that this essay has discussed so far. These indicate a wide variation, although with very high yields holding up the top end of the range. Even the lows (except in two cases) are respectable for the periods concerned.

Table 5.13: The Range of Paddy Yields Per Crop Per Hectare (Summary Table)

		Tons Per Hectare	
Source	*Period*	*Highest*	*Lowest*
Table 5.3 (Pandya/Chola)	945–1300	16.10	1.63
Dharampal I (Jaghire)	1774–76	5.66	2.50
Dharampal II(Jaghire]	1774–76	6.25	5.15
Table 5.5 (Canara)	1800–01	2.30	1.11
Nala-Rayana-Pallyam	1800–01	6.88	3.33
Table 5.11 (Madras)	1853–87	4.11	0.79
Table 5.12 (Telangana)	1875–76	9.13	1.94

Source: Constructed by the author.

The results derived from the data used in this essay depend on: [1] weights for a *kallam* of paddy, [2] the assumption of share of tax in the total output, [3] weights for a Winchester Bushel of paddy, [4] weights for a Madras Measure of paddy, and [5] on the conversion rate of *maunds* of paddy into kilograms. Other assumptions can give different results.

After having examined the data available to us here carefully, the evidence of very high levels of paddy land productivity in some areas of pre-industrial South India is evident. What is interesting about our data set is the apparent continuity of the high level of paddy yields throughout the centuries.[17]

The Way Forward

The above data ensemble and this essay's attempt to carefully analyse and transform it into estimates that are comparable over time and space reveal the difficulties in the process and the ambiguity of the results. The study carried out here can be easily dealt with, elaborated and added to, and it is open for further analysis and future endeavours. A lot more attention and clarification are required before a fair and accurate picture can emerge and its implications can be analysed.

Just like the data sources that examined here, it is very likely that there are many more such sources in the government archives at all levels, including sources such as district settlement surveys and other similar works, which have not received the attention they deserve, either from official or academic circles. The importance of such data-based scholarship needs to be stressed. Much of the information and data available in archival sources needs to be handled carefully and delicately in order to reveal the condition of the land and the people in the past. This approach is not only valid for subjects such as those dealt with here, but also for most subjects concerning India's past.[18]

Notes

1. The state agencies mostly compile these and publish them in four series known as the *South Indian Inscriptions* (SII) and *Annual Report on Epigraphy* (ARE), *Epigraphia Indica* (EI) and *Epigraphia Carnataka* (EC).
2. As Aiyer comments,

   > It is expressly stated that the interest in grain should be paid in heaped measures according to the standard metal measure specially used for the purpose. This is the sense that can be given to the phrase *poli nirai -madi narayan*. Apparently, the ordinary measures differed widely from these special measures; thus while a *kurini* of 'interest' paddy contained 6 *nali* and a *kallam*, 15 *kurini*, the ordinary *kurini* measure had the capacity of 8 *nali* and a *kallam* 12 *kurini*. A *kallam* of 'interest' paddy fell short of the ordinary *kallam* by 6 *nali*. That the measure *[kal]* used for measuring 'interest' paddy had the capacity of 6 *nali* is made clear by another inscription which has the phrase *palisai kuduppadana aru-nali-kkalal* (Aiyer 1930–31: 104–05].

   It therefore seems clear that this is an age-old problem which continues to plague scholars today.
3. This leads to statements like the following:

   > The single greatest demand for agrarian produce was the land tax, *kadamai* or more rarely *irai*. It is currently impossible to determine the percentage of the yield demanded as *kadamai*, but there was an attempt during the eleventh century to standardise the evaluation and measurement of rice land and to impose standard land tax rates in the areas around the Kaveri river (Heitzman 1987: 50).

   He refers to Karashima (2001), but Karashima does not settle the issue (2001: 94–107). With the variation in land productivity and local conditions, it is difficult to assess this issue accurately except in general terms. Also, see Karashima (2008).

4. Since the *kharif* (monsoon) crops may yield as much as 60 per cent more than the *rabi* (winter) crop, this average is an underestimate for the *kharif* crop.
5. Some of these measures were standardised by a reference unit deposited with the temple authorities, and thus, were legitimatised. In some cases, the authorities insisted on the use of a measure stamped by the royal seal. In the British period, the Collectorate maintained the standard measures and stamped the *bazaar* measures with the government seal.
6. From a report of 1782 AD for the five *subahs* of Tanjore which was prepared for the Committee of Secrecy investigating the affairs of the East India Company's administration in the Karnatik. He also uses a paddy-to-rice conversion ratio of 0.60 (Arasaratnam 1968: 210).
7. There is some confusion here, which is difficult to clarify. It would seem more likely the 'Glossary' is correct, and that the errors were made in three similar calculations in his text (Arasaratnam 1968: 210).
8. Maclean (1885) gives the weights for Madras Measures, which vary for each district. Unfortunately, these are in terms of rice, not paddy (1885, Volume 2: 505–20).
9. 'Tables of Weights and Measures & c. and Correct Batty Tables made use of at the Different Ports of East Indies', London 1778; also Madras Almanac, Madras 1795.
10. The following excerpt highlights the nature of this data:

    > The English survey records in the archives were prepared from more detailed Tamil palm-leaf account which, it seems, were kept in every locality of this region.... These palm-leaf manuscripts, probably written in a format similar to the original locality accounts, were deposited with the Collector of Chengalpattu around 1795. A few years ago these and several other eighteenth and nineteenth-century palm-leaf records were acquired by the Department of Palm-Leaf Manuscripts of the Tamil University at Thanjavur (Bajaj and Srinivas 1994).

11. A *kani* is equal to 1.33 acres.
12. There is some confusion here. Dharmapal (1990) refers, in the text, to the years 1762–66 AD, and in the table, to 1762–65 AD, both as five-year periods.
13. The aggregate yields per acre for Tamil Nadu (from 1985–86 to 2011–12) for the three crop seasons (Autumn/*Kuruvai*, Winter/*Samba*, Summer/*Kodai*) also confirm the trend of decreasing yields as the seasons move on, for all but one year: 'The average yield rate of rice per hectare during autumn [monsoon] season is more than in winter and summer seasons in all the pre- and post-hybrid periods' (Sivagnanam 2014: 26).

14. I have, however, selected only two soil types out of the half-a-dozen or so available.
15. Yanagisawa (1996) takes a Madras Measure to be equal to 2.6 lbs, though she claims that other references suggest 2.25, 2.3, 2.48 and 2.66 lbs.
16. A *maund* is 37.32 kilograms.
17. Incidentally, for comparison, figures for over 1,200 years are available for Japanese paddy yields, averaged across a vast acreage. These suggest paddy yields from the period 742–85 AD to 1878–87 AD, ranging from 1.25–2.39 tons per hectare (Ishikawa 1967: 98). This essay, however, indicates much higher paddy yields (over a similar period) in South India than comparable Japanese yields. The quality and quantity of data available for pre-industrial Japan are remarkable. It is likely that similar data for India awaits archival research.
18. In 1866, Max Müller bemoaned the loss of Indian history through the neglect of traditional manuscripts written on palm leaves. These had to be regularly recopied due to their natural deterioration. He ascribed the situation to the loss of power by the *rajahs* and their submission to the British government, which neglected the traditional role of maintaining these archives. He was outraged when the East India Company authorities rejected the offer of the archives (Müller 1903, Volume 1: 345).

References

Adhya, G. L. 1966. *Early Indian Economics: Studies in the Economic Life of Northern and Western India, c. 200 BC–300 AD*. New Delhi: Asia Publishing House.

Aiyer, K. V. Subramaya. 1930–31. 'Tiruchchendur Inscription of Pandyan Varaguna Maharaja [II]', in *Epgraphia Indica*, Volume XXI, eds Hirananda Sastri, K . N. Dixit and N. P. Chakravarti. New Delhi: Manger of Publications, Government of India.

Alaev, L. B. 1984. 'Systems of Agricultural Production: South India', in *The Cambridge Economic History of India, Volume 1, c. 1200–c. 1750*, eds Tapan Raychaudhuri and Irfan Habib. New Delhi: Orient Longman, in association with Cambridge University Press.

Appadorai, Angadipuram. 1936. *Economic Conditions in Southern India [1000–1500 AD]*, 2 Volumes. Madras: University of Madras Press.

Arasaratnam, S. 1968. *Merchants, Companies and Commerce in the Coromandel Coast, 1650–1740*. New Delhi: Oxford University Press.

Ashoka. 289 BC. *Lumbini Pillar Inscription*, trans. S. Dhammika. Available at http://www.cs.colostate.edu/~malaiya/ashoka.html (accessed 8 June 2015).

Bajaj, J. K., and M. D. Srinivas. 1994. *Indian Economy and Polity in the Eighteenth Century: The Chengalpattu Survey: 176–774*. Madras: Center of Policy Studies.

Bajaj, J. K., and M. D. Srinivas. 1996. *Anam Bahu Kurvita: Recollecting the Indian Discipline of Growing and Sharing Food in Plenty*. Madras: Center of Policy Studies.

Buchanan-Hamilton, Francis. 1988[1807]. *A Journey From Madras, etc...*, 3 Volumes. London: T. Cadell and W. Davies. New Delhi: Asian Educational Services.

Dharampal. 1982. 'Indian Agriculture at the Turn of Century', *PPST Bulletin* 2(2). Available at http://ppstbulletins.blogspot.in/2011/09/indianagriculture-at-turn-of-century.html (accessed 23 May 2015).

——. 1990. 'Productivity of Indian Agriculture in Historical Perspective', *PPST Bulletin*, 19–20: 6. Available at http://ppstbulletins.blogspot.in/2011/10/productivity-of-indian-agriculture-in.html (accessed 23 May 2015).

——. 2000. *Indian Science and Technology in the Eighteenth Century: Some Contemporary European Accounts, Collected Works*, Volume 1, Mapusa, Goa: Other Indian Press.

Douie, Sir James McCrone. 1915. *Punjab Settlement Manual*. Lahore: Superintendent, Government Printing.

Dutt, R. C. 1960[1882]. *The Economic History of India*, 2 Volumes. New Delhi: Publication Division, Government of India.

Firminger, W. K. (ed.). 1985. *Fifth Report of the Select Committee on the Affairs of the East India Company, 1812*, 3 Volumes. New Delhi: Neeraj Publishing House.

Guha, Sumit. 1992. 'Growth, Stagnation or Decline?', in *Agricultural Productivity in British India (Oxford in India Readings)*. New Delhi: Oxford University Press.

Gune, V. T. 1974. 'Land Laws', in *History of Medieval Deccan [1295–1724]*, Volume II, eds H. K. Sherwani and P. M. Joshi. Hyderabad: Director of Printing, Government of Andhra Pradesh (GoAP).

Heitzman, James. 1987. 'State Formation in South India 850–1280', *Indian Economic Social History Review* 24(1): 35–61.

Ishikawa, Shigeru. 1967. *Economic Development in Asian Perspective*. Tokyo: Kinokuniya Bookstore.

Karashima, Noburu. 2001. *History and Society in South India: The Cholas to Vijayanagar*. New Delhi: Oxford University Press.

——. 2008. *Epigraphical Study of Ancient and Medieval Villages in the Tamil Country*. Available at http://www.agrarianstudies.org/UserFiles/File/S7_Karashima_Epigraphical_Study_of_Ancient_and_Medievil_Villages_in_the_Tamil_Country.pdf (accessed 15 June 2015).

Koichi, Fujita. 2011. 'Socio-economic Dynamics in a Tank-Irrigated Rural Area in Contemporary Tamil Nadu, India', *Southeast Asian Studies* 49(1): 3–21.

Maclean, C. D. (ed.). 1885. *Manual of the Administration of the Madras Presidency*, 3 Volumes. New Delhi: Asian Educational Series.

Maddison, Angus. 2001. *The World Economy: A Millennial Perspective*. Paris: Organisation for Economic Cooperation and Development (OECD).

——. 2007. *Contours of the World Economy, 1–2030 CE: Essays in Macroeconomic History*. Oxford: Oxford University Press.

Mahdi Ali, Moulvi. 1879. *Memorandum to the Famine Commission*. Bombay: The Times of India Press.

Müller, G. M. 1903. *The Life and Letters of the Right Honourable Friedrich Max Muller*, 2 Volumes. London: Longmans Green.

Munro, Thomas. 1881. *Selections from his Minutes and Other Official Writings*, 2 Volumes, ed. A. Arbuthnot. London: C. Kegan Paul and Co.

Parthasarathy, Venkatesh. 2019. 'Metric Estimate of the Volume Measure used in the Madras Region at the Dawn of the Colonial Era', *Indian Journal of History of Science* 54(2): 209–14.

Rice, Benjamin Lewis. 1878. *Mysore and Coorg: Coorg*, Volume 3. Bangalore: Mysore Government Press.

Sivagnanam, K. Jyothi. 2014. 'Spread of New Varieties of Hybrid Rice and its Impact on the Overall Production and Productivity in Tamil Nadu', *AERC Research Study*, No. 53, Agro-Economic Research Centre, University of Madras, Chennai, 2014. Available at http://www.unom.ac.in/uploads/academics/aerc/Hybrid_Rice.pdf (accessed 28 May 2005).

Sivramkrishna, Sashi. 2015. 'Estimating Agricultural Productivity in Mysore and South Canara from Buchanan's Journey [1800–01]: Positioning India in the Great Divergence Debate', *Economic and Political Weekly* l(6): 66–76.

Stein, Burton (ed.). 1992. *The Making of Agrarian Policy in British India 1770–1900*. New Delhi: Oxford University Press.

Subbarayalu, Y. 2012. *South India under the Cholas*. New Delhi: Oxford University Press.

Voelcker, J. A. 1893. *Report of the Improvement of Indian Agriculture*. London: Eyre and Spottiswoode.

Watters, Thomas. 1904. *On Youang Chawang's Travels in India [629–645 AD]*, eds Rhys Davids and S. W. Bushell. London: Royal Asiatic Society.

Yanagisawa, Haruka. 1996. *A Century of Change: Caste and Irrigated Lands in Tamilnadu 1860s–1970s*. New Delhi: Manohar Publishers.

6

Telangana's Wealth, Income and Taxes (1285 AD–2019)

Telangana was considered poor, underdeveloped, backward, weak, and as a region that needed support from the outside. These are myths about the historical conditions of wealth, income and taxes in Telangana. The credibility of these myths needs to be addressed based on what little historical sources are available from the past and the modern period.

The Kakatiya Kingdom

The Kakatiya kingdom inaugurated the region as an independent political entity around 1175 AD. After a brilliant period of progress and development, it collapsed in 1324 AD when the Delhi Sultan conquered it. This kingdom is the direct ancestor of the Telangana state. That is to say, the present state has almost the same boundaries as the Kakatiya kingdom, and shares in its culture, language, customs and religion. Thus, the people of Telangana are direct descendants of the people of the Kakatiya kingdom. The Kakatiya kingdom was ruled by a dynasty and group of elites who were Telugu-speaking and natives of its land. This period was the first time that the land and people of Telangana were not subject to non-Telugu speaking dynasties and rulers from outside Telangana. With the Muslim conquest of the kingdom in the mid-fourteenth century, the Telangana land and people were ruled by Muslim dynasties for nearly 600 years until Muslim rule ended in 1950. Even under a democratic dispensation, Telangana was dominated politically and socially by Telugu-speaking Andhra elite groups. It is only after 2014 and the formation of a separate state that the Telangana land and people began to be ruled by native political elite groups. There is thus a 700-year gap during which alien rulers ruled Telangana.

A somewhat sketchy economic and financial history of the Kakatiya Kingdom is available from historical sources. The surviving inscriptions and chronicles of its visitors, invaders and conquerors provide some data. This information provides an idea of the state's wealth, income and taxes, considering there is no direct evidence of the condition of the land and the people. Some assumptions have to be made from the wealth of the kingdom, whose resources were entirely was based on the taxes collected from the land and the people, largely from agriculture and partly from manufacture and the export of textiles and the mining of diamonds.

Marco Polo seems to have visited India in around 1285 AD. About the Kakatiya kingdom, which he calls 'Mutifili', he states that the kingdom was ruled by a wise queen for nearly 40 years, who was 'more beloved by her subjects than any Queen, or King has ever been' (Ricci 2002: 307). His description of the kingdom with regard to the details of the operation of the diamond mines is fanciful, but it confirms the importance of this sector. He also states that its textiles are 'the best and most beautiful, and finest' in the world. He argues that the kingdom had the 'biggest sheep in the world' and the people have "great abundance and plenty of all necessaries of life' (ibid.: 308–09).

Marco Polo was an experienced traveller who knew Europe and had come to India after a very long stay in China, where he was the guest of the great (Kublai) Khan. Thus, when he wrote about the Kakatiya kingdom, he had in his mind the comparison with the rest of the world that he knew. The essential facts that struck him about the kingdom at that time was that, first, it was independent and paid no tribute to another kingdom or empire. Second, Queen Rudrama Devi presided for over 40 years of good governance. Third, it was the sole producer of diamonds in the world. Fourth, its textiles were the finest in the world; and fifth, Telangana's animal husbandry was extensive and its sheep were the biggest in the world. Sixth, there was a general availability (and consumption) of all the necessities of life, that is, rice, meat, milk and fruit. This is a phase in Telangana's history that we should be proud of, because of the achievements of its rulers and people.

However, in less than 40 years, Telangana would be conquered by alien Muslims after seven brutal raids and invasions by the armies of the Khilji and Tuglak sultans of Delhi. These were not conquests where the sultan established rule over Telangana, but they were only for the purpose of forcible extraction of conquest loot and subsequent tribute. On this issue of tribute, the traditional Hindu way was to offer presents without being forced by armed attack and the defeat of armies.

However, Koranic traditions and instructions guided the Delhi sultans. It was in keeping with this Koranic policy that Alauddin and his Tughlak successors dealt with the Kakatiya Kingdom. First, of course, there were the raids or invasions. The first raid took place in 1309 AD, largely by horse cavalry, as surprise was essential. However, it failed to succeed in its objective and was defeated. On this, Ferishta writes that the sultan's general, Malik Kafur, had 'issued orders to lay waste to the country with fire and sword. This confounded the inhabitants, who had never injured their wanton enemies'. After Warangal town was 'taken by assault and many of the garrison put to the sword', peace was 'purchased' by presenting 300 elephants, 7,000 horses, and money and jewels up to a large amount; also, agreement was made to pay annual tribute (Briggs 1989, Volume 1: 212–13).

Another chronicler, Abdullah Wassaf, in his work, *Tazjiyatul Amsar Wa Tajjriyatul Asar*, states that '6,000 *kharwars* or loads of gold were dispatched to Delhi'. Moreover, as a result of 'the abundance of diamonds obtained by plunder, they became so cheap that, one weighing a *miskal* (4.25 grams) could be purchased for three dinars' (Elliot 2008, Volume 3: 49). Another chronicler, Amir Khusro, suggests in his work, *Tarikh-i-Allai*, that Malik Kafur left Warangal in 1310 AD, with 'a thousand camels groaned under the weight of the treasures' in his booty (ibid.: 84).

The above extracts indicate the general extent of the accumulated state wealth of Telangana, until the Delhi sultans ravaged and looted it. With this event, the Kakatiya kingdom was committed to paying tribute to Delhi, and when the tribute was not received, the Delhi army came to invade and extract it by force. The objective of citing this account here is to establish the date when the Kakatiya rulers and Telangana lost independence and were forced to pay tribute to alien rulers.

During this period, Prataparudra was buying time and getting his forces organised. In 1312 AD, Prataparudra even sent word that the tribute was ready, and Malik Kafur arrived to collect the tribute and enjoy his hospitality. Moreover, Prataparudra supported and also accompanied the Delhi forces in a raid into the Tamil country. But while the Khilji-Tughlaq bloody transition was underway and Delhi was in crisis, Prataparudra took this opportunity to avoid payment of the annual tribute. When the Tughlaqs consolidated their rule and sent an army to Warangal in 1322 AD, he was successful in beating off the Delhi armies in the sixth invasion. However, as the people of Warangal and their king rejoiced and celebrated, the defeated Delhi armies returned in surprise in three months, and the final conquest of the Kakatiya kingdom took place in 1324 AD.

By 1344 AD, however, Ferishta writes about the alliance with Vijayanagar after the fall of the Kakatiyas, stating that after the fall of Warangal, the Telangana *nayakas*, with encouragement from the Vijayanagar emperor, expelled the Muslim forces from Warangal and forced them to vacate Telangana: 'The confederate Hindoos seized the country occupied by the Mohammedans, in the Deccan, and expelled them, so that within a few months, Mohamed Toghluk had no possessions in that quarter except Dowlatabad' (Briggs 1989, Volume 1: 246–47). This, in fact, marked the end of sultanate rule in Telangana.

Bahmani Telangana

A new chapter now began in Telangana, about which standard history is mostly silent. The establishment of the Vijayanagar empire and the rise of the Muslim Bahmani empire in its turn now saw Telangana divided. Although the raja of Warangal had supported the Bahamani rulers in their fight for independence from the Delhi sultanate, the situation dissolved to hostility soon after. Much of Telangana gradually, and after much warfare, fell under Bahmani domination. River Krishna became the border between the two empires, and the Raichur Doab (the area where the two rivers merged–Gadwal, Raichur and Alampur) became a perennially contested war zone between the two empires. This lasted until the Bahmani collapse and its division into the five successor Deccan sultanates. The sultanate of Golkonda held most of Telangana, while that of Bijapur held Nizamabad (Medak zone). After the collapse of the Vijayanagar empire in 1565 AD, Golkonda consolidated the entire Telangana as well as Coastal Andhra and the Carnatic regions under its rule, while Bijapur occupied Mysore and regions further south and west. Telangana was now firmly part of the Golkonda sultanate.

The Muslim invaders and conquerors carried on a brutal policy of loot, rapine and enslavement. The Muslim tradition of total war and barbaric violence, intended to terrorise the opposition, overrode the Hindu tradition of war, which protected non-combatants and ended battles at sundown. As the Muslim dynasties moved from raiding to ruling, they were forced to realise that random loot, massacres, destruction of standing crops, and laying the country waste were dysfunctional. For in return, the Hindu kings could (and did sometimes) adopt the same practices in Muslim-ruled areas.

Fundamentally, disrupting life and activity of the ordinary people did not yield taxes and tribute, as all economic activity came to a standstill. This change in attitude may be inferred from Muslim chroniclers, who soon stopped reporting massacres of hundreds of thousands as they had done in the early phase of the Muslim onslaught on the Deccan.

The turning point was reached in 1357 AD, when peace was reached after the sultan received 'a large subsidy in gold and jewels–which the Sultan seems to have used to build the Great Mosque of Gulbarga'. This peace broke down in 1371 AD, when the Sultan 'picked a fight with Nagadeo the son of the Rajah of Telangana over a horse and executed the young man in most horrible fashion– 'shot from an engine into a burning pile of wood' (Gribble 2002: 37). The Telangana retaliation was swift. On his way back to Gulbarga, Mohamed Shah's army was attacked by Telangana forces, which 'harassed the Mohammedan army to such an extent that out of four thousand men only fifteen hundred reached Gulbarga, after having lost their tents, baggage, and plunder, with the exception of gold and jewels. The Sultan himself was wounded in the hand and was forced to halt at Kailas' (ibid.: 37).

This defeat resulted in a state of total war, and Mohamed Shah appeared with two armies, one heading for Warangal and the other for Golkonda. After two years of warfare, an agreement was reached, according to which the *raja* of Warangal surrendered Golkonda, along with 300 elephants, 200 horses and Rs 33,00,000 lakh (Gribble 2002, Volume I: 38). A perpetual peace treaty establishing borders and non-interference in Telangana's affairs by the sultan and his successors was signed. The ambassadors of the *raja* of Telangana then presented 'a splendid throne covered with valuable jewels which had been prepared sometime before as a present to the Emperor Mohamed Tughluk Shah'. Gribble says that the throne was later dismantled and was worth Rs 3.5 crores (Gribble 2002, Volume I: 39). As for the perpetual treaty: 'The treaty itself seems to have been faithfully kept, and for many generations, we find no more mention of wars between the Gulbarga and Telangana Princes. It was in this way that Golconda came into the power of the Mohammedans' (ibid.: 38–39).

However, in 1424 AD, after about 50 years, the Bahmani sultan, Ahmed Shah, invaded Telangana, and Warangal itself was taken, and the *raja* was killed. The sultan then took possession of the Warangal treasury and Telangana became part of the Bahmani empire (Gribble 2002, Volume I: 86). This was the end of the quasi-independent Hindu kingdom of Telangana.

Golkonda Telangana

During this period, there is evidence of European travellers writing about the prosperity of Golkonda Telangana. The Frenchman, Jean Baptiste Tavernier, travelled across Golkonda between 1643, 1645, 1651 and 1660 AD. He embarked from Hormuz on a Golkonda ship. In his *Travels in India*, he refers to a large ship, which makes an annual trip to Persia 'laden with muslins and chites or coloured calicoes, the flowered decoration of which is all done by hand–which makes them more beautiful and more expensive than when it is printed' (Ball 1898, Volume I: 255). His travel experience in the region led him to state the following:

> It is not necessary that those who travel in India should provide themselves with food beforehand–especially is this the case with the idolaters, who do not eat anything which has had life–*because even in the smallest villages they always find in abundance rice, flour, butter, milk, beans, and other vegetables, sugar, and other sweetmeats, dry and liquid* (Ball 1898, Volume I: 297) (emphasis added).

His impressions of Golkonda are that it was 'a rich country, abounding in corn, rice, cattle, sheep, fowl, and other commodities necessary to life. As there are numerous tanks, there is also an abundance of good fish' (Ball 1898, Volume I: 150). He also described the tanks upon which agriculture depended. But about the industry, he was very precise:

> The iron at Haidarâbàd, at a very early period, obtained a wide renown, being, in fact, the material which, when made into steel, afforded the source of supply for the manufacture of Damascus blades–the raw material having been exported to Persia and the Panjâb for that purpose. Two villages, situated to the north of Golconda, namely, Nirmal and Indore [Indur–Nizamabad], are specially mentioned in the *Ain-i-Akbari* as producing excellent iron and steel (ibid.: Volume I: 157).

The iron/steel was used to make not only high quality swords, but was also used to make guns:

> They do not have a sabre like the Persians, but they carry a broadsword like the Swiss, with which they both cut and thrust, and they suspend it from a belt. The barrels of their muskets are stronger than ours, and the iron is better and purer; this makes them not liable to burst (ibid.: 157).

He commented on the revenues derived by the government from taxes on the toddy consumed. He saw toddy being transported in leather bags on horseback. He felt that 'it is principally on this account that they allow so many public women, because they are the cause of the consumption of much tari, those who sell it having for this reason their shops in their neighborhood' (Ball 1898, Volume I: 158). Most transportation of goods and people was either by pack-horses or oxen, as the roads were not fit for wheeled wagon movement, and palanquins were used to convey people rather than chariots (ibid.: 175). His interest in diamonds led him to visit the mines, and his description of the mines is illuminating:

> The first time I was at this mine [Kollur] there were close upon 60,000 persons who worked there, including men, women, and children, who were employed in diverse ways, the men digging, the women and children in carrying earth, for they search for stones at this mine in an altogether different manner from that practiced at Ramulkota (Ball 1898, Volume II: 75).

Another traveller was another Frenchman, Jean de Thevenot, who recorded his impressions of his visit in 1663–67 (Lowell 1687). Interestingly, he calls the small Mogul province of Bidar as the province of Telanga and says, 'This Province of Telenga is worth above ten million a year to the Great Mogul' (ibid.: 94). On the way to Hyderabad (Bhagyanagar), he recounts:

> The King of Golconda has vast Revenues .... The Customs of Merchant Goods that pass through the Countery, and of the Ports of Masulipatan and Madraspatan yield him much, and there is hardly any sort of Provisions in his Kingdom from which he hath not considerable dues. The Diamond Mines pay him likewise great revenue, and all they whom he allows to digg in, those that are towards Masulipatan pay him a Pagoda every hour they work there, who daily find near three pounds weight, and nobody diggs there but for the King (Lowell 1687: 102).

These foreign travellers' accounts give an impression of general and widespread prosperity and wealth in Golkonda during the periods of their respective visits.

Mughal Intervention and Eventual Conquest

The Mughal annexation of the sultanate of Bijapur meant that Golkonda now had a potentially hostile neighbour. This sultanate included parts of Telangana, such as modern Adilabad, Medak, Nizamabad, the Raichur Doab, and other territories to the north and west of Hyderabad (the Muslim chroniclers have always considered these areas to be part of 'Tilengana'). Friendly relations between Bijapur and Golkonda, both ruled by Shia Muslim dynasties, were essential for the peace and property of Golkonda. Bijapur had always acted as a buffer and an early warning of any northern attack on Golkonda. However, the Mughal annexation of the sultanate of Bijapur meant that Golkonda now had a dangerous neighbour. Golkonda would from now onwards be subject to direct Mughal military and financial pressure.

Three types of metals were used as currency for this period–gold, silver and copper. The gold coin called *hun* had a gold content of approximately 10.97 grams each, and this amount, at the present price of gold of Rs 4,700 per gram, was worth Rs 52,000 for each current. The silver rupee weighed 11.53 grams, and at today's price of silver, Rs 70 per gram, it was worth Rs 461 per silver rupee current. The dam was worth 20.96 grams of copper, and at the current copper price of Rs 0.72 per gram, the dam was worth Rs 15.10 per current.

In the records of the period of the Mughal emperor Shah Jahan (c. 1656), this '*Suba* of Telangana' yielded a total revenue of 1 crore and 20 lakhs *dams* (Rs 18.14 crores per current). Together with Gulshanabad (the name for Medak), which yielded 96 lakh *dams* (Rs 14.5 crores per current), the Mughal territories of Telangana had revenues of 2 crores for 16 lakhs *dams* (Rs 32.65 crores per current) (Khan 1950: 241).

The Golkonda sultan bought peace from the Mughal emperor by a promise and payment of an annual tribute of 200,000 pagodas. These pagodas were gold pieces, which were worth from 6–7.5 francs of our money, sometimes more and sometimes less (Ball 1898, Volume I: 161). Other reports confirm this assertion: 'According to the 'Document of Submission' [*inqiyad-nama*] acceded by Abdullah Qutb Shah on 23 May 1636, tribute valued at 200,000 gold *hun* or 800,000 silver rupees would be sent yearly to Agra' (Richards 1975: 35). But in 1656 AD, the Mughals invaded Golconda and 'settled terms which required Golconda to pay two million rupees indemnity' (Richards 1975: 38). Vexed with this in 1674 AD, Prime Minister Madanna Pandit persuaded the Golkonda sultan, Abul Hassan, to form an alliance with Shivaji:

> Under the terms of this pact, Golconda sent 100,000 gold *hun* [Rs 403 crores] every year to the Maratha King as a military subsidy .... In 1677 Abul Hassan ventured to subsidise Shivaji's expedition to Tanjore and southern Karnatik. This war yielded large territories formerly considered to be under Bijapur's domination. After the death of Shivaji in 1680 the alliance and subsidy continued under the rule of Shamhaji, his son and successor. A link was established between the Martha kingdom, the most aggressive, and Golconda, the wealthiest and most stable kingdom in the Deccan (Richards 1975: 44–45).

Thus, for 13 years, Golkonda paid the Marathas a total of 13,00,000 gold *huns* (Rs 6,645 crores current) instead of paying the Mughals 26,00,000 gold *huns*. Naturally, this aroused Aurangzeb's, and after his accession to the throne, he decided to crush Golkonda and annex it as a part of his empire in 1687 AD.

Another Muslim chronicler, Muhammad Hashim (Khafi Khan) also records events in Golkonda at the Moghul conquest in his work, *Muntakhabul Lubab* (c. 1732). He provides the following account of the loot of Golkonda that Aurangzeb took away:

> The property of Abul Hasan [The King of Golconda] which was recovered *after its dispersion* amounted to eight *lacs* and fifty-one thousand *huns* [Rs 4,349 crores current] and two *krors* and fifty-three thousand rupees, altogether six *krors* eighty *lacs* and ten thousand rupees [Rs 5,493 crores current], besides jewels, inlaid articles and vessels of gold and silver. The total in dams was one *arab* fifteen *krors* sixteen *lacs* and a fraction [Rs 1,742 crores current], which was the sum entered into the records [grand total of Rs 11,584 current] (Elliot 2008, Volume 7: 207–33) (emphasis added).

For the same figures, Gribble adopts the value of rupees at 7 million sterling and the *dams* (copper coins) at 2.5 million sterling, the total amounting to about 9.5 million sterling (Gribble 2002: 310) The 1924 sterling is worth 54 sterling per current, and the current sterling is worth Rs 100 each; the total of 9.5 million (1924) sterling is worth Rs 5,130 crores per current: As Richards points out:

> Mughal officials spent several weeks inventorying, packing and shipping this treasure to Agra and Delhi. Even depleted, as it must have been, by a year of warfare and siege when normal revenues were cut off, the size and variety of Abul Hasan's treasury testify to the truth behind his reputation for immense wealth [and the economic power which accrued to the state in Golconda (Richards 1975: 54).

However, Richards fails to mention that the land and the people of Golkonda, largely Telangana, paid heavily for this accumulation of Abul Hassan and his predecessors, with an annual land tax of 50 per cent of the total crop output, which the Muslim rulers exacted from their non-Muslim agriculturists.

Data on Golkonda Revenues

The first set of robust data for Golkonda and its administrative units is recorded at the Mughal takeover by Girdhrailal. Girdhrailal recorded

(c. 1771) the account of the revenues of Golkonda as of 1685–86 AD in his work, *AhqarTarikh-i-Zafarah* (quoted in Sherwani 1974: 655). The revenue data for each *sarkar* (an administrative unit consisting of *parganas*) is also given as the number of *parganas* in each *sarkar*. The Telangana *sarkars* and Coastal Andhra *sarkars* are provided separately. This provides a reasonable set of estimates for the two regions from the late-seventeenth century onwards.

Golkonda was divided into 20 *sarkars*, with around 379 *parganas*. Out of the total, Telangana consisted of 13 *sarkars*, comprising 150 *parganas*, while coastal Andhra had 7 *sarkars*, comprising 229 *parganas*. Out of the total Golconda revenue, that is, Rs 1,87,76,919, Telangana contributed Rs 1,32,67,512 (71 per cent), and Coastal Andhra contributed Rs 55,09,407 (29 per cent). The average revenue of a Telangana *pargana* was Rs 88,450, and was higher by 3.67 times than that of the coastal Andhra *pargana* average revenue of Rs 24,059. This higher revenue-bearing capacity and basic higher income of Telangana, when compared to coastal Andhra, is obvious. However, port customs duties of the sea ports located there boosted the revenues of coastal Andhra.

Golkonda Telangana under the Mughals

The Mughal conquest of Golkonda was not easily achieved. While the Fort of Golkonda was under siege, troops loyal to Abul Hasan continued to harass the Mughal army and its logistics, thus disrupting traffic and communications. Golkonda's allies, the Mahrattas and other subsidiary rajas and *nayakas* of Telangana, assisted in the process. As is known, the long siege was unsuccessful until Aurangzeb managed to bribe a Golkonda officer to open a gate and allow the entry of the besieging forces.

The confusion, disruption and violence affected all economic activity so much so that apart from the loot of Golkonda, the hinterland of Telangana was devastated. This situation also resulted in famine, as crops were not sown and agriculture was affected significantly, as aptly captured in Richard's account:

> Under conditions such as these, nearly all economic activity stopped. Even when agricultural production began to pick up in 1688, trade remained frozen; for the roads were uniformly dangerous. At the capital, the greatest market in the province, no business at all was transacted; 'everybody hiding their Diamonds and money'. Diamond production had ceased, and the area around the mines was deserted .... the communities of weavers, bleachers and other craftsmen who had produced cloth for export in better times had

> nearly disappeared. Any who remained would be discouraged from attempts at production by a shortage of raw cotton (Richars 1975: 70).

Aurangzeb further complicated the issue by detaching the Karnatik territories, south of the Krishna and Gundlekamma rivers, from Golkonda (now called Hyderabad) and by creating another entity called the Hyderabad-Karnatik (consisting of the seven districts of Machlipatnam, Nizampatnam, Rajahmundry, Eluru, Murtazanagar, Mustfanagr and Srikakulam). Richards provides the following account in this regard:

> After 1687, tax collections, bribes, tribute, specie for coining, and diamonds from the southern districts moved to the headquarters of the *faujdar* of the Karnatik, not to Hyderabad .... Thus, the wealth of Golconda, including its diamonds, began to be systematically drained .... At the time of annexation, Hyderabad, as the foremost commercial and capital centre in the south had developed a complex economic structure which could not be destroyed overnight. Nevertheless, the events of 1687 and the emperor's administrative choices set off a process of relative decline (Richards 1975: 72).

This Hyderabad-Karnatik region, in fact, became the core area that would later be called Andhra. This region was in some ways a restoration of the old division between Telangana and Warangal, ruled by the Bahmani empire, and with the coastal areas ruled by the Vijayanagar empire. This division now comes in handy because we now have robust data collected by the Mughal administration on both the regions of Golkonda. Richards (1975) provides the figures taken from the Mughal archives. These figures illustrate the quantum and nature of the taxes collected from the Golkonda kingdom, including the previously surrendered 12 Golkonda districts in the Karnatic realising Rs 82.85 lakhs, which added up to Rs 2.20 crores in 1689–90 AD. The total revenues of the Mughal empire amounted to Rs 17.5 crores, and thus, Golconda revenues constituted a 12 per cent increase (1975: 149).

The Mughal data also provides a breakdown by districts, so that the difference between Telangana and Coastal Andhra districts can be observed. Unfortunately, there are no population figures so as to be able to assess the revenue collected per person. Richards also provides the number of villages in Telangana (5,216 villages) and Coastal Andhra (3,648 villages): 'the average *hasil* per village in Andhra was now approximately two-thirds the figure in Telangana whereas before it had been about half' (Richards 1975: 154).

The total figures for 1689–90 AD indicate that Telangana revenues were 95 per cent more than Andhra revenues during the Qutub Shahi period and 79 per cent more after the Mughal settlement (Richards 1975: 152–23). Not only were taxes raised by the Mughal administration, but the mode of collection was changed, bypassing the traditional and largely Hindu elites who acted as intermediaries on behalf of the Golkonda state. Collection rates in coastal Andhra were 100 per cent of the tax demand. In the Telangana region, only three *sarkars*, Kaulas, Malkanur and Nalgonda, reached 100 per cent collection rates; in the latter, two rates exceeded 100 per cent, thereby indicating that the previous year's arrears were also collected that year. Collection in Telangana as a whole at 76 per cent was much lower than coastal Andhra's 100 per cent, suggesting more resistance by the Hindu *nayakas*. The Mughals, for this very reason, were determined to break the hold of the Hindu elites, which had, in the shape of Madanna Pandit and his relations, captured the Golkonda state and crafted an alliance with the Marathas.

Aurangzeb, fanatic Muslim that he was, also ordered the imposition of *jiziya* on the Hindu population, something previously unknown in the Deccan. The Qutub Shahs, in order to maintain good relations with their Hindu feudal supporters and ordinary subjects, had avoided levying this onerous and humiliating Islamic tax. They were more than satisfied with exacting the Islamic canonical tax of 50 per cent of the output from their Hindu cultivators:

> The Emperor Aurangzeb's insistence on the collection of the *jiziya* was a notable deviation from the long-established practice in Golconda. To add to its impact, the *jiziya* had a sharp economic bite which placed another 4 per cent or even more on the assessed taxes of both the Karnatik [Coastal Andhra] and Hyderabad [Telangana]. In the case of the latter region, this was in addition to the 13 per cent rise established by the 1689-90 revenue survey (Richards 1975: 171).

However, achieving this was not as easy as Aurangzeb had thought. For one, his officials in Golconda urged him not to impose *jizya*, as it would lead to resistance and revolt at a time when Mughal rule had not been consolidated. As per Islamic law, *jizya* was a general tax per head on non-Muslims, to be levied by an Islamic state. The amount of annual *jizya* (one *dinar*), as prescribed by Islamic law, was equivalent to 4.24–6.36 grams of gold. Not only was it to be collected compulsorily, but the manner in which it was to be rendered was also intended to humiliate the payer. Hindus had to pay this tax until Akbar abolished it; but afterwards, Aurangzeb reinforced it strictly, which provoked much resistance. The Golkonda administration, therefore, had it incorporated in the increased land revenue collection, which did not follow Quranic directions regarding *jizya*, as it was not just a tax but an acknowledgement of *dhimmi* (subject) status in a Muslim state.

Despite the requirement of Islamic law and Aurangzeb's insistence in enforcing it, local governors were reluctant since it would create problems for their administration. They first pleaded with the emperor to postpone the levy on the grounds that the Hindu population was impoverished due to the invasion and war. They also stated that the Hindu population would desert the cities. This persuaded the emperor to defer the imposition by a year. Both governors of the largest urban centres, Hyderabad and Machlipatnam, were opposed to the imposition. As Richards (1975) writes:

> Both men disliked the reaction the tax aroused and resisted its collection. This must have been an especially sensitive concern for Mughal officials in Hyderabad in the years between 1700 and 1704 when the Mahratta pressure on the province was at its height. Finally, in 1704, the Emperor removed this source of tension between the rulers and ruled by stopping the collection of *jiziya* throughout all provinces of the Mughal Deccan. His action was in response to the Maratha raids (Richards 1975: 207–09).

The stabilisation of Golkonda, which had been achieved by that time, was again disrupted by Aurangzeb's death since following this event the region degenerated into a war zone. This state of affairs brought the Marathas into play, and they exploited the weakness of the imperial administration, thereby gaining substantial revenues and influence in Golkonda. When the Marathas were threatening the very existence of the Delhi emperors, it was not surprising that they conceded as much as they could in Golkonda in order to satisfy and keep Maratha power at bay by granting them the right to collect *chauth* and *sirdeshmukhi* in the entire Deccan in 1719. What is surprising indeed is that the Marathas did not annex Golkonda altogether and extend the Maratha *samaraj* throughout south India. Their attention seems to have mostly drifted northwards instead, and they were content to extract as much as they could from Golkonda and its people.

Hyderabad-Telangana during the Maratha Phase

The conditions in Hyderabad were terrible. In 1725 AD, the Marathas clashed with the Nizam, who refused to pay *chauth* and *sirdeshmukhi* to the Marathas. The war began in August 1727 AD and ended in March

1728 AD. The Nizam suffered a crushing defeat at Palkhed near Daulatabad. According to the Treaty of Munji Shivagaon, the Nizam was forced to abide by the following terms: [1] Chhatrapati Shahu was recognized as the only Maratha ruler, [2] Marathas were confirmed in their right to collect *chauth* and *sirdeshmukhi* of the Deccan, [3] those Maratha revenue collectors who had been driven out would be reappointed, and [4] the balance revenue was to be paid to Chhatrapati Shahu:

> The *surdeshmookee* had also been sanctioned at the same time, but was not levied with the same regularity; in fact, it was part of the Mahratta policy to allow taxes to fall into arrears so as to give them a *casus belli* on some future occasion, when possibly they might have an opportunity of securing more than their just dues by virtue of the sword (Gribble 2002, Volume II: 7–8).

In the war with the Marathas, Nizamul Mulk, as the agent of the emperor of Delhi, not yet ruler of the Deccan, was defeated and forced to negotiate terms with Baji Rao, the Peshwa, as highlighted in the following account:

> At length, Nizam-ul-Mulk submitted to making terms and on the 26th Ramzan 1150 AH [16th January 1738] at Durai [Duraha] *Sarai*, 64 miles from Sironj, a convention was signed. In his own handwriting Nizam-ul-Mulk promised to grant to Baji Rao [1] the whole of Malwa, [2] the complete sovereignty of the territory between the Narmada and the Chambal, [3] to obtain confirmation thereof from the Emperor, and [4] to use his best endeavours to obtain fifty lakhs of Rupees to pay Baji Rao's expenses (Irvine 1922, Volume II: 305).

After losing the war waged by the Marathas on Delhi from 1734 AD till 1738 AD, the Mughal emperor agreed to formally assign the right of the *Surdeshpandya*, or the Inspector of Accounts of the Deccan, to Baji Rao, the Peshwa, with the rights of hereditary succession. Baji Rao paid 6 lakh rupees rupees to attain this right (Gribble 2002, Volume II: 9–10]). With this right conferred by the Mughal emperor, the Marathas became virtual masters of the Mughal *subahs* of the Deccan, including Hyderabad. The drain and loot collected earlier from Golkonda by the Muslim powers in Delhi was now diverted to the Marathas, who collected it with a lot more rigour.

Nizam I, who had initially supported the Marathas against the Mughal emperors, now turned against them and declared independence in 1725 AD, recorded his status as the first point in his 17-point-will:

> Firstly, it behoves the Prince of the Deccan to be at peace with the Mahrattas, who are the Zamindars of this country, to seek peace and agreement with

> them. But he should maintain pre-eminent the dignity and prestige of Islam, and never allow them to overstep the bounds; and guard the principles of righteousness and peace, the best principle of all being that conquest in the Deccan must not be allowed to be made by the armies of these freebooters (Khan 1936: 285).

This injunction was complex and tried to cover too many different issues. First, the acknowledgement of the Marathas as the *zamindars* meant that he conceded territorial rights to them. Second, there is the surprising lack of reference to the payment of nearly 35 per cent of Hyderabad revenues as *chauth* and *sirdeshmukhi* granted by the Mughal emperors in 1719 AD to the Marathas, unless by the first reference to the Marathas as '*zamindars*' included this liability. Third, taking these two above points, it can be concluded that between 1719 AD and 1724 AD, the territory of the state had been reduced by the Maratha victories and had become a tributary of the Marathas. Fourth, maintaining 'the dignity and prestige of Islam' became difficult with the acknowledgement of the overbearing military and financial power of a Hindu state, which treated the Muslim state of Hyderabad as a subordinate entity. This is a feature not in keeping with the dignity and prestige of any state—let alone an Islamic state

Fifth, the reference to the Marathas as freebooters is precisely the same description of the early Muslim invaders of the Deccan, even of the Nizam himself. Not content with this one, the Nizam issued another injunction towards the end of his rule:

> Fifteenth, that the Brahmins of the Deccan, although able, are fit only to be hanged and quartered. It is my own experience, and *Hazart Khuld-Makan* [Emperor Aurangzeb] has also observed the same .... Since the time of *Hazrat Alamgir Padshah*, the standing order has been that wherever a *Zunnardar* [Brahmin] may be found, he should be taken away forthwith and imprisoned (Khan 1936: 289).

This dying statement by the Nizam once again did not make any sense, except indicating a feeling of anger and frustration of a dying man at his critical dependence on the ability and capacity of Brahmins to run his state. It is clear that almost all the officials involved in collecting land revenue, toll and taxes on the road were Brahmins. It was also clear that the Brahmin, Madanna Pandit, and his family had taken over the Golkonda sultanate and had administered it for a decade or so. It was evident to the Nizam that the Peshwa was a Brahmin, and the Maratha state policy was mainly set and administered by Brahmins. In this context, arresting but not killing Brahmins was a non-starter.

The Nizam, in the fifteenth article, referred to two Brahmin 'upsetters of this Muslim State'; he had confined them in Ahmednagar Fort and instructed that they should remain there. Still, one must make allowances for a 77-year old dying man. This is because it was clear that Hyderabad depended on Hindu cooperation and Brahmin officials for its stability, its financial ability to pay the Marathas the tribute, and to administer the state. The complex system of Golkonda was based on the control and protection of the Hindu subjects by their natural leaders–the *rajas*, chiefs and *nayakas*–who had been recognised and confirmed in their jurisdiction formally by the ruling Muslim monarchs in exchange of payment of tribute. The state derived its revenue from the tribute from the feudal *rajas* and land taxes collected from the areas under its direct control. The amounts of revenue derived by Hyderabad are not available for this period.

It seems clear that the Mughal grant of *chauth* and *sirdeshmukhi* of the Deccan amounting to 35 per of Deccan revenues was onerous. Non-payment led to Maratha incursions to forcible collect their demand, and the Nizam was helpless to either pay or defeat the Maratha raids. However, Nizam Ali (Nizam II), assisted by French troops, decided to challenge Maratha power. But in 1760 AD, after his defeat at the Battle of Udgir, Nizam Ali had to yield to the Marathas. The resulting treaty was disastrous for him. He had to give up to the Marathas four major Deccan fortresses and confirm to the Marathas their possession of Ahmednagar, Bijapur, parts of Bidar, and most of Aurangabad. These areas had an annual revenue of more that Rs 62 lakhs (Grant Duff 1852, Volume II: 125).

Undeterred, Nizan II tried once more for a military solution against the Marathas in 1792 AD. But once again at the Battle of Khurdla, he was defeated and was surrounded by the Marathas, when he took refuge at Khurdla. He had then to yield more territory, with revenues of Rs 35 lakhs annually, pay an indemnity of Rs 300 lakhs, and send his Prime Minister to Poona as a hostage (Gribble 2002, Volume II: 91–92). In another incident, Nizam II also gave up two Telangana *parganas*, Indoor (with a revenue of Rs 2,40,813) and Bodun (with revenue of Rs 1,47, 765) (Dighe 1937: 310).

After this, his successor, Nizam III, abandoned the French alliance and made one with the English and Marathas to fight Tippu Sultan. When they defeated Tippu, the division of spoils meant that the Nizam would receive territory with an annual revenue of Rs 25 lakhs. By 1818, 'the total revenue of Hyderabad State could not have been more than a crore and half of rupees, or about one and half million sterling, for the

Marathas continued to levy *chouth* over a considerable portion of the western districts' (Gribble 2002, Volume II: 153).

Following this, Nizam IV allied with the English against the Marathas, and after their defeat at the hands of the combined allies, he received as his share of the spoils the province of Berar, 'the fort of Dowlatabad, the Fort and district of Jalna, some districts lying on the Godavery and the country near the Ajanta Hills' (Gribble 2002, Volume II: 135–36). After this, the Nizam was utterly subject to English power and carried out policy as directed by them.

However, with the English East India Company emerging as the 'Paramount Power', under Minister Chandu Lal (1825–45), Hyderabad went through a period of 25 years of financial stringency, which threatened to plunge the state into insolvency. This required the Nizam to disgorge his personal funds to the extent of Rs 1 crore and 20 lakhs to pay for Hyderabad's debts to English bankers and the East India Company (the real rulers of India until 1860), and maintain the administration, which was falling behind in terms of payments of salaries of their own army, with one-third of the revenues disbursed only to maintain the Hyderabad Contingent that was run, staffed and equipped by English officers to protect the Nizam.

Hyderabad-Telangana under Nawab Sir Salar Jung the Great (1853–83), Dewan of Nizams IV, V and VI

Following the fiscal and political confusion of the early-Nizamate, which almost took the state into bankruptcy, the reforms of Sir Salar Jung the Great ensured a high degree of stability in the civil, military and fiscal situation in Hyderabad-Telangana. This stability took place despite the Wahhabi problems of 1850–60, which disturbed the capital, Hyderabad. By the end of his rule as Dewan, the results of his reforms began to reveal themselves.

1880–81

During 1880–81, the differences in revenue extraction in the two future states of Telangana and Andhra Pradesh were significant. According to Moulavi Chiragh Ali, the land revenue of Telangana was Rs 1.026 crores (Rs 70 crores per current) from a population of 0.30 crores, which means a per capita revenue of Rs 3.42 (Ali 1886: 44). In the 'Memorandum of the Progress of Madras Presidency', the relevant figure for the Andhra region was Rs 2.16 crores revenue from a population of 1.19 crores, or Rs 1.82 per capita revenue. Thus, even in 1880, the per capita revenue from Telangana under the Nizam was 88 per cent more than that of Andhra under the British (Raghavaiyengar 1988: xci, xcvii). Telangana continued, thereafter, to produce enormous revenues for the Nizam, who emerged as the richest prince in India, if not in the world.

Telangana in the Union of India

1948

The Dar Commission, appointed by the Constituent Assembly in 1948, found that the annual revenues during 1945-48, from the Telugu districts of Madras Province, was Rs 12 crores, while their population was 1.88 crores, thereby generating a per capita annual revenue of Rs 6.38. Incidentally, Dar also gave the corresponding revenue figure for the unified Hyderabad state, in which Telangana was the largest region, at Rs 24.63 crores, for a population of 1.63 crores, thereby yielding a per capita revenue of Rs 15.11 (Government of India [GoI] 1948: 43).

1956

The State Reorganization Commission (SRC) found that Telangana revenues yielded Rs 17 crores per annum and its population was 1.13 crores (after the exclusion of Hyderabad's Maratha and Kanada districts). SRC stated that Andhra had annual revenues of Rs 22 crores with a population of 2.09 crores (GoI 1955: 105-06). Thus, the per capita annual revenue from Telangana was Rs 15.04, while that from Andhra was Rs 10.53. This implied that every resident of Telangana (admittedly a poorer region) was taxed at 43 per cent more than every resident of Andhra, which was known to be a rich region with a developed economy. However, despite the SRC recommendation for the statehood of Telangana, and despite the relative fiscal imbalance, Telangana was forcibly merged with Andhra. Promises of fair and equitable fiscal behaviour were made, but were never kept.

1956–68

The First Telangana Agitation in 1969 raised the issue of the diversion of Telangana revenues to the Andhra region. Kumar Lalit of the office of the Comptroller and Auditor General of India reported that for over 12 years (1956-68), the total revenues from Telangana were Rs 514.46 crores, while those from Andhra were Rs 719.01 crores. In the median year of 1961, Telangana's population was 1.46 crores and Andhra's was 2.77 crores; thus, Rs 29.36 per capita revenue was extracted from Telangana annually and Rs 21.63 per capita from Andhra. The First Telangana Movement was subverted and crushed. New promises of fair treatment were made, and as before, were never kept.

2003–07

The Second Telangana Movement began in the 2000s. Replying to a query in the Legislative Assembly, Rosaiah (2007), then Finance Minister, put forward the figures of average annual revenues for the period from 2003–07 for the regions. Excluding the revenue of the 'headaquarters' (Rs 8,108 crores), the state received Rs 5,580 crores of revenue from the Telangana region and its people, and Rs 4,318 crores from the Andhra (including Rayalaseema) region and its people. The 2001 population of Telangana was 2.82 crores, and of Andhra, 4.50 crores. Thus, the government extracted Rs 1978.72 per person from Telangana annually, while Andhra contributed only Rs 959.56 per capita. Telangana therefore contributed more than twice per capita, as compared to Andhra.

2014–15

The truth about the relative revenues of the two states was revealed, after separation, when their Finance Ministers presented the very first full budgets for Telangana and Andhra Pradesh. The revised estimates for 2014–15 of the State Own Receipts (SOR) for Telangana was amounted to Rs 48, 620 crores, while for Andhra, it was Rs 47,397 crores (Government of Andhra Pradesh [GoAP] 2014; Government of Telangana [GoT] 2014]. Considering the 2011 population of Telangana at 3.53 crores, and of Andhra at 4.94 crores, the Telangana revenue receipts were Rs 13,777.30 per capita and for Andhra, they were Rs 9,598.40 per capita.

2015–20

The Fourteenth Finance Commission had projected the position for a five-year period, that is, from 2015–20, for the two states after the demerger. It painted a rosy fiscal picture for Telangana, with revenue surpluses for each of the five years. The Commission predicted a total SOR of Rs 3, 91,256 crores for Telangana and Rs 3, 94, 076 crores for Andhra over the five-year period. This works out to average annual revenue per capita of Rs 22,168 from Telangana and Rs 15,955 from Andhra (GoI 2015: 445, 453).

However, state-owned revenues (2017–18) for Telangana were Rs 64,345 crores, and for Andhra Pradesh, Rs 53,625crores. Given that the estimated population for Telangana for that year was Rs 3.91 crores, and for Andhra, Rs 5.06 crores, per capita state revenues for Telangana was Rs 16,457, and for Andhra, Rs 10,598. The difference between the two states is in the ratio is 1.55:1 in Telangana's favour, which is far more than ever before (Reserve Bank of India 2016–20). To sum up, Table 6.1 below indicates the relative per capita state revenue from both regions over 385 years (1636 AD–2020).

It is clear that over nearly more than 400 years, the people of Telangana have been forced to contribute as taxes between 36 to 106 per cent more revenue per capita than their Andhra counterparts (see Table 6.1). This was why the Telangana 'merger' or 'forced marriage', as it was called, was organised. This was also why Telangana's statehood was subverted in 1969. Even after K. Chandrasekhar Rao's heroic fast-till-death (29 November till 9 December 2009) and the consequent All-Party Agreement for Telangana

Table 6.1: Annual Revenue Contribution from Telangana and Andhra

Period	*Source*	*Telangana*	*Andhra*	*Telangana to Andhra (In Per cent)*
		Total Collection in Rs		
1685	Sherwani 1974: 655	132.67	55.09	240.82
1687-88	Richards 1975: 152–53	82.99	42.60	194.81
1689-90	Richards 1975: 160–61	91.41	51.03	179.13
		Collection in Rs Per Capita		
1880–81	Ali 1886: 2, 86; Raghavaiyangar 1988: xci, ccxli	3.42	1.82	187.91
1945–48	Government of India (GoI) 1948: 43	12.80	6.46	198.14
1955–56	GoI 1955: 101,105, 106,111	15.04	10.53	142.83
1956–68	GoAP 1969: 17	29.36	21.63	135.74
2003–07	Pingle 2014: 266	1979	960	106.21
2014–15	GoAP 2014: 3; GoT 2014: 4	13,777	9,598	143.54
2015–20	GoI 2015: 445, 453	22,168	15,955	138.94
2017–18	GoAP 2019:1; GoT 2019:1	16,457	10,598	155.28

Source: Constructed by the author.

Statehood (2 June 2014), the Centre backtracked for five years. Finally, in 2014, the state of Telangana came into being.

In 2015, the Fourteenth Finance Commission, headed by Y. V. Reddy, former IAS officer, of Andhra Pradesh, acknowledged what had been denied for 68 years—the fact that Telangana had been subsidising Andhra all along and projected it forward from past assumptions. By 2017–18, the revenues of Telangana reached the highest proportion since the merger, as compared to Andhra. Only now, as in Kakatiya Ganapatideva's times, Telangana revenues will be applied to the development of the land and the people of Telangana

References

Ali, Moulavi Cheragh. 1886. 'Hyderabad under Sir Salar Jung'. Bombay: Education Society Press.

Ball, V. (trans.). 1898. *Travels in India by Jean Baptiste Tavernier*, 2 Volumes. London: Macmillan.

Briggs, John. 1989. *History of the Rise of Mohammedan Power in India*, 4 Volumes. New Delhi: Atlantic Publishers.

Dighe, V. G. (ed.). 1937. *Maratha-Nizam Relations 1792–1795*. Bombay: Government Printing Press.

Elliot, H. M., and J. Dowson. 2008. *The History of India as told by its Own Historians*, 8 Volumes. New Delhi: Low Price Publications.

GoI. 1948. *Report of the Linguistic Provinces Commission*. New Delhi: Manager Government of India Press.

——. 1955. *Report of the State's Reorganization Commission*. New Delhi: Manager of Publications, Government of India..

——. 2015. *Report of the 14th Finance Commission*. New Delhi: Director of Publications.

GoAP. 2014. *Budget at a Glance*. Available at https://www.apfinance.gov.in/uploads/budget-2014-15-books/Volume-VI.pdf.

GoT. 2014. *Budget*. Hyderabad: GoT.

Grant-Duff, James. 1852. *A History of the Mahrattas*, Volume II. London: Longman, Rees, Orme, Brown and Green.

Gribble, J. D. B. 2002. *A History of the Deccan*, 2 Volumes. New Delhi: Rupa Publications.

Irvine, William. 1922. *Later Moghuls*, Volume II, ed. Jadunath Sarkar. Calcutta: M. C. Sarkar and Co.

Khan, Yusuf Husain. 1936. *Nizam-ul Mulk, Asaf Jah I- Founder of Hyderabad State*. Mangalore: The Basel Mission Press.

Khan, M. Naseeruddin. 1950. *Selected Documents of Shah Jahan's Reign*. Hyderabad: Daftar I Diwani.

Lowell, A. 1687. *The Travels of Monsieur de Thevenot into the Levant*. London: H. Clarke.

Pingle, Gautam. 2014. *The Fall and Rise of Telangana*, Hyderabad: Orient BlackSwan.

Raghavaiyengar, S. Srinivas. 1988[1893]. *Memorandum of the Progress of Madras Presidency*. New Delhi: Asian Educational Services.

Rao, B. Shiva (ed.). 1967. *The Framing of India's Constitution, Select Documents*, Six Volumes. New Delhi: Universal Law Publishing.

Reserve Bank of India. 2016–20. Handbook of Statistics on Indian States. Available at https://m.rbi.org.in/Scripts/AnnualPublications.aspx?head=Handbook%20of%20Statistics%20on%20Indian%20States.

Ricci, Aldo. 2002. *The Travels of Marco Polo*. New Delhi: Rupa Publications.

Richards, J. F. 1975. *Mughal Administration of Golconda*. Oxford: Clarendon Press.

Rosaiah, K. 2007. 'LAQ No: 7406 [Starred] of the Andhra Pradesh Legislature', Session 9, 21 March 2007.

Sherwani, H. K. 1974. *History of the Qutb Shahi Dynasty*. New Delhi: Munshiram Manoharlal.

7

Sundarlal Report on Post-Police Action Riots

The words we use are a significant way of communication and are critical in conveying meaning. Moreover, a sentence conveys not just meaning, but also implications, depending upon the type and use of words. Especially in writing official reports of important events, words have to be carefully chosen in order to describe and analyse the situation without conveying prejudice and judgment of the author. However, the choice of words and sentence construction depend primarily on the preference of the author. This essay describes how the authors drafted and finalised the extraordinary Sundarlal Report on the communal riots in Hyderabad following the takeover of the state by the Indian army in 1948.

---

* This essay is unusual, and follows a distinct narrative style, whereby the comparison has been carried out in the original voice, by citing the texts, without paraphrasing. This has been done to preserve the authenticity and uniqueness of the original texts, which are rarely available.

The emergence of the Sundarlal Report is a minor saga in itself. It is reported that the entire collection of documents was donated by Pandit Sundarlal's heirs to the Nehru Memorial Museum Library (NMML) in 1968. Thereafter, the final report was published in *Frontline* (Vol. 18, #05, March 3, 2001), and in the same issue A. G. Noorani, referring to it in his article, 'Of a Massacre Untold', stated that Director of Pandit Sundarlal Institute of Asian Studies obtained a copy of the full text for him from NMML. In his 2013 book, *Destruction of Hyderabad*, Noorani provided the text of only of the Final Report and 'Confidential Notes' as Appendices 14 and 15. However, the entire set of documents of 40 pages in raw typescript and handwritten margin notes, including the Draft Report, was published by *Deccan Chronicle* at the same time. The page numbers cited here are those given in the Deccan Chronicle documents.

Draft reports are usually the first cut, revealing the unrestrained expression of the author. Subsequently, changes are made not only to bring grammar and vocabulary into line, but also to modulate, temper and make the narrative acceptable to the higher leadership.

A few changes were made in draft report [A] itself. More radical changes were carried into the final report [B].

A. 'It is a very significant fact that out of these eight, the four worst affected districts [Osmanbad, Gulbarga, Bidar and Nander] had been the great strongholds of the Razakars at whose hands the people therein Hindus there had suffered to the greatest extent in the whole State' (*Deccan Chronicle* 2013: 3).

Here the words 'therein Hindus' was left out of the draft itself, and with other changes, the paragraph emerged thus:

B. 'It is a very significant fact that out of these eight, the four worst affected districts [Osmanbad, Gulbarga, Bidar and Nander] had been the great strongholds of the Razakars and the people of these four districts had been the worst sufferers at the hands of the Razakars' (*Deccan Chronicle* 2013: 16).

Thus, the target of the Razakars was no longer 'Hindus', but the 'people', and the specificity of the word used no longer informed the reader fully. When it came to identifying the perpetrators of the post-police action violence, the draft itself went through alteration:

A. 'The perpetrators of these atrocities were *unfortunately* not limited to those who had suffered at the hands of the Razakars, nor *only* to *the entire population of* non-Muslims of Hyderabad state. These latter were aided and abetted by bands, with and without arms, who had infiltrated into the state in the wake of the Indian Army *from Indian territory* across the border' (*Deccan Chronicle* 2013: 3).

B. 'The perpetrators of these atrocities were not limited to those who had suffered at the hands of the Razakars, nor to the non-Muslims of Hyderabad state. These latter were aided and abetted by *individuals* and bands of people, with and without arms, from across the border who had infiltrated *through* in the wake of the Indian Army' (*Deccan Chronicle* 2013: 16) (emphasis added).

Therefore, the report suggests that neither did Hindus individually take revenge for the atrocities committed against them, nor did the Hyderabadi Hindus who had been subject to the Razakar atrocities take any action. However, it also suggested that it was Hindus who had come from outside Hyderabad, who could not have had any experience of Razakar atrocities, but were rather just there for loot, rape and murder. Another issue was the problem of perception by the Muslims of the future under Indian rule:

A. '*These happenings* followed close on the heels of the Police Action and the consequent collapse of the Razakars organization which had, in the Muslim mind, stood as an effective barrier against the establishment of a Hindu Raj, the latter being synonymous to the average Hyderabadi Muslim with the demand of responsible government *by the State Congress* as it would in effect be based on the will of the Hindu majority' (*Deccan Chronicle* 2013: 6).

B. '*This communal trouble* followed close on the heels of the Police Action and the consequent collapse of the Razakars organization which had stood, in the Muslim mind, as an effective barrier against the establishment of responsible government which was synonymous to the average Hyderabadi Muslim with Hindu Raj, because it would be based on the will of the Hindu majority' (*Deccan Chronicle* 2013: 18) (emphasis added).

Not only were 'these happenings' replaced by 'this communal trouble' but 'Hindu Raj' also became synonymous with the demand for a 'responsible government' by the 'State Congress'. As regards the Muslim population and their attitude after the takeover by the Indian army:

A. 'A few complaints/cases might have had some little substance, but these have been magnified and used as examples and proofs positive of the hardships inflicted upon Muslim State employees simply because they were Muslims by the Administration now running the State for which the Indian Government is responsible. The literate section of a community being the most intelligent is usually the most vocal and the community as a whole implicitly believes what it is repeatedly told by its so-called intelligentsia with or without ulterior and selfish motives. The Hyderabad Muslims were no exception. It is not to be wondered

> therefore that Hyderabad Muslims reeling and dazed under severe retaliatory/repeated blows (could not think clearly even if they can think that all) have not been able to recover their mental balance. It is not to be wondered therefore that even though the outrages to which they were subjected have ceased thanks to the strong prompt and effective measures promptly taken by the present administration' (*Deccan Chronicle* 2013: 7–8).

In the draft itself, the criticism of the Hyderabad Muslim literati and intelligentsia was left out and the whole paragraph was eliminated in the final report. It is fascinating to note that there was extensive praise of the Military Governor, Major- General Chaudhri, in the draft, but it finds no place in the final report. Also, a description of the atrocities and loot by Indian army personnel with specific reference to the Sikh soldiers' criminal activity in the draft did not find a place in the final report. These soldiers had come from Punjab, which had not only seen widespread massacres of Hindus and Muslims, but had also forced the movement of Hindus from Pakistan to India and of Muslims from India to Pakistan.

One of the most critical political elements of this report was a recommendation, which the Committee itself was very hesitant in putting forward, but nevertheless did present it: 'Not without some hesitation we are perhaps overstepping our legitimate province by touching on the subject of future administrative changes':

A. 'We have already drawn attention to the very real fear in the Muslim mind that a responsible Government in Hyderabad State *meaning* as it does a government under the will of the Hindu majority is likely to be of little short of a *calamity—in view of* the strained relations between the communities in the present' (*Deccan Chronicle* 2013: 10) (emphasis added).
B. 'We have already drawn attention to the very real fear in the Muslim mind that a responsible Government in Hyderabad *implying* as it does, a government under the will of the Hindu majority, is likely to be little short of *disaster considering* the present strained relations of the two communities, *besides a cleavage in the Congress ranks. We are constrained to remark that the State Congress has failed to give an absolutely satisfactory account*

> *of itself during the period of trouble*' (*Deccan Chronicle* 2013: 22) (emphasis added).

Given the concerns of the Muslim population as well as the problematic conditions between the two religious communities, compounded with the problem that the State Congress leadership was divided (without explaining why it was divided), the Committee went on to suggest regulatory strategies for the future.

A. 'The time, therefore, for any radical changes in the form of government or in the administration does not appear to be propitious. We would respectfully suggest that their postponement for at least *three* years, *if not more*. For allied reasons we would also suggest the inclusion of at least two Muslims enjoying the confidence of their co-religionists, in the Administrative set up of the State at the highest level and in an effective capacity' (*Deccan Chronicle* 2013: 11).

B. 'Therefore the time for any radical changes in the form of government does not appear to be propitious. We would respectfully suggest that their postponement for at least *some* years *to come*. For allied reasons, we would also suggest the inclusion of at least two more Muslims enjoying the confidence of their co-religionists, in the Administrative set up of the State at the highest level and in an effective capacity' (*Deccan Chronicle* 2013: 22) (emphasis added).

Thus, the Committee felt that there should be no radical changes either in government or in the administration. It also advised in favour of the appointment of additional Muslim members at the highest level of the administrative set-up, which had already been revamped after Police Action. This deferment of change, in fact, was to last for 'at least three years or more' (as in the draft) or for 'some years to come' (as in the final report). This proposition was extraordinary, as the Hindus of Hyderabad had been promised self-rule through a democratic process. The Committee neglected to appreciate that Hyderabad had been ruled for nearly 600 years by a Muslim ruling elite. The recommendation implied that 85 per cent of the population, which was Hindu and had been 'liberated' from autocracy by the Indian army, were to wait for another three years or more for their cherished and promised objective.

In a parallel and preceding case of the annexation of the princely state of Jammu and Kashmir, the Indian authorities had persuaded Maharaja Hari Singh to release the opposition leader, Sheikh Mohammed Abdullah, and appoint him as the Emergency Administrator of the state on 30 October 30 1947. He was appointed as the Prime Minister of an Interim government of the state of Jammu and Kashmir on 5 March 1948. Thus, in a sense, the Government of India was prepared to introduce or impose popular rule in a Muslim-dominated state, which was ruled by a Hindu ruler, but the Committee was not prepared to advise the same when it came to a Hindu-dominated state ruled by a Muslim ruler. Moreover, the Committee recommended two additional Muslim members to be appointed to a high level when the Executive Council already had two Muslim members and three Hindus, apart from three Indian government representatives.

The government of India followed the accommodations of this Committee and continued to retain General Chaudhri as Military Governor and B. S. Bakle, Indian Civil Service (ICS), as Chief Civil Administrator. The Nizam had adopted the Constitution of India as the Constitution of Hyderabad on 26 November 1949. The Constitution of India came into force on 26 January 1950. Thus, the Nizam of Hyderabad continued to be the legal ruler of the state till 26 January 1950. During the period between 17 September 1948 and 26 January 1950, all actions taken by the government of Hyderabad were made nominally in the name of His Exalted Highness the Nizam of Hyderabad. When the matter came before the Supreme Court, it decided the issue:

> After the Police action in the State of Hyderabad in August, 1948, the Nizam, by a *Farman* dated September 19, 1948, invested the Military Governor 'with all authority for the administration of the State "and by a later *Farman* declared that' the said authority includes and has always included authority to make Regulations. 'By virtue of the said powers, the Military Governor promulgated the Hyderabad [Abolition of *Jagirs*] Regulations of 1358 *Fasli*. Thereafter on the termination of the appointment of the Military Governor, the Nizam by another *Farman* appointed Mr. Vellodi as his Chief Minister and directed that 'all the powers of administration, vested in the Military Governor before the said date are exercisable by the Chief Minister.... There can be no question that the Nizam, at the time when he executed the *Farmans* and prior to it, was an absolute ruler vested with all authority executive, legislative and judicial and had unquestionable powers to modify

> or extinguish any of the rights of his subjects and the language of the *Farmans* leaves no manner of doubt that he hereby delegated the entirety of his authority and powers to the Military Governor and thereafter to the Prime [*sic.* Chief] Minister.... On December 1, 1949, another *Farman* was issued by His Exalted Highness the Nizam which provided as follows: 'Whereas the General Officer Commanding in Chief Southern Army has as from the 1st December, 1949, terminated the appointment of Major General Chaudary, OBE, to be the Military Governor for the Hyderabad State; And whereas it is necessary to make other arrangements for the administration of the State as from the said date; Now, therefore, I hereby appoint as from the said date Mr M. K. Vellodi, CIE, ICS, to be my Chief Minister and ... I further direct that all the powers of administration, vested in the Military Governor before the said date are exercisable by the Chief Minister' (Supreme Court of India 1960).

Even after the promulgation of the Constitution of India and the declaration of the Republic on 26 January 1950, Hyderabad continued to be administered by the Union Government, which now re-appointed the M. K. Vellodi, ICS, as Chief Minister of Hyderabad. It was only possible to make such an appointment with regard to the exercise of powers under Article 356 of the Constitution. Thus, it was only after the General Election of 1952 that Hyderabad attained democratic self-rule.

In this matter, therefore, the Sundarlal Committee played a decisive role in delaying self-rule for the people of Hyderabad. The two reports, draft and final, illustrate how secret reports of so-called independent committees can be decisive and effective in altering public policy discreetly and confidentially. Whether the changes were a result of the Committee's own volition or were 'advised' by higher authorities is a matter of speculation. It is no surprise that this report was kept a secret till 2001, and only then the attention was more on the number of Muslims murdered immediately after Police Action than the significant issue of delay in introducing a democratic rule, the purpose for which the Indian army had taken over Hyderabad.

Readers may like to compare the two versions of the Sundarlal Report below and come to their conclusions on the way reports are significantly altered by the authors themselves (see Table 7.1).

Table 7.1: A Comparison of the Draft and Final Versions of the Sundarlal Report

Paragraph	*Final Report*	*Draft Report*
1	To: (1) the Honorable the Prime Minister, Government of India, New Delhi (2) The Honorable State's Minister, Government of India, New Delhi	
	Sir	*Dear* Sir
	We were asked by the Government of India to proceed to Hyderabad State on a goodwill mission. *After completing our task there we now* and beg to submit our Report.	We were asked by the Government of India to proceed to Hyderabad State on a goodwill mission and beg to submit our Report.
2	**Introductory**	
	[1] The delegation consisting of Pandit Sundarlal, Kazi Abdul Ghaffar and Maulana Abdullah Misri arrived in Hyderabad on the *29th* of November and left for Delhi on the *21st* of December 1948. During this period we toured through 9 out of the 16 districts of the state, visiting 7 District headquarters, 21 towns, and 23 importance villages. In addition, we *interviewed* over 500 people from 109 *such* villages *as we did not visit.*	The delegation consisting of Pandit Sundarlal, Kazi Abdul Ghaffar and Maulana Abdullah Misri arrived in Hyderabad on the [blank] of November and left for Delhi on the [blank] of December 1948. During this period we toured through 9 out of the 16 districts of the state, visiting 7 District headquarters, 21 towns, and 23 importance villages. In addition, we *met* over 500 people from 109 villages *which we had not visited.*
3	Further 31 public meetings and 27 private gatherings of Hindus. Muslims, Congressmen, Officials, members of the Jamiat-ul-Ulema and the Ittehad-ul-Muslameen, the staffs and students of many educational institutions, members	Further thirty-one public meetings and 27 private gatherings of Hindus, Muslims, Congressmen, Officials, members of the Jamiat-ul-Ulema and the Ittehad-ul-Muslameen, the staffs and students of many educational institutions, members of

(*Contd.*)

Table 7.1: (*Contd.*)

Paragraph	*Final Report*	*Draft Report*
	of the Progressive Writers' Association and the Hindustani Prachar Sabha etc were addressed by members of the *delegation.*	the Progressive Writers' Association and the Hindustani Prachar Sabha etc were addressed by members of the *Mission.*
4	Amongst the important personages met and interviewed by us may be mentioned H.E.H the Nizam, H.H the Prince of Berar, Major-General J.N.Chaudhari, Mr. D.S. Bakhle, the Chief Civil Administrator, Swami Ramananda Tirtha, Dr Melkote, Messers Ramchander Rao, Ramachari, K Vaidya, Venkat Rao, *and Abul Hasan Syed Ali, Nawab Ali Yavar Jug, Nawab Zain Yar Jung. Raja Dhone Raj, Maulana Abu Yousuf, Moulvi Abul Khair and Moulvi Hameeduddin Qmar Farooqi*	Amongst the important personages met and interviewed by us may be mentioned H.E.H the Nizam, H.H the Prince of Berar, Swami Ramananda Tirtha, Major-General J.N.Chaudhari, Mr. D.S.Bakhle, the Chief Civil Administrator, Dr Melkote, Messers Ramchander Rao, Ramachari, K Vaidya, Venkat Rao ...
5	At all these meetings, gatherings and interviews the main *problem* was the creation and maintenance of cordial relations between the communities. Appeals were made to the people to forget the past and to work unremittingly for the establishment of peace and harmony amongst themselves. The aim and policy of the Indian Union was also explained to them and *special emphasis was laid on* the objective *which* was *the establishment* of a secular government for the people of Hyderabad in which all of them, irrespective of religion, faith or creed will enjoy equal	At all these meetings, gatherings and interviews the main *theme* was the creation and maintenance of cordial relations between the communities. Appeals were made to the people to forget the past and to work unremittingly for the establishment of peace and harmony amongst themselves. The aim and policy of the Indian Union was also *fully* explained to them and *it was emphasized that* the objective was *to provide for the people of Hyderabad a* secular government in which all of them, irrespective of religion, faith or creed will enjoy equal freedom and civil rights and will have the

(*Contd.*)

Table 7.1: (*Contd.*)

Paragraph	*Final Report*	*Draft Report*
	freedom and civil rights and will have the same opportunities for development and progress. It was made perfectly clear that the Military Administration has been charged with the duty of *implementing* that policy.	same opportunities for development and progress. It was made perfectly clear that Military Administration has been charged with the duty of *carrying out* that policy *in actual practice.*
6	*We clarified our position*, whenever the opportunity presented itself, that ours was not a Commission of Investigation or Inquiry into the events preceding or following the Police Action *and that ours was merely a goodwill mission charged with the task of restoring better communal relations. All the same, we feel it our duty to bring to your notice what we what we saw and gathered in our touring, as it has, in our opinion, an importance all of its own.*	*We understood it perfectly and pointedly made it clear*, whenever the opportunity presented itself, that ours was *not* a Commission of Investigation or Inquiry into the events preceding or following the Police Action. *All the same, what we saw and what we were told whilst on our tours and in Hyderabad itself have to our mind an importance of their own, and we feel that we would not be doing our duty were we to fail to bring to your notice what we learnt there.*
7	**Killing and Looting** [2]Hyderabad state has 16 districts, comprising of *nearly* than 22,000 villages. Out of *them*, only three *districts* remained practically, though not wholly free, of communal trouble which affected the state first during the militant activities of the Razakars and then during the reprisals that followed the collapse of that organisation. In another four **districts** the trouble had been more serious but nothing like the havoc that overtook the *remaining eight*	Hyderabad state has *[not counting the Atraf-i-balda, i.e., Hyderabad and its suburbs]* 16 districts [comprising of *no less* than 22,000 villages] out of *which* only three remained practically, though not wholly free, of communal trouble which affected the state first during the militant activities of the Razakars and then during the reprisals that followed the collapse of that organization. In another four the trouble had been more serious but nothing like the *terrible* havoc that overtook the *other* eight.

(Contd.)

Table 7.1: (*Contd.*)

Paragraph	*Final Report*	*Draft Report*
8	Out of these *again*, the worst sufferers *have been the districts* of Osmanabad, Gulbarga, Bidar and Nanded in which **four the** number of people killed in the disturbances during and after police action, was not much less, if not more, than 18,000. In the other four districts, of Aurangabad, Bir, Nalgonda and Medak those who lost their lives numbered *at least 5 thousand. We can say at a very conservative estimate that in the whole state at least 27 to 40 thousand people lost their lives during and after police action.*	Out of these, *four had been* the worst sufferers of *namely* Osmanabad, Gulbarga, Bidar and Nanded in which the number of people killed in the disturbances during and after police action, was not much less, if not more, than 18,000. In the other four districts, of Aurangabad, Bir, Nalgonda and Medak those who lost their lives numbered *between* 3,500 individuals *to* 4,000. *So that out of the total of 25 to 30 thousand which at a very conservative estimate is a safe figure of killed in the whole state, these eight districts account for not less than 90 per cent.*
9	We were *informed* by the authorities that these *eight* were the most affected districts and needed most the good offices of our delegation. We, therefore, concentrated on these, and succeeded, we might say, *to some extent at least*, in dispelling the atmosphere of mutual hostility and distrust.	On *arrival in Hyderabad,* we were *told* by the authorities that these were the worst affected districts and needed most the good offices of our delegation. We, therefore, concentrated on these, and succeeded, if we might say *so, to a not inconsiderable extent,* in dispelling the atmosphere of mutual hostility and distrust.
10	It is a very significant fact that out of these eight, the four worst affected districts [Osmanbad, Gulbarga, Bidar and Nander] had been the *main* strongholds of the Razakars and the people of these four districts *had been the worst sufferers at the hands of the Razakars*	It is a very significant fact that out of these eight, the four worst affected districts [Osmanbad, Gulbarga, Bidar and Nander] had been the *great* strongholds of the Razakars *at whose hands* the people [' therein Hindus there' has been xxed out in the draft] *had suffered to the greatest extent in the whole State*
11	In the town of Latur–the home of Kasim Razvi–which has been a big business centre with rich	In the town of Latur–the home of Kasim Razvi–which has been a big business centre with rich Kutchi

(*Contd.*)

Table 7.1: (*Contd.*)

Paragraph	*Final Report*	*Draft Report*
	Kutchi Muslim merchants the killings continued for *over* 20 days. Out of a population of about ten thousand Muslims, we found barely three *thousand* still in the town. *Over a thousand* had been killed, and the rest had run away with little else besides their lives and *completely* ruined financially.	Muslim merchants the killings continued *for* 20 days. Out of a population of about 10 thousand Muslims, we found barely three still there. *Two to three thousand* had been killed, and the rest had run away *escaping* with little else besides their lives and ruined financially
12	**The Crimes**	
	[3] *Almost everywhere* in the affected areas of the State, communal frenzy did not exhaust itself in murder alone in which *at some places even women and children were not spared.*	*In these districts as everywhere else* in the affected areas of the State, communal frenzy did not exhaust itself in murder alone–murder which *does not appear to have spared women or children.*
	Rape, abductions of women [sometimes out of the State *to Indian towns such as Sholapur and Nagpur*], loot, arson, desecration of mosques, forcible conversions, seizure of houses and lands followed or accompanied the killings.	Loot, Arson, desecration of mosques, forcible 'conversions', rape, abductions of women [sometimes outside the State], seizure of houses and lands followed or accompanied the killings.
13	Tens of crores worth of property were looted or destroyed. The sufferers were Muslims *who formed a* hopeless minority *in rural areas.*	Tens of crores worth of property have been looted, destroyed *or seized from their owners.* The sufferers *everywhere* were Muslims–in *the* hopeless minority *of nearly 1 to 10.*
	The perpetrators of these atrocities were not limited to those who had suffered at the hands of the Razakars, not [nor?] to the non-Muslims of Hyderabad state. These latter were aided and abetted by *individuals and* bands of people, with and without	The perpetrators of these atrocities were *unfortunately* not limited to those who had suffered at the hands of the Razakars, nor *only* to the non-Muslims of Hyderabad state. These latter were aided and abetted by bands of people, with and without arms, who had infiltrated through

(*Contd.*)

Table 7.1: (*Contd.*)

Paragraph	*Final Report*	*Draft Report*
	arms, *from across the border*, who had infiltrated through in the wake of the Indian Army. We found definite indications that a number of armed and trained men belonging to a well-known *Hindu* communal organisation from Sholapur and other *Indian* towns, as also quite a few of local and outside Communists participated in *these riots* and in some cases actually led the rioters.	in the wake of the Indian Army *from Indian territory across the border*. We found definite indications that a number of armed and trained men belonging to a well-known *[?Notorious]* communal [Hindu] Organization from Sholapur and other towns *on the Indian side of the border*, as also quite a few of local and outside Communists participated and in some cases actually led the rioters, *killers and abductors*.
14	**The Army and the Police**	
	[4] Duty compels us to add that we had absolutely unimpeachable evidence to the effect that there were instances in which men belonging to the Indian Army and also the local police took part in looting and even other crimes	*Duty compels us to add that we were informed by unimpeachable and independent parties, of instances - happily isolated ones - in which men belonging to the Indian Army and the local police were seen taking part and sharing the loot!*
15	*During our tour, we gathered, at not a few places, that soldiers encouraged, persuaded and, in a few cases, even compelled the Hindu mob to loot Muslim shops and houses. At one district town, the present Hindu head of the administration told us that there was a general loot of Muslim shops by the military. In another district, a Munsiff's house, among others, was looted by soldiers and a Tahsildar's wife molested. Complaints of molestation and abduction of girls, against Sikh soldiers particularly, were by no means rare. We were generally told that at many places out of the looted property, cash, gold and silver was taken away by the military*	

(*Contd.*)

Table 7.1: (Contd.)

Paragraph	Final Report	Draft Report
	while other articles fell to the share of the mob. Unfortunately, there was a certain element in the Army which was not free from communal feelings probably because some of them could not forget the atrocities committed elsewhere on their own kith and kin.	
16	Lest we might be understood to imply a slur on the Indian Army, we hasten to record our considered opinion of the Indian Army [in Hyderabad], and its officers *generally maintained a high standard of discipline and sense of duty. In General Chaudhri, a firm disciplinarian and thorough gentleman.*	Lest we might be understood by our last statement to imply a slur on the Indian Army, we hasten to record here and now our considered opinion of the Indian Army [in Hyderabad] and its officers *headed by their capable Chief, Major General Chaudhri. Indeed in the latter, we found a man without the slightest tinge of communal prejudice.*
17		*We found him genuinely anxious and going all out to carry out the settled and declared policy of his Government for the establishment of peace and harmony between the communities and for suppression of all lawlessness with a firm hand and as quickly as humanly possible. He and his officers and the Indian Army, on the whole, are unremitting in their efforts to that end. Under his able directions and the cooperation of his officers by far, the largest portion of the immovable property of which the Muslims were deprived and a vast majority of abducted women have already been recovered and restored to their rightful owners and guardians. The work is still going on apace. The Military Governor and the Chief Civil Administrator as also most of their colleague officers and subordinates are*

(Contd.)

Table 7.1: (*Contd.*)

Paragraph	*Final Report*	*Draft Report*
		doing their level best to hold the scales even between the communities. So far as it lay with them, they have succeeded and have done splendidly. But we have no doubt that there was a section in the Army itself not equally free from communal hostility—particularly where it was born out of suffering and calamities on near and dear ones in Pakistan. That this hostility did find vent in criminal acts could hardly be questioned —as little perhaps as the incidents could be helped.
18	From this depressing picture *presented in the foregoing pages*, we turn to incidents that do stand for the silver lining to the dark clouds *of communal strife*. We were given instances by Muslims where Hindus had defended and given protection to *their* Muslim *neighbours*, men and women, *even* at the cost of their own lives	From this *intensely* depressing picture we turn to incidents, *not many, unfortunately*, that do stand for the silver lining to the *very* dark clouds. We were given instances by Muslims where Hindus had defended and given protection to Muslim men and women at the cost of their own lives
19	Before concluding this summary of atrocities committed, we *would like to* affirm that we have not made any of the above statements lightly or without realising to the full our responsibility in making them. What we have seen with our own eyes and what we were told not only by the sufferers and their friends but by reliable parties both Hindus and Muslims, by the known Hindu supporters of the Congress and by the equally known Muslim opponents of the Razakars, *by officials of the past and present administrations and*	Before concluding the summary of the story of the atrocities committed *on the Muslims*, we *must* affirm that we have not made any of the above statements lightly or without realising to the full our responsibility in making them. What we have seen with our own eyes and what we were told not only by the sufferers and their friends but by reliable parties both Hindus and Muslims, by the known Hindu supporters of the Congress and by the equally known Muslim opponents of the Razakars.

(*Contd.*)

Table 7.1: (*Contd.*)

Paragraph	*Final Report*	*Draft Report*
	by responsible individuals has been carefully sifted and discounted by us before arriving at our conclusions. We have refrained from entering into the details of the evidence on which our conclusions are based, but if so desired we are prepared to place before you all the relevant material collected by us.	
20	*In some professions, the fellow feeling was particularly marked. For instance, at places,* Hindu weavers defended Muslim weavers against Hindus and protected them often at a very heavy cost [including the loss of life] to themselves. Many Hindus helped and cooperated in the recovery of abducted Muslim women.	The Hindu weavers *invariably* defended Muslim weavers against Hindus and protected them often at a very heavy cost [including the loss of life] to themselves. Many Hindus helped and cooperated in the recovery of abducted Muslim women
21	**Hindu Raj and Muslim Raj**	
	[5] *This communal trouble* followed close on the heels of the Police Action and the consequent collapse of the Razakars organization which had stood, in the Muslim mind, as an effective barrier against *the establishment of responsible government which was synonymous to the average Hyderabadi Muslim with Hindu Raj,* because it would be based on the will of the Hindu majority	*These happenings* followed close on the heels of the Police Action and the consequent collapse of the Razakars organization which had, in the Muslim mind, stood as an effective barrier against *the establishment of a Hindu Raj, the latter being* synonymous to the average Hyderabadi Muslim *with the demand of responsible government by the State Congress as it would in effect* be based on the will of the Hindu majority.
22	The Muslim masses generally were slow to realise that their sufferings were the inevitable *repercussions* to the atrocities committed on *the Hindus* only, a few *days* before,	The Muslim masses generally were slow to realise that their sufferings were the inevitable *reprisals of the Hindu masses* to the atrocities committed on *the latter* only a

(*Contd.*)

Table 7.1: (*Contd.*)

Paragraph	*Final Report*	*Draft Report*
	by the Razakars. *The Razakar movement had the sympathy of a good number of Muslimans in Hyderabad.*	few *weeks* before *[as they themselves declared]* by the Razakars *who had the active sympathy of practically every Musliman in Hyderabad.*
23	*Such of them as dared to publicly oppose or even criticise the Razakar activities paid heavily for their temerity, so much so that one of them fell before the bullet of an assassin.*	*There are some exceptions of course, but it is doubtful if they number more than a few dozens and such of them as dared to publicly oppose or even criticise the Razakar activities paid heavily for their temerity—in one recorded case one of them with his life.* *Even those Muslims who traced these happenings to their original cause—the Razakars—considered the Police Action as their immediate cause for which they held the Indian Government responsible.*
24	Like the Razakars the perpetrators of these crimes against the Muslims encouraged the belief that they had the backing of the *authorities*. Colour was lent to this belief, as mentioned before by some actions and omissions of *such* people in authority as had been unable to purge their minds of the communal *virus*. Suspicions *thus created* as regards the good faith of Indian Government were not the unnatural outcome of the sufferings of hundreds of thousands of *people* in which tens of thousands lost their lives and others practically all that makes life worth living. *In this campaign of retaliation, at least a hundred were made to suffer for the sins of each guilty individual.*	Like the Razakars the perpetrators of these crimes against the Muslims *actively* encouraged the belief that they had the backing of the *Administration of the day. Unfortunately*, colour was lent to this belief, as mentioned before by some actions and omissions *of the* people in present authority *and their helpers* as had been unable to purge their minds of the communal *hostility*. *The* suspicions as regards the good faith *and impartiality* of Indian Government *as between Hindus and the Muslims, however baseless* were *thus* not the unnatural outcome of *their indiscriminate* sufferings of hundreds of thousands of *Muslims* in which tens of thousands lost their lives and others practically all that makes life worth living *and in which along*

(*Contd.*)

Table 7.1: (*Contd.*)

Paragraph	*Final Report*	*Draft Report*
		with it may be one guilty individual a hundred innocent persons appear to have paid the penalty.
25	**The State Congress** *(6) Unfortunately, during the days of the trouble, the conduct of some of the Congressmen added to the distrust of the Muslim population. We mention a few instances of what we heard about the conduct of some persons posing as Congressmen. It was reported to us during our tour that at many places persons claiming to be Congressmen took law in their own hands an adopted various devices of extracting money from panicky Musulmans. At several places, we heard the complaint that such persons were going about approaching Muslims who had not left their homes or those who had returned extracting money from them against promises of so-called protection. At one place the D.S of Police complained that these Congress people were making administration difficult by such conduct. At one important town a rich Kachhi merchant whose shop had been looted and partly burnt complained to us that he could get back possession of his buildings only after passing a cheque of 15,000 and paying 10,000 in cash, to some Congresswalas. We were told that Congressmen had auctioned cultivable land left behind by Muslims on condition that half the crops were to be handed over to the Congress. Now that the affairs of the State*	

(Contd.)

Table 7.1: (*Contd.*)

Paragraph	*Final Report*	*Draft Report*
	Congress are under consideration of the Congress High Command we hope that for the sake of the good name of the National Congress, the Hyderabad State Congress will be purged of these defects and recurrence of such conduct will be made impossible.	
26	**Services**	
	[7]*Doubts* and suspicions in the minds of the literate Muslims were aggravated by yet another factor, namely the complaints of those who were in State service before Police Action *and who had lost their jobs. We have received a long list of names of persons dismissed, degraded suspended or otherwise penalised in various departments.*	*These* suspicions were *still further* aggravated in the minds of literate Muslims, by yet another factor, namely the *grievances and* complaints of those who were in State service before Police Action. We *are appending* a list [Appendix -] of those which were mentioned to us.
	We are quite prepared to believe that some of these were men who could not be allowed to continue in the best interests of administration. But we have reason to believe that a large number have suffered and are suffering for no fault of theirs there may be cases of mere suspicion or false accusation. In fact, we have incontrovertible evidence of the innocence of some of these men. We are sure that these men can be depended upon for their loyalty to the new regime. The fact also remains that these readjustments have landed a very large number of Muslim families in considerable economic difficulties. We feel that all such state servants unless they are definitely	*A few complaints/cases might have had some little substance, but these have been magnified and used as examples and proofs positive of the hardships inflicted upon Muslim employees of the State simply because they were Muslims. The Hyderabad Muslims reeling and dazed under severe retaliatory and repeated blows have not yet been able to recover their normal mental balance even though the outrages to which they were subjected have ceased thanks to the strong prompt and effective measures promptly taken by the present administration. Although comparatively free from fear they yet are not entirely free from suspicions as regards the ultimate intentions of the Government of India in whose hands their future lies.*

(*Contd.*)

Table 7.1: (*Contd.*)

Paragraph	*Final Report*	*Draft Report*
	proved guilty, should be reinstated as early as possible.	
	The fact is that bitter experience has rought home *to the Hyderabadi Muslims* the dire consequences of communalism. Naturally, they now want to live and let live. *We believe that they would be perfectly happy and contented if they can be taken out of the present atmosphere of distrust and frustration.*	*On the other hand,* bitter experience has brought home to *them* the dire consequences of communalism. Naturally, they now want to live and let live. *They would be happy indeed to get rid of their distrust in the present regime and have faith in its declared future policy. That faith had its birth in the protection they have received from the administration of Major General Chaudhri, and its growth has been materially helped by sending of the Goodwill Mission. But something more is definitely indicated if that faith is not to be a stillborn child*
27	**Suggestions**	
	[7] *In view of the foregoing observations,* we *take* the liberty of *submitting the following suggestions*—which in our *opinion would help in* the establishment of communal peace and harmony in Hyderabad	We *are therefore taking* the liberty of submitting *a few—for whatever they may be worth*—which in our *view go further* the establishment of communal peace and harmony in Hyderabad
28	We do not mean to imply that none of the measures indicated in the following suggestions has yet engaged the attention of the present administration. But we are *presenting a* list of *problems* which we are convinced *deserve consideration.* We mention them in order of priority which, in our view, they deserve:-	We do not mean to imply that none of the measures indicated in the following suggestions has yet engaged the attention of the present administration. *Very probably most of them have.* But *even so,* we are *submitting as comprehensive* list of *matters* which we are convinced *may not be overlooked.* We mention them in order of priority which, in our view, they deserve:-
29	[i] The foremost and immediate need is that those who have suffered should receive all reasonable relief; e.g.	[1] The foremost and immediate need is that those who have suffered should receive all reasonable relief; e.g.

(*Contd.*)

Table 7.1: (*Contd.*)

Paragraph	*Final Report*	*Draft Report*
	a) Houses and land from which Muslims have been dispossessed and which have not yet been restored *to the rightful owners should be restored* to them by the ejectment, if necessary, of those in *possession at present.*	a) Houses and land from which Muslims have been dispossessed should be restored to them by the ejectment, if necessary, of those in present occupation.
	b) Houses which have been damaged should be repaired and made habitable.	b) Houses which have been damaged should be repaired and made habitable.
	c) Abducted women, girls and children *who have not been recovered from places both inside and outside the state [like Sholapur, and Nagpur]* should be recovered and restored to their lawful guardians and, in case the latter cannot be found, provision should be made for their maintenance, employment and training in some means of earning their livelihood.	c) Abducted women, girls and children *or* should be recovered *wherever they may be whether in State jurisdiction or Indian towns,* eg., Sholapur, Nagpur *or elsewhere* and restored to their lawful guardians and, in case the latter cannot be found, provision should be made for their maintenance, employment and training in some means of earning their livelihood.
	d) Work should be provided for those that have lost their means of livelihood or their breadwinners or are otherwise reduced destitute, including the establishment of handicrafts and cottage industries, the provision of capital, implements of trade etc.; as also the provision for maintenance in deserving cases.	d) Work *and maintenance* should be provided for those that have lost their livelihoods or their breadwinners or are otherwise reduced destitute, including the establishment of handicrafts and cottage industries, the provision of *some* capital, implements of trade etc.; as also the provision for *their* maintenance in deserving cases *till they are able to earn for six months whichever is longer.*
	e) Needy agriculturists should be subsidised and given all necessary help for the resumption of their occupation	e) Needy agriculturists should be subsidised and given all necessary help for the resumption of their occupation

(*Contd.*)

Table 7.1: (*Contd.*)

Paragraph	*Final Report*	*Draft Report*
30	[ii] Mosques should be restored to those entitled to look after them, and wherever idols have been installed in mosques they should be removed	[2] Mosques should be restored *after repairs wherever necessary* to those entitled to look after them, and wherever idols have been installed in mosques they should be removed
	[iii] All conversions to another faith *brought about* during this period should be declared null and void in law	[3] All *forcible* conversions to another faith made during this period should be declared null and void in law
	[iv] For the implementation of the above, we would respectfully suggest that a mixed Committee of officials and non-officials both Hindus and Muslims should be immediately appointed	For the implementation of the above, we would respectfully suggest that a mixed Committee *composed* of officials and non-officials both Hindus and Muslims should be immediately appointed *enjoying the confidence of their communities and charged with the rehabilitation of the sufferers mentioned and allied ways and matters*
31	[v] Our second suggestion in this behalf is the HEH the Nizam should be pressed to contribute from his private purse for the relief and rehabilitation of his subjects. Pandit Sundarlal who was invited by the Nizam for an interview has already made the suggestion to HEH personally	Our second suggestion in this behalf is the HEH the Nizam should be *asked and* pressed to contribute from his private purse for the relief and rehabilitation of his *Muslim* subjects *who have suffered so heavily.* Pandit Sundarlal who was invited by the Nizam for an interview has already made the suggestion to HEH personally, *and the latter did not reject it out of hand.*
32	*We are definitely informed that a large number of persons who took part in these atrocities and even led the mob are still at large in various districts. We know that rounding up of miscreants and the muzzling of all disruptive elements is already*	*The rounding-up and the effective muzzling of all wrongdoers and disruptive elements and of activities jeopardizing the communal peace is already engaging the unremitting attention of the Military Governor ably seconded by his colleague the Chief Civil Administration and we*

(Contd.)

Table 7.1: (*Contd.*)

Paragraph	*Final Report*	*Draft Report*
	engaging the attention of the Military Governor; therefore we need only emphasise the necessity of accelerating and supplementing these measures wherever necessary	*need only emphasize the necessity of not only no relaxation in the measures adopted by them but of supplementing them unhesitatingly whenever and wherever necessary.*
33	[vii] Not *without some hesitation, we are perhaps* overstepping our legitimate province *by touching on the subject of future administrative changes*. The fact that we have decided to take that risk is a measure of the importance that we attach to the *subject:-*	*Our next proposals are submitted* not without some hesitation as *might be considered to be* overstepping our legitimate province. But the fact that we have decided to take that risk is a measure of the importance that we attach to the *following further suggestions:-*
34	We have already drawn attention to the very real fear in the Muslim mind that a responsible Government in Hyderabad *implying* as it does, a government under the will of the Hindu majority, is likely to be little short *of disaster considering the* present strained relations of the two communities, *besides a cleavage in the Congress ranks. We are constrained to remark that the State Congress has failed to give an absolutely satisfactory account of itself during the period of trouble.*	We have already drawn attention to the very real fear in the Muslim mind that a responsible Government in Hyderabad state *meaning* as it does a government under the will of the Hindu majority is likely to be of little short of a *calamity—in view of the* strained relations between the communities in the present.
35	Therefore the time for any radical changes in the form of government does not appear to be propitious. We would respectfully suggest that their postponement for at least *some years to come*. For allied reasons, we would also suggest the inclusion of at least two *more* Muslims enjoying the confidence of their co-religionists,	The time, therefore, for any radical changes in the form of government *or in the administration* does not appear to be propitious. We would respectfully suggest that their postponement for at least *three years, if not more*. For allied reasons, we would also suggest the inclusion of at least two Muslims enjoying the confidence of their co-religionists,

(*Contd.*)

Table 7.1: (*Contd.*)

Paragraph	*Final Report*	*Draft Report*
	in the Administrative set up of the State at the highest level and in an effective capacity.	in the Administrative set up of the State at the highest level and in an effective capacity.
36	[viii] Whilst we realise the necessity of retaining and employing in the services only dependable personnel, we would still urge the advisability of caution in making such changes as might lend colour to the existence of anti-Muslim or anti-Hyderabadi bias in the minds of the authorities.	Whilst we realise the necessity of retaining and employing in the services only dependable personnel, we would still urge the advisability of caution in making such changes as might lend colour to the *alleged* existence of anti-Muslim or anti-Hyderabadi bias in the minds of the authorities.
37	[ix] Lastly, we would suggest that mercy should be allowed to temper justice to the fullest extent in the punishment of wrongdoers. We know that the Military Governor is setting suspected Razakars free and is favourably considering the release of all but the very worst and proved *lawbreakers*. *May* we *also* recommend that all those who publicly recant and repent should be pardoned with as few exemptions *as possible? In cases where the imposition of the extreme penalty of law is clearly justified, it may not be imposed. Such* humane acts of forbearance would remove suspicions, *win hearts and* complete the good work- so well begun - of establishing *permanent* peace and harmony between the communities.	Lastly, we would suggest that mercy should be allowed to temper justice to the fullest extent in the punishment of wrongdoers *more highly placed*. The Military Governor is setting suspected Razakars free and is favourably considering the release of all but the very worst and proved *wrongdoers*. We recommend that all those who publicly recant and repent should be pardoned a*nd even* in cases where the imposition of the extreme penalty of law is clearly justified it may *be replaced by a reprieve. These* humane acts of forbearance would remove *once and for all* suspicions *of vindictiveness or anti-Muslim bias and undue pressure on Muslims on part of the Indian Government and so* complete the good work- so well begun - of establishing *permanently further the establishment of communal* peace and harmony between the communities *which were in the previous regime literately flying at the throats of each other.*

(Contd.)

Table 7.1: (*Contd.*)

Paragraph	*Final Report*	*Draft Report*
38	*Before closing, we must gratefully acknowledge the valuable help and willing cooperation given us by the Military Administration in Hyderabad, by Government officials in the districts we visited, by public workers and prominent citizens and lastly by our two secretaries Messers Furruk Sayer and P. P. Ambulkar.*	

Note: All italicised parts in the draft and final reports presented in the table above suggest emphasis, either in original or added by the author.

Source: Constructed by the author from *Deccan Chronicle* 2013: 14–23, 1–11 (Final Report) and Draft Report.

As mentioned earlier in this essay, the Sundarlal Committee also prepared 'confidential notes', consisting of 14 pages, but without a date and an appendix. It is most likely that these notes were the basis for both the draft and the final report. It is interesting to note that the authors of these notes did not pay much attention to grammar or sentence construction. The following sections, not found in the reports, have been extracted. These are important eyewitness reports that bring to light the actual situation prevailing in the affected districts two-and-a-half months after the Indian army had taken control.

> Bold Arya Samajist's entered the State from outside. They asserted their freedom of speech and freedom of practice. Their poignant criticism of other faiths and especially of Islam aroused indignation in highest quarters. Learned Moulvis from other parts of India followed in the wake of the Arya Samajists. There were speeches and counter speeches. The Government had to curtail freedom of speech etc. Their Orders and Ordinances applied to all, but under the prevailing circumstances, naturally enough while Muslims could easily get permission for meetings and processions, the Hindus or Arya Samajists could not. Then followed the Arya Samajist Satyagraha of 1935. It was a fight for civil and religious liberty. Exaggerated, though by no means baseless, accounts of religious intolerance in Hyderabad were spread all over India. Somehow the Satyagraha ended.
>
> There was a section of the population that wanted to start a movement for responsible government on absolutely non-communal lines. Mahatma Gandhi deliberately kept them back, so that their movement may not get mixed up

with a communal movement then going on. Soon after, the State Congress movement for responsible government followed. Naturally, the Nizam tried to suppress it. Again the Hindus in the State were 85 per cent of the total population. Communal antagonism and distrust of each other prevailing in the rest of India could not leave Hyderabad unaffected.

The Muslims were afraid that responsible government in Hyderabad meant the rule of the majority that is the Hindu Raj. The Muslims generally opposed the State Congress movement. To exactly the same extent, the State Congress movement began, in practice, a communal aspect. Suppressed inside, they organised their centres in places within the Indian border outside the State, and from there attacked Octroi posts and Police Chowkis inside the State. The State Congress movement in Hyderabad was admittedly a violent movement. They used arms and ammunition, explosives and dynamite. The Secretary has admitted in his official report that as a result of the movement over 2000 of the enemy lost their lives. Violence spread communalism and communalism encouraged violence.

The Ittehad-ul-Musalmin which was originally a religious and social reform movement became a mainly political movement, its main objective being resisting the Hindu demand for democratic government. The Razakars were the military wing of the Ittehad-ul-Musalmin. Thus the sweet relation that existed between the two communities in the State gradually vanished and Hyderabad became one of the hotbeds of communal tension (*Deccan Chronicle* 2013: 28–29).

The main period of Razakar atrocities was between 15 August 1947 and the Indian Union Police Action of September 1948. Their atrocities chiefly consisted of levying monthly amounts on every town and village. Wherever these amounts were willingly paid, there was generally no further trouble. But at places, they were resisted. Loot followed. If there was no resistance during the loot, the trouble is generally ended in the removal of the looted property, sometimes in motor trucks. But whenever there was further resistance, arson, murder, desecration of temples and even the rape and abduction of women followed. The police and administration manned mostly by Muslims either connived at these atrocities or willingly cooperated with the Razakars in all of these lawless activities because they believe that the Razakars alone could save them from the Hindu Raj and as such had the support of the Nizam's government. A few officials who thought otherwise found themselves helpless. The accounts of these atrocities appear in a section of the Indian and Foreign Press in an exaggerated form. Side by side with the Razakars openly lawless activities, the new movement was started by the Muslims, which gained momentum rapidly. It consisted of systematised efforts to induce Muslims from the neighbouring Indian Provinces to migrate to the State and settle there so that in the course of time, the small Muslim minority might be converted–if not into a majority–at least into a formidable minority. Hundreds of thousands of Muslims were thus inveigled into Hyderabad, and some of them are still there (*Deccan Chronicle* 2013: 30).

Then came the Police Action. Thousands of Hindus who had in the regime immediately preceding left their hearth and homes either on account of Razakar atrocities or through sheer panic and had taken refuge in the adjoining Indian Territories came back to their homes in the State, as soon as they heard of the achievements of the Indian Army. Thousands of others who had continued to live inside the state but had all along been feeling the weight of the Razakar regime welcomed the Indian Army as their saviours and heaved a sigh of relief. Both these sections of the Hindu populace were more or less saturated with communal venom. Many of them had actually suffered at the hands of the Razakars and their supporters, the Nizam administration.

The settled and declared policy of the Indian Government was the establishment of peace and the suppression of all lawlessness. Many officers and men acted up to it. Yet there were many others who are allowed their suppressed communal feelings full play. We are also informed that a number of trained and armed men belonging to a well-known Hindu communal organisation filtered into the State along with the Indian Army from Sholapur and other towns on this side of the border. The Muslim population naturally felt panicky at the advent of the Indian Army (*Deccan Chronicle* 2013: 31).

In connection with this killing, we might just mention a few more facts. It appears that as the Muslim population fled in panic towards the headquarters of the state or towards other villages which they thought might be safer, a very large number was killed on the way and in the jungles. In many places, we were shown wells or *bawaris* still full of corpses which were rotting. In one such, we counted 11 bodies which included that of a woman with a small child sticking to her breast. In another, we saw that earth had been thrown over the bodies thrown into the well, and absolutely incontrovertible evidence of the horror that had been committed was scattered all around. We saw several more such wells. We saw remnants of corpses lying in ditches. At several places, the bodies had been burnt, and we would see the charred bones and skulls still lying there. At these spots, we also heard the statements accompanied with weeping and crying of widows and destitute women and children in whose presence the male members of their families had been thus killed and burnt. We tried to console them by telling them that the responsibility for all their misfortunes lay on the shoulders of those of their co-religionists who had established a reign of terror for the Hindus and assuring them that the new government wanted all Hindus and Muslims to live once more in peace like good neighbours and brothers (*Deccan Chronicle* 2013: 34–35).

At most places arson was also the order of the day. Crimes against women were by no means uncommon. We have it again on incontrovertible evidence that many women threw themselves into wells to save their honour. Sometimes they first threw their children and jumped in themselves.

> Many women were forcibly taken away from their homes, kept for a number of days and then sent back to their homes. This happened in every district that we visited. We were also informed that a few Muslim women were still in the houses of Hindus. As also at several places Muslim property, Muslim houses and Muslims were still in illegal possession of the Hindus. But we must hasten to state that by far the largest portion of such immovable property and such women, though not of movable property, have been returned to the Muslims.
>
> As for forcible conversions this too was a universal factor almost everywhere we went. After the adult males of a locality had been killed, the women and children were generally 'persuaded' to adopt the Hindu faith. We came across hundreds of Muslim women who had been forcibly tattooed on their forehead right in the orthodox Hindu style as a mark of their conversion. Some had even that new Hindu names tattooed on their forearms. We saw children whose ears had been freshly bored in the Hindu style. Beards had been shaved off, and *chotties* kept. We saw the sacred thread hanging around the necks of Muslims. We were told at several places that a certain 'Mantri ji' had gone about from place to place converting such helpless women and children into Hinduism and distributing the sacred thread etc. Here also we must add that with the exception of a small number of Muslim women still in Hindu homes all such forcible conversions have become null and void in practice.
>
> In one important town, we were pained to notice that a prominent Arya Samajist took the law into his own hands. He converted the local Arya Samaj Mandir into a sub-jail. Arrested on his own authority Muslims from his own and adjoining villages, kept them for 4 or 5 days in a sub-jail and then either released them on getting some money from them or handed them over to the police as Razakars. This went on for about a month. When the Arya Samaj building proved insufficient for the purpose, another building in the vicinity was also availed off. We visited both these buildings and made enquiries on the spot. At some places, we were informed that the victims were removed to some adjoining temple and then finished off in the sacred precincts (*Deccan Chronicle* 2013: 35–37).

It is clear from reading the reports as well as the 'confidential notes' that the Committee had neglected several points while preparing their final report. First, the account of the run-up from 1930 onwards up to the crisis of 1948, including the political activities of the Arya Samaj, State Congress, Ittehad-ul-Musalmin and Razakars, was worth taking into account in the record.

Second, the activities of the Arya Samaj movement have been totally left out of the report, except for a reference to a 'well-known Hindu communal organisation'. It seems clear that the Arya Samajists played a significant and devastating role in the atrocities committed against Muslims after Police Action. The fact that the Arya Samaj was dominant in the Marathwada districts, which bore the brunt of atrocities against Muslims, is also a significant omission by the Committee, although it does hint at the connection. The four Marathwada districts and the three Karnatik districts were allotted to the share of the Nizam by the British after their final allied victory over the Maratha Confederacy and Tippu, respectively. They do not constitute the core of Hyderabad state, which consists of the 10 Telangana districts. Third, the report does not mention the eyewitness description of the corpses or any other evidence of massacre, or even the description of the evidence given to them by the families of the murdered Muslims or by other people.

Fourth, the complicity of the state Congress Party in acts of violence and terror in the run-up to the Police Action, and the provocations they initiated are well described in the 'confidential notes', but are not accounted for in the report. The share-out of the loot and extractions from Muslims, which were distributed amongn the perpetrators, police and the Congress Party, have been left out of the account. Fifth, it can also be inferred from the 'confidential notes' and other evidence elsewhere that the state Congress Party had Arya Samajist members, apart from non-violent and secular Congressmen. This meant that the party most likely to govern Hyderabad was riven by significant division, which may have made it difficult for the national leadership to rely on the objectivity of the state Congress in governing Hyderabad. This probably explains, but does not excuse the recommendation of the Committee to defer popular rule and administration in Hyderabad. On the whole, the analysis of the Sundarlal Committee draft and final report, along with its 'confidential notes' illustrates how inquiry committees often reveal or do not reveal the evidence, data and impressions that they collected in their inquiry. It is a point well worth keeping in mind when considering the reports of other committees in the past, present and future.

References

Deccan Chronicle. 2013. *Exclusive Sundarlal Report on Hyderabad Police Action*, 30 November 2013, Updated on 18 March 2019. Available at https://www.deccanchronicle.com/131129/news-current-affairs/article/exclusive-sundarlal-report-police-action.

Noorani, A. G. 2013. *The Destruction of Hyderabad*. New Delhi: Tulika Books.

Supreme Court of India, 'Sarwarlal and Others vs The State of Hyderabad', 1960 AIR 862, 1960 SCR [3] 311, 16 March 1960. Available at https://indiankanoon.org/doc/618203/.

8

Mulki Riots

The Historical Background

The Muslim conquerors of India were an assorted sort. Their motives were greed and lust, which was legitimised by the religious direction to conquer the world and convert all its inhabitants to Islam. While the first motive was intended to satisfy their impulsive pleasures, the religious sanction justified the terror, brutality, murder and enslavement, or the conversion of a non-Muslim population. In this dangerous venture, small groups of invaders risked their lives in order to conquer an alien population. In case of their death in the Holy War, their religion guaranteed [*sic.*] them a heavenly paradise beyond the dreams of any earthly experience. These two elements–greed and religion–allowed for cooperation and collaboration of Muslims belonging to all races, sects, language and culture. Thus, it incorporated those converted to Islam either voluntarily or by force. Purchased slaves and captured young children soon became incorporated in the *Umma*. This movement, in its initial drive, was powerful and unstoppable. But conquest was one thing and governance yet another.

When it came to governance, the Muslim ruling elite tended to fall apart, as the divisions of race, language, culture and birth surfaced and manifested in the creation of factions. The Muslim rulers played one faction against the other in order to maintain control of the whole. This divide-and-rule policy did not work all the time, and most of the times it worked to the the detriment of the ruler himself, who was either

---

* This chapter takes a unique approach towards the Sundarlal Report and Justice Pingle Jaganmohan Reddy's reports, citing them in the original without any paraphrasing. These reports have been missing for six decades, and the author feels that altering the language or changing them in any way would raise questions of interpretation. The decision to retain the original voices verbatim are to preserve authenticity and uniqueness.

assassinated or dethroned by one faction or the other supporting a rival claimant to the throne.

Divisions based on race (Arab, Persian, Turk, Mongol, Turkmen, Uzbek, Tajik, Abyssinian, African, etc.), sect (Sunni, Shia or Sufi), language (Arabic, Turkic, Persian, Dakhani, etc.), religion (by virtue of birth, conversion or enslavement), were too much to be united by Islam. These fissures manifested themselves when it came to the allocation of loot, slaves, honours, posts, estates and power by the ruler.

In the case of the Bahmani ruling establishment, while the rulers seem to be of Turkish origin, their elite was composed of Turk, Persian and Arab immigrants. But as the influx of immigration continued, the rift between native-born or converted elements (Dakhani and foreign-born (*Afaqi*) made it difficult to achieve long-run stability, and resulted in massacres, coups and rebellion. The Bahmani tradition continued in its successors—the five Deccan Sultanates—and continued into the modern phase of the Nizam's rule over Hyderabad. The Nizam complicated matters further by importing not only Muslims, but also Hindus from northern India, and granting them honours, posts and estates. Leonard (2014) sets the context of the late Nizam state and the divisions in the elite between Mulki [that is, native] and non-Mulki (2014: 46–89). This division, based on origin by birth, continued to plague Hyderabad even after Independence. Also, even the linguistic state of Andhra Pradesh was affected, and was troubled by this issue, which was not resolved till the creation of a separate Telangana state.

Crisis in Hyderabad

With the takeover of Hyderabad by the Indian Army in 1948, the first set of moves resulted in the demobilisation of the Hyderabad state army, consisting of 24,000 personnel and the sacking of about 15,000 Muslim bureaucrats and officials. The Nizam's government abolished the *jagirs* and *zamindaris* in 1950, and nominal compensation in bonds and periodic cash installments was paid to those who lost their primary income as well as status. This radical change affected both Muslim and Hindu *jagirdars*. The Hyderabad Tenancy and Agricultural Lands Act arbitrarily conveyed property rights to tenant farmers, and dispossessed the entire upper section of the Muslim and Hindu landed aristocracy and feudal families, who had been the main bulwark and support of the Nizamate.

The Pandit Sundarlal report gives us a picture of the immediate situation in late 1948. The Pandit Sundarlal Committee was asked by the

Indian government to go on a goodwill visit to the riot-affected areas of Hyderabad, with a mandate to help to restore better communal relations. Strangely, neither was this Committee's report published, nor was it made available either to the public or the Parliament. The report was discovered in Pandit Sundarlal's private papers in the Nehru Memorial Library.[1] The findings are the first estimates of the massacres, which followed the takeover of the state by the Indian Army:

> Hyderabad state has 16 districts, comprising of nearly than 22,000 villages. Out of them, only three districts remained practically, though not wholly free, of communal trouble which affected the state first during the militant activities of the Razakars and then during the reprisals that followed the collapse of that organisation. In another four districts the trouble had been more severe but nothing like the havoc that overtook the remaining eight.
>
> Out of these again, the worst sufferers have been the districts of Osmanabad, Gulbarga, Bidar and Nanded in which the number of people killed in the disturbances during and after Police Action, was not much less, if not more, than 18,000. In the other four districts, of Aurangabad, Bir, Nalgonda and Medak those who lost their lives numbered at least 5 thousand. We can say at a very conservative estimate that in the whole state at least 27 to 40 thousand people lost their lives during and after Police Action ...
>
> It is a very significant fact that out of these eight, the four worst affected districts [Osmanbad, Gulbarga, Bidar and Nander] had been the main strongholds of the Razakars and the people of these four districts had been the worst sufferers at the hands of the Razakars (*Deccan Chronicle* 2013: 15).

The Report goes on to give further details:

> Almost everywhere in the affected areas of the State, communal frenzy did not exhaust itself in murder alone in which at some places even women and children were not spared.
>
> Rape, abductions of women [sometimes out of the State to Indian towns such as Sholapur and Nagpur], loot, arson, desecration of mosques, forcible conversions, seizure of houses and lands followed or accompanied the killings.
>
> Tens of crores worth of property were looted or destroyed. The sufferers were Muslims who formed a hopeless minority in rural areas (ibid.: 16).

It also describes the general attitude of Muslims at that time:

> This communal trouble followed close on the heels of the Police Action and the consequent collapse of the Razakars organization which had stood, in the Muslim mind, had stood as an effective barrier against the establishment of

> responsible government which was synonymous to the average Hyderabadi Muslim with Hindu Raj, because it would be based on the will of the Hindu majority.
>
> The Muslim masses generally were slow to realise that their sufferings were the inevitable repercussions to the atrocities committed on the Hindus only, a few days before, by the Razakars. The Razakar movement had the sympathy of a good number of Muslimans in Hyderabad. Such of them as dared to publicly oppose or even criticise the Razakar activities paid heavily for their temerity, so much so that one of them fell before the bullet of an assassin (ibid.: 18).

This general political collapse of 600 years of Muslim rule in Hyderabad state was accompanied by the collapse of the Muslim ruling elite:

> Doubts and suspicions in the minds of the literate Muslims were aggravated by yet another factor, namely the complaints of those who were in State service before Police Action and who had lost their jobs. We have received a long list of names of persons dismissed, degraded suspended or otherwise penalised in various departments (ibid.: 19–20).

While it is also clear that much of the atrocities in the form of massacres seem to have been concentrated in the Marathwada districts of Hyderabad, the memory of those massacres was clearly visible within the Muslim population of Telangana, especially in the Muslim population concentrated in the Old City of Hyderabad. Many factors were involved in this: first, the immediate effects of Indian Army's intervention; second, the resolution of that year's war between India and Pakistan over the accession of Kashmir to India; third, the idea of Pakistan as a bulwark of Muslims in the subcontinent, including India; fourth, the massacre of many tens of thousands of fellow Muslims in the eastern districts in the wake of the invading Indian Army; fifth the removal of 15,000 Muslim officials; sixth, the demobilisation of the 24,000 Hyderabad state force manned, as of 1941, by Muslims (55 per cent) and led by 1,268 Muslims officers in a total officer corps of 1,765. Combined with all these factors was the general realisation among Muslim that the 600 years of Muslim rule over Telangana and its Hindus had ended ignominiously, and their king, the richest man in the world, had humiliated himself before the new rulers of India. All of these were traumatic experiences for Muslims in Telangana. This angst was waiting for release, which came with the Mulki riots.

The Mulki Riots of 1952 loom large in Telangana's collective memory. No one knows till today what the whole affair was really about. This ignorance is because the critical 'Mulki Riots Report' has been missing from official archives, even though it was placed before the Hyderabad state Legislative Assembly. I eventually found this Report in the University of Wisconsin Library in the US. Justice Pingle Jaganmohan Reddy, then the junior-most judge of the Hyderabad High Court, was appointed to carry out the Inquiry. The Mulki Riots Report is well-worth a close reading for those interested in the factual position.

After the takeover of Hyderabad by the Indian Army, the state was under military rule. The Indian Army first dismantled the terroristic Razakar force and then eliminated the armed insurgency initiated by the Communist Party of India (CPI). The demobilisation of the Hyderabad state army meant that an estimated 24,000 officers and men (mostly Muslims) lost their jobs. Nearly 15,000 Muslim officials were dismissed from the official establishment of the Nizam's government. Instead, the Indian government sent its own officers on deputation from outside the state. Justice Reddy writes in his work, *The Judiciary I Served:*

> These disturbances arose out of the growing frustration of Hyderabad consequent on the wholesale import of officers and staff from the neighbouring states namely; the composite states of Madras and Bombay, and other states like Madhya Pradesh and Uttar Pradesh etc. The behaviour of the personnel from Madras [including the Andhra region] was the worst. The Chief Minister of Madras in order to get rid of those found to be not up to the mark either in efficiency or integrity or in the manner of their behaviour took the opportunity to send them to Hyderabad. In contrast, the states other than Madras chose and sent their best personnel. These officials did not cause any trouble, but those from composite Madras did. The people of Hyderabad were used to being dealt with in a decent and cultured manner by those exercising power (Reddy 2014: 59).

C. Rajagopalcahri, the clever fox that he was, seems to have anticipated the Andhra-Telangana merger, and therefore, sent his undesirable Telugu officials from the Tamil region to Hyderabad.

During the four years of the Indian government's indirect rule (1948–52), Telangana experienced the bad behaviour of the imported officials, the lack of new employment opportunities for locals, the dismay of Muslims over the collapse of minority rule, and the general loss of enthusiasm for the 'liberators' of Hyderabad from the majority Hindu population. This was made worse when the promised democratic elections were delayed and held only in 1952, when the Congress government of Ramakrishna Rao came into office.

Many questions were asked in the Hyderabad Legislative Assembly about non-Mulkis, especially Sindhis and Punjabi refugees, who were employed in government service; other questions were related to the repatriation of deputed officers back to their home states. The Chief Minister replied to such queries thus:

> A large number of policemen were recruited to the Police department from among non-Mulkis .... [where] a little over three thousand [3,111] persons have been recruited from Madras Province .... Most of the Tahsildars and Deputy Civil Administrators who came from outside were repatriated, and a good portion of police forces had also had been reptriated (Reddy 1952: 21).

As Justice Reddy states,

> For two years before Police Action, i.e., from 1946 onward till September 1948 there had been a great deal of employment of non-Mulki Muslims in an acute form particularly in the Police and Army of Hyderabad. After the Police Action as a consequence of the new set up that followed in its wake a good many Muslims were thrown out of employment ... (ibid.: 19).

Every government needs to ensure the police are 'their' men: first, the non-Mulki Muslims were employed under the Nizam, and then the non-Mulki Andhras under the Military/Civil Administration. By 1952, the Military government had ended, and the first General Elections under the adult franchise had brought in a democratic government under the new Constitution. The democratic government was staffed with inexperienced politicians from the three distinct regions of Hyderabad state, all pulling in different directions. Naturally, the situation came to a head and resulted in a crisis.

The Crisis Begins

A student agitation in Warangal triggered the Mulki Agitation. About this, Justice Reddy wrote in his Mulki Riots Report:

> The causes of the Warangal strike appear to me, from the evidence, to have originated in a wholesale transfer of about 180 teachers by Mr Parthasarathy, the Divisional Inspector of Schools and a dispute between him and Mr Hygrivachari, Secretary of the local District Congress Committee with respect to the said transfers. It is unfortunate that this dispute between two individuals over the alleged transfer of teachers and disciplinary action against

> some of them by Mr Parthasarathy should have had such unwholesome and tragic consequences (Reddy 1952: 17).

He continues thus:

> In the propaganda started against Mr Parthasarathy, I have no doubt that Mr. Hygrivachari and eight or nine teachers had a hand and were responsible for the feelings created against him. I have equally no doubt that Shri Parthasarathy was engaged in counter propaganda against Mr Hygrivachari and the eight teachers with the net result that the students of Warangal were completely worked up by this propaganda and counter- propaganda. Mr Hygrivachari denied his having used the teachers in the Municipal Elections, but Mr Satyanarayanamurti, whom he admits having seen regarding the promotion of the two teachers, in a letter to Mr Parthasarathy, has clearly stated that Mr Hygrivachari, accompanied by two persons viz., Venkatnarayana and Venkateswarlu, had come to see him and wanted him to speak to Mr Parthasarathy to promote these two teachers who had helped him in the recent Municipal Elections. I am not prepared to accept the version of Mr Hygrivachari when he says that it is only because Mr Parthasarathy told him to give instances of seniors being superseded by juniors that he sent Exhibit 92 [letter] and later sent word through Mr Satyanarayanamurti about the two teachers who according to him were senior and whose claims were overlooked. There is nothing in Exhibit 92 to convey that meaning. On the other hand, it is quite clear that Mr Hygrivachari wanted some favour to be done for these two people who were certainly neither qualified nor seniors, for being given a higher grade (ibid.: 26).

He further states:

> It is a matter of regret that persons well placed in political organisations such as Mr Hygrivachari should attempt to interfere in the day-to-day administration of Government and to bring undue political pressure upon persons in the employment of the Government in a manner calculated to demoralise the services. Such an attitude would encourage Government servants also to approach well-placed leaders of the ruling party to bestow favors or to grant some benefits to them, thereby directly encouraging and creating indiscipline in the services which must at all costs be kept free from political influence, if democracy is to function in our country (ibid.: 27).

This type of behaviour is, of course, now the standard operating procedure of the education, and all other departments, and their effects are as predicted, and worse than anticipated.

The immediate cause, however, was a petty, unscrupulous and failed attempt at manipulation of the promotion of two undeserving teachers who had assisted the leading light of the Congress Party in the Warangal Municipal Election. *This issue, then, was the beginning of the Mulki Agitation, which spread to Hyderabad and other places.* Oddly, the non-Telangana districts were unaffected. Mobs of 20,000–40,000 people, the mass of whom were clearly not students, gathered in the Old City on the banks of the Musi and rioted. The police, with a total force of only 4000 for the city, was short of men needed to handle the situation. It exercised restraint as the do-goody politicians were trying to negotiate with the mob. When the politicians gave up, the mob let loose, and the police opened fire, which resulted in the deaths of eight persons in Hyderabad; but none of them was a student. Justice Reddy concluded in the aftermath of the event:

> Lastly I should like to say that, from the evidence of the incidents both on the 3rd and 4th of September 1952, though the students had taken the initiative into forming themselves into unlawful assemblies and processions, they happily dissociated themselves at the crucial time when violent acts of arson and pelting of stones were being indulged in, necessitating the dispersal by use of firearms ...

He further stated:

> These facts show clearly that the crowd of anti-social and goonda elements in the City of Hyderabad had taken over control, and there is also evidence that some anti-national forces were also involved as evidenced by the shouting of the crowd that 'Pakistan was moving forward' and 'Hindustan was retreating' (Reddy 1952: 86).

What started as a petty political manoeuvre, quickly transformed into the Mulki Movement, and further deteriorated into an anti-social and anti-national riot, which expressed the frustration of the lower orders of the Muslim minority. The failure of the Ramakrishna Rao government to handle this and other issues indicated to national political leadership the weakness of the Hyderabad state administration, which they themselves had so deliberately undermined by the wholesale dismissal of an age-old ruling elite without its replacement by a locally-born and well-trained alternative. Such was the politics of Hyderabad city and Telangana.

The Political Issues

The Mulki agitation during the Nizam's rule had targeted Muslim non-Mulkis who were recruited from outside the state to reinforce the ruling

Muslim elite. Mostly it was a Muslim–Muslim affair, with a Shia–Sunni subtext. After the mass removal of the Muslim officials after Police Action, the government of India had deputed officials from other states to administer Hyderabad state. This deputation was to be temporary, and repatriation was intended. As Justice Reddy pointed out in the Mulki Riots Report:

> It is evident from these statements that the repatriation of non-Mulkis in Government service had already commenced even before the popular Government took over after the General Election, on 7th March 1952. After the installation of the popular Government, the policy of repatriation has been continued. It is also evident that in the State Assembly, the question of employment of non-Mulkis in the Government services were also the subject matter of interpellations.... I am satisfied that while this general feeling was present in the background among the educated classes, it *was not intense or critical*, particularly after questions in the Assembly when the whole matter was thrashed out and necessary information placed before the public, *as to cause a spontaneous strike* among the Warangal students as is alleged to have been the case (Reddy 1952: 22).

What was the role of the People's Democratic Front (PDF), the official Opposition in the Assembly? (The PDF was a front for the CPI, which had been banned for its armed warfare against the state). The Warangal strike was entirely due to the machinations of Hygrivachari, the rising star of the Congress Party. The strikes went on intermittently from 26 July till 22 August, when the Chief Minister visited Warangal and spoke to the strike leaders. They asked for the formation of a Cabinet Sub-Committee to investigate the Mulki issue. On 26 August, he announced the formation of this Cabinet Sub-Committee. This announcement failed to end the strike, which had by then taken a life of its own. As Justice Reddy remarked:

> These facts clearly show that the strike towards the end of August was organised on All-Telangana basis.... If the demand of the students was only for the appointment of a Sub-Committee that Sub-Committee was appointed by 26th and, after that, there was no purpose in the continuation of the strike for so many days even after taking into consideration the cane-charge of the police on 28th August in Warangal (Reddy 1952: 31).

On 29 and 30 August, the strike spread to Hyderabad city, starting in the Abids and Saifabad areas, and moving towards the Old City, where it received support from tens of thousands of the Old City masses and the *madrasa* students. In the Abids/Saifabad areas, the police had been quiet and meekly followed the students as they broke into schools and damaged property. By the time the action shifted to the Old City, the matter had become acute and tense. The Police Commissioner was attacked and had to be rescued, police *thanas* (police stations) and buses were burnt, and rescuing fire trucks were damaged. The Chief Minister's parked car was also burnt in Sultan Bazaar, having brought the CM's wife to a public meeting, which was also disrupted.

The police opened fire on 3 September, killing Mohamed Kassim, factory-worker aged 22 years; Shaik Mahboob, a rickshaw-puller aged 30 years, Jamaluddin, private servant aged 40 years, and Ramulu, private employee, aged 18 years. One of them, Shaik Mahboob, was killed while he was burning a bus. None of the casualties were students.

A public meeting in Fateh Maidan was called the next day to plan the next moves. At this point, the Chief Minister swung into action and summoned the Leader of the Opposition, V. K. Deshpande (PDF Member of Legislative Assembly [MLA]), and V. K. Dhage. The Chief Minister informed them of the events to the extent he knew, and asked them to attend the meeting and state that the government would hold a judicial inquiry into the firings. At the meeting, however, Deshpande did not disclose the imminent judicial inquiry already decided by the Chief Minister. Instead, he demanded a judicial inquiry on behalf of the PDF; others echoed the demand.

While the Chief Minister told them that only two individuals, neither of whom was a student, were killed, Deshpande declared that eight people had been shot dead, while the CM informed him that only six were injured. It was clear that the Leader of the Opposition was lying, as Dhage confirmed the Chief Minister's statement, and the Chief Minister himself stated the same in the witness box. Neither did Deshpande appear before the Commission on the plea of ill health, nor did he allow himself to be examined at home. Wise move! Justice Reddy quotes Konda Laxman, the Congress MLA from Asifabad:

> The people of Hyderabad even now do not want all the non-Mulkis to go back. They want some of the police, and some of the civilians should go back because they were treating the local people badly and were behaving with an air of superiority and were indulging in malpractices and that he had spoken on this question in the Assembly also (Reddy 1952: 21).

Therefore, as evident, the ruling Congress Party was speaking in different voices. The main opposition, the CPI, also took different stands. The CPI issued a pamphlet which said: 'The students were committing acts of violence upon the petty Government servants who have come to earn their live-hood from Andhradesa ...' It demanded that the police take action to prevent this anarchy! It also specified that the student strike was being 'encouraged to oppose the united agitation for the establishment of Vishalandhra' (Reddy 1952: 29). This was only to be expected from a party with its top leadership based in Vijayawada and staffed by Andhras! However, another stand was taken by Maqdoom Mohiuddin, a CPI Leader based in Hyderabad, who made a speech on 10 August 1952, in which he stated:

> As was before, the Government is recruiting Panjabis and thereby marring the chances of Hyderabadis .... Sindhis and Punjabis are enemies of each other [*sic.*] .... Brothers, your slogan demanding Punjabis to go back is justified.... Not only Punjabis but all other outside officers imported into the State should go back. The people of UP, Bengal, Madras and Punjab who are holding high posts here want to recruit candidates of their own provinces in Government offices here ... (Reddy 1952: 29–30).

His primary target seems to have been Panjabi and Sindhi refugees from Pakistan who were looking for a livelihood.

The events of 4 September unfolded, and despite all the negotiation by people like Dr Jaisoorya (PDF MLA) and Padmaja Naidu (both children of Sarojini Naidu), and repeated police caning and even firing, the mob went on a rampage.

The Mulki Riots Report indicates the degree of immaturity and inefficiency of the Chief Minister and his administration, and the culpability of the Leader of the Opposition. The situation was rapidly transformed from a petty quarrel about teachers promotions and transfers, to a Telangana-wide Mulki Agitation, and then, finally into a confrontation by a 20,000–40,000 people forming a mob of of Old City *goondas* and rowdies. The mystery is that the agitation did not affect the Marathwada and Kannada regions of Hyderabad, but only of Telangana. Were the people of Telangana more aware, or more immature?

Note

1. The facsimile of the final report, and also the draft, are available on the internet (Deccan Chronicle 2013).

References

Deccan Chronicle. 2013. *Exclusive Sundarlal Report on Hyderabad Police Action*, 30 November 2013, Updated on 18 March 2019. Available at https://www.deccanchronicle.com/131129/news-current-affairs/article/exclusive-sundarlal-report-police-action.

Leonard, Karen. 2014. *Hyderabad and the Hyderabadis*. New Delhi: Manohar Books.

Reddy, Pingle Jaganmohan. 1952. *Inquiry Relating to the Firing in the City of Hyderabad on 3rd and 4th September 1952*. Hyderabad; Government of Hyderabad.

——. 2014. *The Judiciary I served*. Hyderabad: Orient BlackSwan.

Noorani, A. G. 2013. *The Destruction of Hyderabad*. New Delhi: Tulika Books.

9
Hindu–Muslim Household Income Comparisons

There has been a trend in India of dealing with per capita estimates of expenditure, calorie intake, and other indicators of welfare. This use of per capita estimates followed the approach of the international community. However, most Indian data is based on household surveys by individual researchers, the National Sample Survey Organisation (NSSO) and similar institutions. The household data is then converted into per capita terms and used as indicators of poverty, nutrition and well-being. This conversion poses specific methodological issues, which have not been recognised by the policymakers, although they are evident. Taking per capita figures into consideration is to assume that there are no differences between members of the household, whether it is gender differences, the presence of children, or old and working members. In the joint family system in India and elsewhere, this is not true. The joint family households fortunately compensate and cooperate among their members. It is in this context that this essay examines the data on Hindu-Muslim incomes.

Expenditure Profile of Muslim and Hindu Households

The status of minorities in India has always been an important subject. Keeping track of their progress is no easy task. The 'High-Level Committee Report on Social, Economic and Educational Status of the Muslim Community of India' (Sachar 2006; henceforth referred to as the 'Sachar Committee Report') was the first comprehensive attempt at this task. Not only did it present data about Muslims, but it also provided comparative data on the Hindu majority. It generated widespread interest both in the academic and political, and among civil society. It stimulated policy initiatives by the Union and state governments. This essay aims at analysing the relative economic status of Hindu and Muslim households, as indicated in the Sachar Report, which used raw data from the sixty-first NSSO Round (NSSO 2004–05; 2007). We shall also present the data gathered from surveys of 42 Minority Concentration Districts, the Post-Sachar Commission Report, and the comprehensive and methodologically sound Sudhir Commission survey of Telangana Muslims.

Data Issues

Sachar used data in a collateral manner, that is, derived from NSSO data sets that were not intended to address the Hindu/Muslim differentials *per se*. As such, the sampling process, which was geared towards generating a representative sample of the entire population, will not yield a correct statistical representation of the Muslim population. The NSSO itself cautions us against this:

> We would like to sound a note of caution at the outset that reported religion of household was a by-product of a general household sample survey aimed at estimating salient characteristics of employment and unemployment of the general population and was not specifically designed for collecting information on economic conditions of specific religious communities (NSSO 2007: 3).

Sachar provides the All-India Monthly Per Capita Expenditure (MPCE)[1] averages for Muslims and Hindus by dividing the household data by the number of family members in the household (NSSO: 2007; Sachar 2006: 212). The consequence is that the size of the family critically determines the MPCE estimates.

Hindu populations have a much more significant proportion of Scheduled Castes (SCs) and Scheduled Tribes (STs) than the Muslim population, while Muslims have twice the proportion of 'Other' Castes (presumably upper castes) than Hindus. This differential will affect the expenditure averages for both All-Hindu data (downwards) and All-Muslim data (upwards). Both Hindus and Muslims have a similar proportion of Backward Castes (BCs), and therefore, this sub-group may not have a distorting element in the overall comparative estimates (see Table 9.1). Here we will use the Sachar data relevant to the All-Hindu category, including all Hindu social groups, and compare it to the All-Muslim category, including all Muslim social groups, undifferentiated by any factor other than their religious affiliation.

Table 9.1: All-India Religious Population by Caste Categories

Religion	*SCs*	*STs*	*BCs*	*Others*	*All*
Hindu	22.2	9.1	42.8	26	100
Muslim	0.8	0.5	39.2	59.5	100
Christian	9	32.8	24.8	33.3	100
Sikhs	30.7	0.9	22.4	46.1	100
Buddhists	89.5	7.4	0.4	2.7	100
Jains		2.6	3	94.3	100
Zoroastrians		15.9	13.7	70.4	100
Others	2.6	82.5	6.2	8.7	100
Total	19.7	8.5	41.1	30.8	100

Source: Sachar 2006: 7.

Results: Rural Data (Table 9.2)

When we examine data from rural areas across different states, the ratio of annual household expenditure of Muslims and Hindus can be seen as not significantly different. Apart from three states, West Bengal, Assam and Haryana, in all other states, Muslim household expenditure in rural areas is above 90 per cent of Hindu household expenditure. The lowest ratio is for Haryana, where rural Muslim expenditure is only 66 per cent of Hindu rural expenditure. The case of Delhi's rural Muslims, who have 166 per cent of Hindu expenditures, is extreme; but this estimate is based on a sample size of only two households having one member each.

Results: Urban Data (Table 9.3)

Muslim/Hindu ratios for annual household expenditure in urban areas provide the lowest ratio, at 52 per cent for Himachal Pradesh, with Punjab at 61 per cent, the second-lowest. All the others are above 70 per cent. In eight states, Muslim urban household expenditure is more than 90 per cent of Hindu urban household expenditure. However, Muslim household expenditure relative to Hindu ones tends to be lower in urban areas in many states. If anything, the problem of disparities between the two religious communities is in urban, and *not* in rural areas (emphasis added).

Table 9.2: Rural Annual Household Expenditure in Rupees

	Hindu			*Muslim*			*Muslim/Hindu (in Per cent)*	
	MPCE	*Household Size*	*Household expenditure*	MPCE	*Household Size*	*Household expenditure*	*Household expenditure*	MPCE
All-India	568	4.9	33705	553	5.6	37051	110	97
West Bengal	610	4.7	34586	501	5.2	31146	90	82
Kerala	970	4.1	47549	968	5.3	61082	128	100
Uttar Pradesh	544	6	38951	509	6.3	38337	98	94
Bihar	448	5.4	29155	426	5.4	27570	95	95
Assam	615	4.9	36446	511	5.6	34045	93	83
Jammu & Kashmir	840	5	50706	776	6.1	57046	113	92
Jharkhand	448	5.2	27728	423	5.8	29276	106	94
Karnataka	526	4.7	29860	532	5.1	32398	108	101
Uttaranchal	652	5	38787	600	5.9	42336	109	92
Delhi	1023	4.4	53963	1696	1	20352	38	166
Maharashtra	603	4.8	35011	576	5.5	38360	110	96
Andhra Pradesh	604	4	29307	610	4.5	33258	113	101

(*Contd*)

Table 9.2: (*Contd*)

	Hindu			*Muslim*			*Muslim/Hindu (in Per cent)*	
	MPCE	*Household Size*	*Household expenditure*	MPCE	*Household Size*	*Household expenditure*	*Household expenditure*	MPCE
Gujarat	644	5	38272	668	5.5	44453	116	104
Rajasthan	593	5.6	39819	611	6.3	46436	117	103
Madhya Pradesh	458	5.5	30175	475	5.9	33368	111	104
Haryana	913	5.4	59700	605	6.8	49285	83	66
Tamil Nadu	597	3.8	27561	724	4.1	35981	131	121
Orissa	424	4.9	24811	447	6.3	33628	136	105
Himachal Pradesh	834	4.8	47640	798	6.3	60561	127	96
Chattisgarh	445	5.3	28401	473	5.9	33677	119	106
Punjab	852	5	51423	777	5.7	53075	103	91

Sources: NSSO 2007: 36–37; Sachar 2006: 364.

Table 9.3: Urban Annual Household Expenditure in Rupees

	Hindus			*Muslims*			*Muslim/Hindu (in Per cent)*	
States	MPCE	*Household Size*	*Household expenditure*	MPCE	*Household Size*	*Household expenditure*	*Household expenditure*	MPCE
All-India	1139	4.4	59575	804	5.4	51832	87	71
West Bengal	1214	4.1	59908	748	4.7	41865	70	62
Kerala	1363	4.4	71214	1081	5.3	68139	96	79
Uttar Pradesh	976	5.2	60439	662	6.2	49285	82	68
Bihar	768	5.1	46961	559	5.7	38273	81	73
Assam	1113	4.2	55748	1199	4.9	70366	126	108
J &K	1323	4.5	71423	991	5.2	61615	86	75
Jharkhand	1038	4.8	59801	727	5.5	48102	80	70
Karnataka	1201	4.1	58412	837	5.2	52668	90	70
Uttaranchal	1033	4.6	56439	753	5	44800	79	73
Delhi	1423	4.1	69571	1051	4.3	54745	79	74
Maharashtra	1278	4.4	66776	921	5.4	59857	90	72
Andhra Pradesh	1134	4	54104	803	5.2	50048	93	71
Gujarat	1227	4.6	67049	875	5.2	54771	82	71

(*Contd*)

Table 9.3: (*Contd*)

	Hindus			*Muslims*			*Muslim/Hindu (in Per cent)*	
States	MPCE	*Household Size*	*Household expenditure*	MPCE	*Household Size*	*Household expenditure*	*Household expenditure*	MPCE
Rajasthan	979	4.8	56588	685	5.9	48679	86	70
Madhya Pradesh	902	4.9	53429	669	6.1	48867	91	74
Haryana	1155	4.7	65551	1105	5.3	70720	108	96
Tamil Nadu	1166	3.7	51777	1020	4.1	50212	97	87
Orissa	795	4.5	43250	785	4.6	43795	101	99
Himachal Pradesh	1487	3.7	65175	869	3.2	33601	52	58
Chattisgarh	956	4.5	51958	590	5.9	41514	80	62
Punjab	1241	4.7	70372	811	4.4	42655	61	65

Source: NSSO 2007: 36–37; Sachar 2006: 364.

Peculiar Cases

The Assam figures are peculiar. The Muslim–Hindu rural household expenditure ratio there (at 93 per cent of Hindu expenditure) is matched by a much higher expenditure for urban households (at 126 per cent). Assam therefore seems to defy comparison with other states. The size of the urban Muslim population in Assam is relatively small, amounting in 2001 to only 5 lakhs, as compared to the rural Muslim population of 77 lakhs.

Another peculiar case is the urban figures for Jammu and Kashmir. One would have expected Jammu and Kashmir (a Muslim majority state) to show better all-round results for Muslim household expenditure, but it does not; in fact, urban Muslims fare worse there (86 per cent of Hindu households) than in many other states. Rural Muslim households, on the other hand, do better (by 113 per cent) than Hindu rural households. This result may, however, be a consequence of regional variations between the Muslim-majority Kashmir valley and the Hindu-dominated Jammu region. There is an obvious need to look at state data on a regional basis.

Some Explanations

Differences in the age structure of the households, with more young and older members (see Table 9.4) affect income-generation and expenditure. Hindu households with larger proportions of persons in the 15–54-year age-group have a higher potential supply of family labour and income-earning capacity. Conversely, a higher proportion of non-working section of the Muslim households (especially those below 15 years) means not only lower income, but also higher expenditure than Hindu households.

It is also clear that the All-India Labor Force Participation Rates (LFPR) for Muslim women are substantially lower both in rural (52 per cent) and urban areas (70 per cent) than for Hindu women (NSSO 2007: 26, 44–45, 47–48). This implies that the incomes generated by Hindu women at work contribute to raising their household incomes and expenditures, as compared to their Muslim sisters. However, among the different states, there are vast differences when with regard to the issue of employment (see Table 9.5).

While there are Hindu–Muslim differences in the case of males as well in rural areas, these differences are not as dramatic as in the case of females. In the rural areas, the differences in female employment between the two communities are also not so acute and may well contribute to

Table 9.4: All-India Household Age Profile

	Females				*Males*			
	Rural		*Urban*		*Rural*		*Urban*	
	Hindus	*Muslims*	*Hindus*	*Muslims*	*Hindus*	*Muslims*	*Hindus*	*Muslims*
Below 15 years	341	394	273	356	359	428	276	357
15–54	560	530	616	559	539	493	628	568
55 and Above	99	76	110	85	102	79	97	77
Total	1000	1000	999	1000	1000	1000	1001	1002

Source: Data consolidated by the author (NSSO 2007: A-7, A-8, A-10, A-11).

Table 9.5: The Proportion of Persons (Per 1,000) Employed According to the Usual Principal and Subsidiary Status

	Rural				*Urban*			
	Male		*Female*		*Male*		*Female*	
States	*Hindu*	*Muslim*	*Hindu*	*Muslim*	*Hindu*	*Muslim*	*Hindu*	*Muslim*
All-India	553	495	344	178	555	526	174	121
West Bengal	591	541	194	131	593	599	155	152
Kerala	596	448	302	124	574	464	247	81
Uttar Pradesh	504	450	249	190	534	506	104	147
Bihar	487	413	150	74	443	503	64	77
Assam	561	535	252	131	549	571	118	56
Jammu & Kashmir	580	538	395	202	520	532	117	108
Jharkhand	552	440	302	267	467	502	127	93
Karnataka	625	600	470	348	584	553	200	119
Uttaranchal	524	520	445	148	508	570	136	46
Delhi	489	1000	49	0	535	604	96	11
Maharashtra	572	476	480	280	570	533	202	126
Andhra Pradesh	609	538	490	397	567	539	246	108

(*Contd*)

Table 9.5: (*Contd*)

	Rural				*Urban*			
	Male		*Female*		*Male*		*Female*	
States	*Hindu*	*Muslim*	*Hindu*	*Muslim*	*Hindu*	*Muslim*	*Hindu*	*Muslim*
Gujarat	590	619	436	322	585	531	168	82
Rajasthan	509	481	411	236	505	482	189	126
Madhya Pradesh	544	535	370	279	520	517	159	142
Haryana	524	471	321	277	511	534	130	14
Tamil Nadu	605	460	475	141	606	499	254	120
Orissa	587	477	319	254	507	465	149	42
Himachal Pradesh	555	590	505	516	627	811	240	48
Chattisgarh	563	600	459	75	531	564	188	114
Punjab	544	606	202	472	582	641	122	118

Source: NSSO 2007: 50–51, 53–54.

towards equalisation of their household expenditure.[2] However, in urban areas, women are generally employed to a lesser extent than in rural areas, irrespective of their religion.

The size and structure of the household, and the participation of women in income-generating work are mostly matters arising out of household decisions. These could have a significant effect on household income altogether. It also seems to have a significant effect on the substantially lower infant mortality rates (IMR) among Muslims than those of Hindus (Bhalotra 2010). It is assumed that Muslim women, along with their infants, in the safety of their homes, are less likely to be in harm's way. In this sense, Muslim women are 'trading off' the survival of their infants against possible income earned by wage labour.

It seems clear that in rural areas, Muslim households are on par with Hindu households. The differences in urban areas are significant, but not uniform across states. After examining this data, it is therefore difficult to conclude that Hindu–Muslim rural differentials in household expenditure are fixed across the country. If anything, rural Muslims households seem to be doing better than the rural Hindu households. However, this is not the case in urban areas, where Muslim household expenditure levels are much lower than Hindu household expenditure.

Minority Concentration Districts Programme

As a response to the Sachar Report, the Indian government undertook the task of accelerating development in the Minority Concentration Districts (MCDs). The MCDs were defined as those areas that had a substantial proportion, that is, at least 25 per cent, of all religious minorities–namely Muslims, Sikhs, Christians, Buddhists and Zoroastrians (Parsis), as notified under Section 2 [c] of the National Commission for Minorities Act, 1992.

However, the 89 MCDs, which were selected by the Ministry of Minority Affairs, were mostly those districts where Muslims formed a substantial share of the population. The Ministry commissioned baseline surveys of MCDs, which were completed in 2008 as preparatory to funding the development of these districts.[3] These surveys were conducted by independent organisations, using a common methodology prescribed by the Ministry. The MCDs mostly had a large share of Muslim population, although, as can be seen, there are many districts where their share is well below the national average, let alone the defining 25 per cent. The surveys commenced in 2007 and were completed in 2008.

Thus, the data is dated four years later than the data used in the Sachar Report.

The Indian Council of Social Science Research (ICSSR) guided the Surveys and subcontracted them to research institutions in the states. Under the overall coordination of the ICSSR, the survey work was conducted by: [i] the Centre for Studies in Social Sciences, Calcutta (CSSSC), [ii] Giri Institute for Development Studies (GIDS), Lucknow, [iii] OKD Institute for Social Change and Development, Guwahati, and [iv] the Institute for Human Development (IHD), New Delhi; [v] the Aligarh Muslim University, and [vi] Jamia Millia Islamia.

Despite all this, however, their quality is somewhat variable, and not all are comparable with each other. Only 42 out of the 89 surveys seem to have reported income levels for Muslims and Hindus. This is a vital omission.[4] A report by D. Narasimha Reddy, commissioned by the ICSSR as an 'Overview of the Findings', deals with some of these issues and shortcomings. Neither the reports nor the 'Overview' seems to consider income differentials that are significant, in as much as no attention is paid to that data. This data is significant, as it was intended to provide a baseline for comparison after the investment in these MCDs are completed.

Table 9.6 presents the figures for Hindu and Muslim household income per annum, and Muslim incomes as a percentage of Hindu incomes in the 42 MCDs. These figures vary considerably. The lowest figures can be found in Sirsa, Haryana (51 per cent), Uddham Singh Nagar in Uttaranchal (52 per cent) and Mamit in Mizoram (58 per cent). Another six districts indicate that Muslim incomes are 60–70 per cent of Hindu incomes, nine districts indicate that Muslim incomes are between 70 and 90 per cent, and eight districts are with Muslim incomes at 90 per cent or more of Hindu incomes. In 16 MCDs, Muslim household incomes are higher than Hindu household incomes. This uneven pattern implies that there can be no firm conclusions drawn about the condition of the Muslim community across these 42 districts (see Pingle 2014).

Post-Sachar/MCD Results

The Post-Sachar Evaluation Committee (Kundu Committee), appointed by the Ministry of Minority Affairs, Government of India reported back in 2014 (Government of India [GoI] 2014). It tabulated the MPCE data for Hindus and Muslims, which were derived from the NSSO over three

Table 9.6: Average Annual Household Income in MCDs 2007–08 (in Rupees)

Serial	*District*	*State*	*Muslim Population (in Per cent)*	*Hindu*	*Muslim*	*Hindu/ Muslim (in Per cent)*
1	Bahraich	UP	34.8	30153	28224	94
2	Balrampur	UP	36.7	46333	41341	89
3	Barabanki	UP	22.0	32195	26306	82
4	Muzzafarnagar	UP	38.1	43665	37975	87
5	Bijnor	UP	41.7	30948	25994	84
6	Baduan	UP	21.3	23737	26341	111
7	Bagpat	UP	24.7	44735	30498	68
8	Saharanpur	UP	39.1	61017	66457	109
9	Bulandshar	UP	21.1	52985	35482	67
10	Lucknow	UP	20.5	34068	45557	134
11	Moradabad	UP	45.5	40625	41637	102
12	Siddharthanagar	UP	29.4	31712	39406	124
13	JP Nagar	UP	39.4	50987	50842	100
14	Lashmipur Keri	UP	19.1	30970	24730	80
15	Shrawasti	UP	21.6	41876	37107	89
16	Bareilly	UP	33.9	27534	25278	92
17	Rampur	UP	49.1	42940	45699	106
18	Hardwar	Uttarkhand	37.7	42840	37636	88
19	U Singh Nagar	Uttarkhand	16.2	84796	43985	52
20	Dharbhanga	Bihar	22.3	33174	32149	97
21	P- Chamaparan	Bihar	21.7	25148	33398	133
22	Kishangunj	Bihar	74.1	34291	38020	111
23	Katihar	Bihar	44.8	26065	27966	107
24	Araria	Bihar	41.4	32065	31012	97
25	Purnia	Bihar	38.1	32055	28891	90
26	Sitamarhi	Bihar	21.4	32804	29951	91
27	Gumla	Jharkhand	3.6	18996	29004	153
28	Pakur	Jharkhand	32.7	29070	38438	132
29	Ranchi	Jharkhand	10.2	33565	33426	100
30	Sahibganj	Jharkhand	32.4	33051	35216	107
31	Parbhani	Mah	6.6	52013	32002	62
32	Hingol	Mah	6.1	62503	37864	61

(Contd)

Table 9.6: (*Contd*)

Serial	*District*	*State*	*Muslim Population (in Per cent)*	*Hindu*	*Muslim*	*Hindu/ Muslim (in Per cent)*
33	Washi	Mah	6.5	55461	48445	87
34	Bhuldana	Mah	9.1	50898	32876	65
35	Sirsa	Haryana	negl	86375	44063	51
36	Mewat	Haryana	74.2	34798	48580	140
37	Leh	J&K	12.9	83079	76527	92
38	Bidar	Karnataka	12.2	48324	43539	90
39	Gulbarga	Karnataka	11.6	49150	40251	82
40	Mamit	Mizoram	1.8	58006	33627	58
41	Lawngtlai	Mizoram	0.3	51203	35254	69
42	Wynad	Kerala	26.5	44446	56802	128

Source: ICSSR Website, 'The List of Districts'.

periods, from 2004-05, 2009-10, and 2011-12 (the first on which Sachar based its conclusions). As in the case of the Sachar Committee Report, its consumption/income data was in per capita terms, and the household size data is missing. However, taking into account the household size from the relevant NSSO reports of the same rounds, I have put together in Table 9.7 the consumption/income per household for the three periods, for both All- Hindus and All-Muslim households.

In terms of the proportionate differences between the two communities, Table 9.8 provides the relevant data. Table 9.8 indicates that in rural areas, Muslim household incomes are higher than Hindu household incomes. More importantly, the proportionate gap between Muslim household income and Hindu household income in urban areas is reducing over time. Much of this effect is due to the reduction in Muslim household size over the three periods. Over time, this effect will tend to equalise the two sets of household incomes, as also per capita incomes. If the WPR for Muslim women in urban areas improves, then it is quite likely that Muslim household incomes will achieve parity, and probably also exceed Hindu household incomes nationwide.

As far as 'wealth' is concerned, there exists some interesting data from the National Family Health Surveys (NFHS). The distribution of total 'wealth' (as defined by NFHS) across the Hindu and Muslim population is surprisingly uniform across quintiles for both religious groups. In this

Table 9.7: Post-Sachar Evaluation

	Rural						*Urban*					
	All Hindu			*Muslim*			*All Hindu*			*All Muslim*		
Year	MPCE	*Household Size*	*Household Income*	MPCE	*Household Size*	*Household Income*	MPCE	*Household Size*	*Household Income*	MPCE	*Household Size*	*Household Income*
2004–05	178.2	4.95	882.09	173.2	5.59	968.188	336.9	4.36	1468.884	237.9	5.37	1277.523
2009–10	190.1	4.5	855.45	178.4	4.9	874.16	382.2	4.0	1528.8	264.8	4.8	1271.04
2011–12	218.8	4.4	962.72	207.9	5.0	1039.5	429.9	3.9	1676.61	297.6	5.0	1488.0

Source: GoI 2014: 35–36. For household size, see NSSO 2007; 2013; 2015.

Table 9.8: Ratio of Muslim to Hindu Incomes

	Rural	*Urban*	*Rural*	*Urban*
	MPCE		*Household Income*	
Year	*Muslim/Hindu*	*Muslim/Hindu*	*Muslim/Hindu*	*Muslim/Hindu*
2004–05	0.97	0.71	1.10	0.87
2009–10	0.94	0.69	1.02	0.83
2011–12	0.95	0.69	1.08	0.89

Source: Based on the author's calculations.

Table 9.9: Per Cent Distribution by Wealth Quintiles

	NHFS 3 (2005–06)		*NHFS 4 (2015–16)*	
	Hindu	*Muslim*	*Hindu*	*Muslim*
First	20.7	18.9	21	18
Second	20.6	19.7	20.4	20.3
Third	20.2	20.6	20.2	20
Fourth	19.2	23.6	19.3	22.9
Fifth	19.2	17.2	19.1	18.8
	100	100	100	100

Source: Inernational Institution of Population Sciences (IIPS) 2007: India, 45; 2017: India, 31.

respect, there also seems to be hardly any difference in the distribution pattern between Hindus and Muslims (see Table 9.9).

Telangana Data

The Telangana government issued detailed terms of reference to the Sudhir Commission, tasking it to prepare a comprehensive study on the social, educational and economic status of Muslims in Telangana (Sudhir 2016). The Sudhir Commission decided to get a sample survey conducted in all the 10 districts of the state, and gather first-hand information from households. A sample of 4,348 Muslim households was considered adequate for the sample survey. A sample of 3,131 Hindu households was included to represent the population of Hindus in the state.

Significant Findings

In conformity with the All-India data, household size differs, with Muslim households having significantly larger families than Hindu households in Telangana (see Table 9.10).

Table 9.10: Average Household Size

	Hindu	*Muslim*	*All*
Rural	4.5	5.4	4.8
Urban	4.6	5.5	5.2
All	4.6	5.5	5.0

Source: Sudhir 2016: Table 2.2.

Also, the same phenomenon, again, as apparent in the national figures, show a much lower female work participation ratios for Muslim women than Hindu women (see Table 9.11), indicating lower Muslim female income generation through paid labour.

However, the levels of household incomes do not differ at all between the two religious communities. It is clear from Table 9.12 that Muslim households in all locations in Telangana are doing as well as, or better than, Hindu households in terms of income. However, Muslim households have a substantially higher expenditure than Hindu households in all locations.

The data for nutrition also indicates near parity in Telangana between Hindus and Muslims in either rural or urban areas (see Table 9.13).

In fact, taking into account the fact that Muslim household size is larger than Hindu household size, the per capita estimates (derived from household total consumption) are creditable. A robust state-level survey, explicitly aimed at the condition of the Muslim population, has led to an extraordinary result. The problem, if at all, seems to be more on the

Table 9.11: Work Participation Ratios (15–64 Years) 2012–13 (in Per Cent)

Location	*Gender*	*Hindu*	*Muslim*	*All*
Rural	Male	80	75	79
	Female	65	47	63
Urban	Male	76	69	74
	Female	25	8	21

Source: Sudhir 2016: Table 2.2.

Table 9.12: Hindu–Muslim Monthly Household Income and Expenditure

	Income		*Expenditure*	
Location	*Hindu*	*Muslim*	*Hindu*	*Muslim*
Rural	10,887	10,372	4,400	5,295
Urban	12,938	13,742	5,838	7,086
All	11,587	12,848	4,892	6,615
GHMC	14,198	14,474	6,570	7,738
NON-GHMC	11,342	11,785	4,734	5,880

Source: Sudhir 2016: Tables A. 5.14; A. 5.15.

Table 9.13: Average Daily Consumption per capita

	Hindu		*Muslim*	
	Rural	*Urban*	*Rural*	*Urban*
Calories in Kcal	2123.8	1994.1	2081.5	1883.6
Protein in Grams	51.1	49.4	50.7	47.7
Fat in Grams	43.1	46.1	40.9	43.8

Source: Kumar 2018: 154; NSSO 2011-12.

expenditure side than the income generation angle, and is likely to be due to larger Muslim families. Despite these factors, Muslim households in Telangana have higher incomes than Hindu households, suggesting that they have made significant efforts to overcome any disabilities or disadvantages that Muslim minorities may have had since 1948, when Muslim rule in Telangana ended after nearly 600 years.

Conclusion

This essay does not substantiate the currently held notion of fixed and firm Muslim expenditure/income differences, as compared to the Hindu majority. On the other hand, it argues that the comparative level of expenditure/income of Muslims is substantially better than is otherwise assumed. This achievement by the Muslim community, despite its loss of power and any current disadvantages, is a result of the efforts of individual Muslim households, especially in rural areas of Telangana. In this respect, Muslims in Telangana are ahead of their community in other states. This needs to be recognised and lauded.

Notes

1. The NSSO collects expenditure data rather than income data, as the former is more reliable and credible. The expenditure figures are a proxy for income, and in most cases, are underestimates of income. In the narrative, however, expenditure is used interchangeably with income.
2. Rural Muslim women in Punjab have an LFPR that is 2.33 times that of rural Hindu women. This is, however, likely to be a statistical issue, as figures are based on samples of 26 rural Muslim households, as compared to 473 rural Hindu households. In the urban sample, male LFPR for Muslims is 11 per cent higher than Hindu men, but again, this is based on 47 Muslim sample households and 1,195 Hindu households.

3. For all 89 reports, see the ICSSR website.
4. This failure in collecting and reporting the most critical baseline data is somewhat difficult to understand.

References

Bhalotra, Sonia, Christine Valente and Arthur van Soest. 2010. 'Religion and Childhood Death in India', in *Handbook of Muslims in India*, eds A. Sharif and R. Basant. Oxford University Press.

GoI. 2014. 'Post Sachar Evaluation Committee, [Kundu Committee] Ministry of Minority Affairs'. Available at http://iosworld.org/download/Post_Sachar_Evaluation_Committee.pdf.

ICSSR Website. Available at https://www.icssr.org/Overview%20Report.pdf.

——. 'The List of Districts'. Available at https://icssr.org/list-districts.

IIPS. 2007. National Family Health Survey [NFHS-3], 2005–06, India, Volume 1. Mumbai: IIPS. Available at http://rchiips.org/nfhs/NFHS-3%20Data/VOL-1/India_volume_I_corrected_17oct08.pdf.

Kumar, Rishi. 2018. 'Gender Analysis of Nutrition in Telangana', in *Telangana Social Development Report 2018: Gender, Access and Well Being*, eds Kalpana Kannabiran, Padmini Swaminathan and J. Jeyarajan. Hyderabad: Council for Social Development.

NSSO. 2004–05. Sixty-First Round. Employment and Unemployment Situation among Major Religious Groups in India 2004–05, Report No. 515. New Delhi: NSSO, GoI.

——. 2007. Sixty-First Round. *Employment and Unemployment Situation among Major Religious Groups in India 2004–2005*, Report No. 521.

——. 2011–12. Sixty-Eighth Round. *Employment and Unemployment Situation among Major Religious Groups in India 2011–2012*, Report No. 568.

——. 2013. Sixty-Sixth Round. *Employment and Unemployment Situation among Major Religious Groups in India 2009–2010*, Report No. 552.

——. 2015. Sixty-Eighth Round. *Employment and Unemployment Situation among Major Religious Groups in India 2011–2012*, Report No. 568.

Pingle, Gautam. 2014. 'Hindu–Muslim Rural Household Comparisons', *Journal of Indian School of Political Economy*, 26(1–4). Available at https://www.researchgate.net/publication/321796617_HINDU-MUSLIM_RURAL_HOUSEHOLD_COMPARISONS.

Sachar, Rajinder. 2006. *High-Level Committee Report on Social, Economic and Educational Status of the Muslim Community of India*. New Delhi: GoI.

Sudhir Commission. 2016. *Report of the Commission of Inquiry on Socio-Economic and Educational Conditions of Muslims*. Hyderabad: Government of Telangana (GoT).

Conclusion

The nine essays in this book set out to explore the development of the land of Telangana and its people for over 700 years. The essays are not exhaustive, and sometimes, the linkages between them may be lacking. Scholars will hopefully try and compensate for the deficiency as well as elaborate on this picture of the past. Indian history is a work-in-progress. Many more inscriptions need translation and analysis, and their information needs to be incorporated and used to correct, alter, or add to existing knowledge. The general lack of interest in history in India has been commented on, especially by foreign observers. The current interest in the idea of the nation and the nation-state may spur new interest and understanding of the past and how we got to the present. However, it seems incumbent that we draw some general hypotheses from the essays here, although may not be appropriate to call them conclusions, as they are tentative and need to be discussed, elaborated upon, and accepted.

It seems obvious that the Kakatiya state, from its very origins expanded to include most of the Telugu-speaking people and the lands they inhabited. A classic monarchical–feudal model drove the expansion of the Kakatiya state. It was extremely successful in the same way that it was successful in Japan or Europe. The combination of secular power and religious sanction captured the imagination and loyalty of the vassals as well as the general population. For 200 years, the Kakatiya state progressed despite challenges and setbacks, in order to provide to its people a degree of prosperity, peace and social harmony. However, its leadership was unable to understand and meet the challenge that came from outside their cognitive universe.

It is clear that the Muslim invasions, conquest, and the rule of the Indian subcontinent were a set of traumatic experiences, which were beyond the comprehension of the Hindu leadership and population. The levels of violence that Hindu society experienced at the hands of its Muslim victors and rulers was by any account unprecedented. An unbridgeable racial and religious division between the Islamic rulers, on the one hand, and the Hindu elite and population, on the other, manifested itself.

Understanding the ideological and religious drives of the Muslim invaders and rulers was not within the cognitive capacity of the Hindu elite and population. The Hindus had been indoctrinated and raised for millennia by a relatively tolerant religion, polity and society. Hindu society sought to include all it diverse groups within a hierarchical social and political order.

Today, we can understand the iconoclastic drive of Islam, fuelled by its Semitic legacy. The aggression behind this drive is also apparent. The need to exercise terror by a racial and religious minority over an overwhelming majority seems logical, although not excusable. The destruction of temples, the massacre of civilian populations, the enslavement of women and children, and the deliberate use of terror as a public policy shook the ancient Hindu civilisation to its core. Inevitably, when confrontation failed, the Hindu elite and population developed various forms of accommodation with their Muslim rulers.

On the other hand, Muslim conquerors realised that they had to rule a hostile, alien and resentful population, which they did not understand nor seek to understand. When wholesale conversion to Islam did not succeed as it did in other geographies, Islam in India reached for accommodation with the Hindu elite as well as with the general population. As the Islamic religious policy failed to yield results, what remained was the Muslim ruler's desire to extract as much surplus from the population as possible.

Islamic *Sharia* and Koranic injunctions dictated that those who did not convert to Islam had to pay the *jizya* religious tax and the onerous land tax. Non-Muslim agriculturists were taxed at 50 per cent of the land output, while Muslims paid only 10 per cent. This extraordinary and confiscatory tax rate was in contrast with the Hindu canonical rate of 16.6 per cent of the land output. The differential in taxation applied to Muslims and non-Muslims in other economic sectors such as trade and tolls. The taxes were collected either directly by Muslim rulers, or through the agency of the Hindu elite and vassals. The past prosperity of the land and its people ended, and the consequent prosperity of the Muslim rulers and their state commenced. This situation was certainly not a way of winning the hearts and minds of the subject people, even though there was reluctant compliance.

These essays indicate the erosion and moderation of the Islamic drive of the Muslim rulers and the beginnings of a secular understanding of the nature of power and the problems of governance over a racially and religiously different population. By the time Muslim power crossed south of the Vindhya mountain range, there had been 200 years of Islamic conquest and rule of Northern India. While the Khilji and the Tughlak invaders, and the conquerors of Telangana were much in the early Islamic model of conquerors, this model did not succeed in subjugating the people, and only aroused constant resistance and warfare. Their Bahmani successors, after the initial brutality, came to an accommodation with the Vijayanagar Empire and the Telangana people.

The Kakatiya model was the basis for the Vijayanagar empire, which, during the 200 years of its existence, prevented Muslim power from crossing the south of the Tungabhadra–Krishna river border. The relative peace assured by the Vijayanagar empire ensured the continued development of the traditional Hindu model based on toleration and inclusion as well as the low rate of tax on agriculture. It is interesting to note that in Travancore and Cochin, the land tax rate was 10 per cent or nil. It is difficult not to conclude that this factor, and the fact that these two geographies never experienced alien rule of any kind, were the historical antecedents for the much appreciated 'Kerala Model'. The past determines much of the present.

The relative tranquillity and peace in South India probably also explains the extraordinary high yields of paddy in the current period. In pre-modern South India, the high paddy yields, combined with light taxation, determined the level of development of the land and its people and cultural and religious growth. The great temples and the extraordinary spread of irrigation projects of the South, as well as its trade links with Southeast Asia and the Persian Gulf are indicators of endogenous growth.

As we set foot into the modern period, the last three essays attempt to understand the implications of the collapse of Muslim rule in Telangana and the traumatc consequences of the Police Action and its aftermath. The ability of the Muslim population, not only in Telangana, but also across the country, to cope with the effects of Independence and what they perceived as Hindu Raj, has been extraordinary. The effort Muslims have had to make to achieve substantial household incomes and material prosperity is remarkable. One of the most positive features of a democratic India is that that the Muslim minority has been able to take care of itself and achieve prosperity without the exercise of state power.

These essays, especially those on land tax, paddy yields, semi-feudal tenure, and the wealth and income in Telangana, indicate the potential and the reality of the capacity of the land and people of Telangana that were required to achieve a high degree of prosperity and material progress.

The fact that it had not happened for 700 years is not the fault of the land and its people. For this extraordinarily long period, Telangana was subjected to a governing order that was ruled by, and benefitted, an alien ruling class and elite. Since 1324 AD, the native Telangana elite has coped heroically with great sacrifices in terms of its loss of pride, honour, self-respect and independence. On the positive side, the Telangana elite has maintained the integrity and autonomy of the village society, its cultural and religious traditions, and its agricultural potential. The Telangana elite extracted the onerous taxes required to accommodate and keep an alien ruling class at a distance. The price of continued existence has been high, but the elite and people of Telangana have demonstrated their capacity to meet existential challenges over time.

From 2014 onwards, Telangana has been ruled by a democratically elected elite originating from its land and people. Telangana's future progress will depend partly on the motivations, behaviour and action of its governing elite. More fundamentally, it will depend on the liberation of the potential of the land and its people to achieve material prosperity, and social and cultural development. Whether the outcome will result in *Bangaru* (Golden) Telangana remains to be seen, but the prognosis is favourable.

Index